Art in Education: An International Perspective

Robert W. Ott
Al Hurwitz
Editors

The Pennsylvania State University Press
University Park and London

Library of Congress Cataloging in Publication Data

Main entry under title:

Art in education.

Includes index.
1. Art—Study and teaching—Addresses, essays, lectures. I. Ott, Robert.
II. Hurwitz, Al.
N85.A657 1984   707   83-43226
ISBN 0-271-00372-3

To the members and officers of INSEA (The International Society for Education through Art) and of CECA/ICOM (The Committee for Education and Cultural Action of The International Council of Museums) who have served to develop these organizations to facilitate communication among art educators concerning the meaning of art in the lives of children, adolescents, and adults throughout the world. INSEA and CECA offer art educators a humane forum that remains unsurpassed in the history of art education. To those dedicated educators who continue to demonstrate their involvement in mankind as citizens of the world through these organizations . . . we dedicate this book.

Contents

About the Authors

ROBERT W. OTT, Doctorate, Penn State University, where he is a professor of Art Education. Chairman of Training Working Party for CECA/ICOM and editor of *The Museologist* for NEMC/AAM. Editor, *Art in Education: An International Perspective.*

AL HURWITZ, Doctorate, Penn State University. Head of the Department of Art Education, Maryland Institute of Art. Past president of INSEA (International Society for Education Through Art) and author of *Children and Their Art, The Joyous Vision,* and *Programs of Promise.* Editor, *Art in Education: An International Perspective.*

BRIAN ALLISON, Doctorate, University of Leeds. President of The International Society for Education Through Art. Head of the Department of Art Education, Leicester Polytechnic, Great Britain.

FRANCES E. ANDERSON, Doctorate, New York University. Assistant Professor of Education, Illinois State University. Has done research in Special Education.

ANA MAE T.B. BARBOSA, Doctorate, Boston University. Professor of Art Education, University of Sao Paulo, Brazil.

MAHMOUD EL-BASSIOUNY, Doctorate, Ohio State University. Head of the Department of Art Education, University of Qatar. Formerly head of Art at Helwan College of Education, University of Cairo.

WILLIAM BRADLEY, Doctorate, University of Minnesota. Associate Professor, School of Visual Arts, Penn State University. Author of *Art: Magic, Impulse and Control.*

JOHN CONDOUS, Inspector of Art, South Australia. Past president of INSEA.

BEN CROSSKELL, Formerly an art inspector in Australia, having also been a secondary school art teacher. His main interests have been in art curricula.

ELLIOT EISNER, Doctorate, University of Chicago. Professor of Education, Stanford University. Past president of The National Art Education Association. Author of *Readings in Art Education; The Arts: Human Development and Education; The Education of Vision;* and *The Educational Imagination.*

HOWARD GARDNER, Doctorate, Harvard University. Director of Project Zero, Harvard University. Author of *Artful Scribbles* and *The Arts and Human Development.*

HARRIET GOITEIN, Staff, Youth Wing, Israel Museum.

JOHN W. GROSSERT, Doctorate, University of Wittwatersrand. Formerly an art inspector, Natal, South Africa.

S. WILLIAM IVES, Doctorate, Harvard University. Involved in Project Zero, Harvard University. Associate Professor of Education, Wheelock College, Boston. Formerly Professor, Massachusetts College of Art.

LOIS SWAN JONES, Doctorate, Associate Professor of Art, North Texas State University. Author of *Art: Research Methods and Resources.*

HETA KAUPPINEN, Doctorate, Penn State University. Chief Inspector of Art Education for the National Board of General Education, Finland. Has taught at the University of Iowa and Colorado State University.

MAX KLAGER, Doctorate, University of Minnesota. Professor of Art Education, University of Heidelberg. Author of *Das Bild und Die Welt des Kinder* and *Seh Weisen: Kunst Geistig Behind.*

BRENDA LANSDOWN, Graduate degree candidate, University of Wisconsin. Art teacher with extensive travel in the Orient.

ARLINE J. LEDERMAN, Doctoral Candidate, New York University. Head of Department of Art Education, Montclair State College, New Jersey.

EMMANUEL C. NYARKOH, Doctorate, Ohio State University. Head of Department of Art, University of Ghana.

RUTH C. OMABEGHO, Doctorate, New York University. Professor of Art Education, University of Lagos, Nigeria.

DENNIS SCHAPEL, Master of Fine Arts, Maryland Institute of Art. Head of Art Department, Darwin Community College, Northern Territory, Australia.

PROMILA SEN, Doctorate, University of North Carolina. Professor of Art Education, Winston-Salem College. UNESCO Special Projects consultant.

THOMAS SLETTEHAUGH, Doctorate, Penn State University. Professor of Art Education, University of Minnesota. Formerly Art Education Head, Mississippi College for Women.

MAARTEN TAMSMA, Editor, *Zienswek*, Dutch Journal for Art Education. A secondary school art teacher in Amsterdam.

MARIA VIDA-SZEKACS, Formerly a professor of Education, University of Budapest, Hungary. Author of *Art Education in Japan*.

FRANK WACHOWIAK, Formerly a professor of Art, University of Georgia. Author of *Emphasis Art* and *Art in Depth*.

BRENT WILSON, Doctorate, University of Iowa. Professor of Art Education, Penn State University. Author of *Teaching Children to Draw* and *Kuvaama Taidon Didaktiikka*. Director of National Assessment Programs in Art.

MARJORIE WILSON, Doctorate, Penn State University. Formerly a professor of Art, Florida State University and Frostburg State College, Maryland. Author of *Teaching Children to Draw*.

IRENA WOJNAR, Doctorate, University of Warsaw. Chairperson of the National Committee on Aesthetic Education (Poland). Author of six books on Aesthetic Education; editor of *Paedeia*, Journal of Art Education.

SHIRLEY WOOD, Doctorate, Michigan State University. Professor, Henan University, People's Republic of China, since 1948.

BORIS YUSOV, Curriculum Specialist in Art Education for the Central Committee for Culture and Education, The United Soviet Socialist Republic.

Acknowledgments

The editors are grateful to the staff of The Pennsylvania State University Press and their advisors for their dedicated support and expert help in the preparation of this book. During the planning and drafting stages John M. Pickering of the Press showed unusual sensitivity to the needs and goals of art education throughout the world, and Patricia A. Coryell gave valuable assistance at the final editorial stage. The Press staff received expert guidance from Professor Dale B. Harris of Penn State and Professor Elliot W. Eisner of Stanford.

Special thanks also are extended to the contributors and to the organizations and individuals who provided textual and illustrative materials and permission to print them. In particular, the editors thank the Soenaid Robertson Child Art Collection, the Penn State International Art Education Collection, and the Hurwitz Collection of Children's Art for the numerous illustrations that enhance this book. Two esteemed publications, *Art Education* (the Journal of the National Art Education Association) and *Studies in Art Education*, graciously permitted republication of material originally appearing in their columns.

Introduction   International Art Education

Art in Education: An International Perspective proposes to fill a void in an area of growing concern among educators both in the United States and abroad—that of knowledge about art education throughout the world. Art in the educational systems of nations seeks to excite the consciousness of students to the heritage of symbols within the culture of that nation and often of other nations as well. Art teachers in many nations throughout the world are motivating their students toward appreciation, participation, and the rewards of personal fulfillment that come to individuals when they contribute artistically to their heritage and to the world.

American art teachers have begun to realize that for many of them, the time has come to break out of their cultural and professional isolation and to learn how others are teaching art and accomplishing art education goals. Some of these teachers are curious about practical solutions to their own problems, while others reflect the kind of professional curiosity that any practitioners may have about their field. In all cases these art teachers, who are open to foreign perspectives on their own, are dispelling the kind of cultural arrogance of which Americans are so often accused. There is, after all, no set of values so flexible that they do not present their own boundaries. The purpose of this book is to assist these teachers in venturing beyond the paradigms that have been set by their own training, culture, and practices and in so doing permit a re-study of their own beliefs and a relationship to those of others.

The study of comparative education is in itself a recognized scholarly activity, yet art education as an area of this study has been largely neglected. Educational provincialism, in other disciplines, has rapidly diminished thanks to the increased knowledge of the education patterns of other nations. Art, however, even with its elements of universality, has not achieved this breadth, especially in the areas of the practice and teaching of art. All too often art education continues its preoccupation with individual systems and societies, and perpetuates its isolation through excuses about problems of language or about difficulties in gaining support for travel, translations, communications, and technological development.

The shrinkage, however, in the amount of time it takes to travel from one country to another and the expansion of technologies throughout the world are facts which are bringing more cultures, and should bring more art educators, into direct contact with each other rather than promote isolation. As a result, there remains today a need for the marked accelerations of interest in international art education by the practicing art teacher.

This expanding area of professional concern is also reflected and documented in an increase in the current literature on cross-cultural issues in both commercial and official U.S. publications. An acceleration of exchange of art teachers from the United States to foreign countries, moreover, has been one answer. So also is the number of students from abroad who are seeking graduate studies in art education in the United States, particularly from Great Britain and African and Islamic countries. A few U.S. universities, such as Penn State, Ohio State, and Illinois State universities, are actively encouraging foreign students to study in their programs and have thus become unofficial centers for students seeking graduate work in cross-cultural art education studies in this country. These remain, sadly, too few.

Some steadily growing professional art education societies which offer international formats have indicated that cross-cultural issues are areas wherein art teachers are finding new knowledge. The International Society for Education Through Art (INSEA) and the Committee for Education and Cultural Action (CECA) of the International Council of Museums provide annual meetings for an ever-increasing population of art educators in attendance at their impressive convocations. In this country, the U.S. Society for Education through Art (USSEA) conducts two conferences a year and presently publishes its own research journal. Similar national art education organizations dedicated to cross-cultural study are also thriving in numerous countries throughout the world.

International publications on art education classroom practices have also begun to appear but remain too few and too limited in their distribution. These publications reveal that their readerships have a need for information about international art teaching practices and are trying to meet the challenge. *School Arts* magazine, for example, has published several special issues on cross-cultural art education practices, but other than such an isolated example, the publication field remains limited.

A growing trend for the study of art education from an international viewpoint is, however, a definite need, and this need extends from the level of scholarly research as reflected in the subjects of doctoral dissertations, to the classroom teacher who is now willing to consider shared goals within the profession of art education. There remains the problem of appropriate attitudes one must maintain when confronting viewpoints of other countries which differ from one's own traditions, but in order to maintain proper empathy, art teachers have temporarily set aside some of their cherished sets of beliefs and have found that being different does not imply inferiority of any sort. When considering and studying the programs, goals, and values of another country, the art teacher is professionally critical on one hand, and at the same time maintains an ability to shift his or her basic orientation in order to empathize with what may be a radically different frame of reference. This may appear to be contradictory, but it is the best way to describe a stance that is both analytical yet open, that is fair to others. Art teachers today are showing that they are willing to do this. They are beginning to find considerable satisfaction in the study of cross-cultural art education because of both the pleasure of satisfied curiosity and the realization that much can be learned from foreign approaches to the practice of teaching art.

COMMONALITY AMONG ART EDUCATORS

Although the impulse to create or respond to art is universal, art itself is not an international or universal language since perceptions and actions can clearly be shaped by culture and the environment. Because early forms of comparative education often proved to be a search for institutional practices that could be transplanted from one culture to another, cross-cultural art education had little significance for art teachers in past decades. Outright borrowing, we have learned from others in education, has contained dangerous implications for educational practices, especially when they lack cultural roots. This, for example, has been realized from such practices imposed on certain African colonies by their European rulers. Despite the differences which do exist among the world's educational systems, there is, however, an essential and consistently articulated core of beliefs that art teachers are finding sharable with artists and art teachers from all cultures—essentially that art education is a basic human study throughout the world. INSEA presidents Brian Allison and Al Hurwitz, concurring during prominent international conferences, have remarked on art and international cooperation. As Allison stated: "Creative activity in the arts is a basic need common to all people, for Art is one of man's highest forms of expression and communication.

Association on a worldwide basis of those concerned with education through art is necessary in order that they may *share experiences, improve practices, and strengthen the position of art in relation to all education."*

Whatever its national context, art continues to enter as an entree into the curricula of every society. Wherever art exists, certain classic issues continue to concern the thoughtful and dedicated art educator. Art teachers in Ghana, Austria, or Eastern Europe must confront similar questions: Why is art worth the time and expense that it requires? How is it to be taught? Indeed, how shall it be defined in view of the increasing philosophical pluralism of many countries like Holland, Germany, and the United States? Other questions arise as to the context of art instruction. Art educators are asking, How can institutions of higher education prepare teachers to deal with the development of goals, with the methodology of instruction, and with curriculum development in an ever-changing world?

Persons in each society search for answers within their own traditions and attitudes and within the constraints placed upon such commonly shared problems as priorities, economics, and resource availability. These problems are of major concern to the contemporary individual art educator because each society is a unique complex of issues. Every country responds to pressures from within as well as beyond the realm of art education. The USSR and Japan have centralized approaches to art curriculums, while the United States and India are a maze of independent configurations. Great Britain continues its emphasis upon national examinations, while the United States has yet to honor art as being even worthy of examinations or as an issue to be considered. The American art teacher worries about survival in a profession threatened by inflation, a shrinking population, and declining academic scores, while a minister of culture in an African nation is concerned about the short supply of art teachers in the elementary grades. The nature of curricula, however, bedevils both U.S. and African secondary teachers, who must search for art lessons which are substantive yet relevant to the culture of black students in both countries. In Holland, the USSR, and West Germany, Marxist aesthetics have different meanings, while in the United States an art teacher may engage in an art lesson totally unaware of its context in another society.

The following few terms teachers will find occurring with predictable frequency in cross-cultural studies in the chapters that relate to these issues in international art education. Indeed, it is difficult to conduct a dialogue on cross-cultural art education without referring to such basic concepts as "society," "civilization," and "culture."

"Society" can be defined as a group of human beings distinguished from other groups by such factors as shared values, social structure, and arts expression. In a narrow sense, a society is also a professional organization; in broader terms, it can be a tribe such as the Bedouin. America could be viewed as a megasociety composed of subcultures.

"Civilization," the most encompassing term in this book, suggests some phase of a society's development (as in the Roman and Greek civilizations) and implies some stage of improvement in material terms, or, as Herbert Read puts it in *The Grass Roots of Art*, "the sum total of the products and amenities of a given social organization, its wealth, customs, and material achievements." A civilization may, in term, encompass within its parameters an array of cultures which, in turn, reflect styles of social and artistic expression peculiar to a group.

"Culture" refers to systems of behavior acquired and transmitted by means of symbols and other forms of aesthetic artifacts which may include literary, mimetic, and musical as well as visual products. The cultures developed by immigrants to America, which contain European sources with American overtones, differ vastly from the culture of the Gulas in the Louisiana bayou area to the suburbanites of Northeastern coastal cities. Both are part of the American society, since they share a broader set of values and submit to a common legal and political system. Culture is, however, where the state of a civilization can be studied through the level of achievement of societies within its boundaries. The study of cultures reveals the aesthetic and intellectual nature of groups within a given society.

The terms "civilization" and "culture" also take on a normative character when a "civilized" and "cultured" person is assumed to have achieved more elevated levels of development. The values held by these terms set the stage for the goals and forms of education that, in turn, determine what teachers do with their students when educating them in the arts. Such concepts are not abstractions but have, therefore, very tangible connections to the classroom. It is difficult to envision a system of education that does not reflect these concerns. Systems do indeed proceed vertically from a central power base (as in Soviet Russia and Japan), while others move laterally at certain points in the continuum, as in the case of Great Britain and the United States.

Education itself does not do badly when placed in the broader perspective of global issues such as energy, nutrition, war, and human rights. Art education, when studied in relation to education in general, drops considerably in parity with other subjects; indeed, one is impelled to speculate as to the reason for art's existence in the curricula throughout the world, since decision makers in education rarely, if ever, have a personal history of involvement in the arts. The fact that art does exist in the schools of many countries must be attributed to the persistence of art itself. What, after all, does the artist share with the child? The artist, as Hayman has noted, is one who uses art to intensify experience, to express and communicate ideas. Artists are people who interpret, reform, and enhance life and who order experience. There are other characteristics to be sure, but these have been singled out because they are behaviors that teachers can engender in children and that are dealt with in ways which differ from culture to culture.

The works of children, like those of professionals, are objects that are open to interpretations. Although a painting by a child in Qatar or a sculpture by Henry Moore may be easier to describe than to analyze and judge, there is always the possibility that we do learn from each other and that cultures as well as teachers and children extend the perception of one's profession. The Japanese can teach us to draw upon our own traditions for sustenance; the Soviets can show us how special agencies can better serve the gifted. The Americans, the British, and the Dutch have a growing number of models that demonstrate new uses of museums as agencies of art educators, while the Brazilians have shown us that art education is possible in the poorest of isolated areas. No one country has all the answers, nor can any one society be singled out as maintaining a full or adequate array of support for the aesthetic needs of all of its children. This book, therefore, provides the mosaic of ideas and concepts presently in existence, and it compels the reader, after studying its concepts, to test a few ideas to enrich a particular corner of any art teacher's world.

Eisner and Ecker have observed that some art educators would claim that the basic problems of art education transcend national boundaries. If human nature, including the need for aesthetic experience and the growth of artistic expression, cuts across borders and languages and seemingly demonstrates the unity of art, then a good case can be made that the resolution of problems in art education would apply universally. There are others, however, who see the problem in a different light, claiming that art is a cultural phenomenon bound in time and place to social and aesthetic conditions idiosyncratic to the culture. If this point of view is correct, then it may be difficult, if not impossible, to arrive at universally acceptable solutions to the problems of art education.

In a statement prepared for a special journal on international art education, Hurwitz noted:

> I have searched for a core of beliefs regarding art education shared by all art teachers regardless of where they reside. Based upon countless conversations with teachers and examinations of curriculum materials, I think I can safely say that there are a few points of consensus which exist despite national differences.

—Art teachers seem to believe that we are by nature shapers, formers, decorators. The process of creating form is a natural and desirable function of humans, and is an appropriate area of study in the schools.

—It is possible to derive pleasure from each other's art work even when we do not completely understand it. Art education can improve our understanding and therefore should be included as a part of general education.

—All of us are thinking, feeling, expressive beings. Art can direct us to a more complete realization of our humanity.

—Although ideas of what is pleasing or beautiful may differ from culture to culture, all art teachers believe that such concepts do exist and should be taught. We believe that these are related to aesthetic experience, and in some cases even to moral and ethical considerations. (As an example, the European Marxist sees beauty in a minipark arising out of a slum area and regards it as more moral than a painting made for personal pleasure.)

The claim that the study of art is a humanizing process capable of making us more whole, more compassionate, and more sensitive to one another has yet to be proved to anyone's satisfaction, yet it is a belief to which art teachers often subscribe. You might say this is a part of an internationally shared mystique that surrounds art education and that it has to do with a sense of mission. ("The Global Classroom," *School Arts Magazine* [March 1983])

At this point it is essential to make a distinction between the *evolution* of the image-making process and the *forms* that images take. It can be stated, with some authority, that graphic development does indeed follow broad, universal patterns. Children do scribble before they arrive at some symbolic rendering of their environment, and their symbols are scattered before they achieve some semblance of coherency through the handling of space, size, proximity, and so on. The *forms* of the shapes, from earliest symbol to more fully developed subjects, can and do differ markedly, not only from country to country but within a shared culture.

Gardner and Ives report that "nearly all experts who have considered the early evolution of children's drawings find quite striking parallels across the full range of human cultures"; yet they go on to report other research showing that children's artistic expressions are affected by the available media (pens, brushes, clay, beads, and such), by cultural conventions (modes of handwriting, printing, building, and other activities), and by adults' attitudes toward cultural referents (indifference, fear, approval, disapproval, or whatever). Wilson and Wilson also present data in this book that show how children from four cultures differ in their drawing styles. Art education clearly then must reflect both universal and cultural influences upon the characteristics of children's artistic expression. However, the need for "unusual solutions" may not be realistic or even pressing in the minds of still others. Kafka's protagonists never reach "The Castle" and Chekhov's "Three Sisters" dream of Moscow for three acts without ever reaching the city of their dreams, but it is the reach for the ideal that supplies the substance of both literary works.

Effective teachers have always known that not all of the answers to their problems reside in their own classrooms. Currently, many art teachers are beginning to realize that some answers may lie beyond the borders of their own countries. When art teachers fight a sense of isolation, they usually go through certain stages. They begin with regional meetings and they may read the newsletters and journals of their state and national organizations. They may also stage regional and national conferences. The final phase of communication is the world at large, for whenever art educators venture beyond the boundaries of their own culture, they are on their way to becoming citizens of the world through their professions.

Art in Education: An International Perspective was written to serve the contemporary art teacher as a guide to the world of their colleagues, who, despite differences in geography and even in ideology, share their many concerns.

I
Backgrounds to Cross-Cultural Study

The beginning section of this book presents reasons for involvement through an inquiry process into art as it is taught in other countries. Through the following accounts, a direction is presented for the eventual use of this book by suggesting a basis for a practical means for inquiry into art education through cross-cultural research.

Three articles are included to promote research information and to serve as a stimulus towards identifying a need for inquiring into the works of others, into other formal modes of art instruction, and into other stimulations, influences, and intrusions that affect art teaching in various countries.

In *I Was Just Thinking* Robert Lynd discusses the experience of entering into other environments about which one is not completely knowledgeable or may feel to some extent ignorant. He suggests that "the great pleasure of ignorance is the pleasure of asking questions. The man who has lost this pleasure or exchanged it for the pleasure of dogma, which is the pleasure of answering, is already beginning to stiffen." In the following articles Ives and Gardner, Wilson and Wilson, and Elliot Eisner encourage questions about and inquiry into cross-cultural research.

Ives and Gardner relate that all children "are acted upon" or influenced by their teachers and parents and by their particular environments. Reviewing the history and philosophy of the developmental approach to teaching art, they point out that the developmental stages unfold as a result of children's interactions with the world around them. Children therefore must, in turn, act upon the particular culture in which they live. The authors emphasize that there is a distinct role within the developmental framework for the effect of the culture on the child and, further, this role too often goes unappreciated by the art teacher who has not inquired deeply enough for more definite answers to the role of culture in the child's production of drawings.

A schoolboy in Afghanistan studies the traditional weaver's craft. Photo by Arline Lederman.

Ives and Gardner suggest that a combination of the existing information on children's drawings with the organizational perspective provided by the developmental framework will allow art teachers to obtain some preliminary responses to questions they might like to ask. The authors provide a particular research viewpoint in art education that permits questions to be asked so that more definite answers concerning cultural influences on children's drawings can be made, this by recognizing that all knowledge proceeds from an interaction with the environment.

The cultural referents of children's artistic expression are both chance and choice—usually choice by adults—as this section will demonstrate. Chance, at least so far as the individual child is concerned, determines whether a child's environment is rural or urban; agricultural or industrial; desert, woodland, savanna, or seacoast; temperate, arctic, or tropical. Choice determines the emphases, attitudes, and values reflected in each child's work. An art activity may be assigned to or selected by the child. In either case, the way in which an art experience is dealt with will reflect the child both as a genetically unique individual and as a member of a particular society and a partner in its culture.

The child's choices are affected—indeed, often determined—by limits set by teachers, parents, school board members and officials, government agencies, and "opinion makers." As this book's nineteen national profiles will make clear in the next section, the ways in which societies affect a child's choice of referents—directly or indirectly, obviously or subtly—are many and varied. All societies encourage certain values and attitudes and discourage others, whether by governmental fiat or social pressure. Competitive societies encourage competition; cooperative societies urge cooperation; stability or change is invited according to how revolutionary a society considers itself; and self-protection is emphasized in proportion to perceived danger. Societies that were formerly colonial, as in the cases of Nigeria and Ghana, are understandably ambivalent toward the cultures of the one-time colonizers. In the most avowedly revolutionary societies, those of the Soviet Union and the People's Republic of China, art educators are usually under special constraints. In considering profiles of differing modes of art education, responsible art educators should never adopt the ways of others and completely abandon their own.

The reader will appreciate the analysis of the developmental stages that Ives and Gardner present, with emphasis upon the earlier stages, when children's art resembles the most treasured of adult forms; there are developmental periods when children turn to others to observe and copy them faithfully, so that as young adults they can produce in an acceptable manner. Ives and Gardner arouse in the reader questions concerning the degree to which different cultures influence children and their art. Moreover, they suggest questions that come to the art teacher's mind concerning artistic development across the cultures.

Wilson and Wilson present an inquiry that relates a process by which children learn about their culturally unique world; this process is one of reinvention, in which the symbolic artifacts are received and recycled in the children's own play, dramas, and drawings. The Wilsons describe their mode of inquiry as they ask a set of questions concerning the pervasiveness of the contemporary culture on children's drawings. In so doing, they provide for the teacher a method of inquiry for cross-cultural research which focuses on the differences rather than the similarities in children's drawings. Such differences reveal the diverse worlds into which children enculturate themselves and which they are conceptualizing in their narrative drawings. This interest in questioning these differences causes the authors to remark about art teachers: "One frequently hears art educators say that children's art is the same all over the world, that it is, in fact, a universal language. Our data present quite another picture—one in which children from diverse cultures draw with distinct cultural styles in order to depict particular symbolic versions of vastly different worlds."

After these two articles, which provoke the art teacher to begin asking questions, Eisner completes this section of the book with an article that focuses the art educator's attention onto the essential concerns of any form of cross-cultural research, inquiry, or questioning. He does not hesitate to say that research is systematic, is composed of careful inquiry, and is wider than quantification or empiricism. Like the Wilsons, Eisner declares that it is the differences among the cultures and modes of art teaching that the art teacher inquires into to see what makes cross-cultural research actually cross-cultural. It is cross-cultural research that takes the art teacher out of familiar contexts and shows different settings for art teaching and classroom approaches that are guided by ideas and practices which are based upon other assumptions. In so doing, cross-cultural research provides art teachers with the opportunity to test and refine their own beliefs by checking them against the performances of art teachers in different cultures.

Part I of this book, therefore, provides formats which teachers can understand as a basis for inquiry into cross-cultural research; it also supplies models for inquiry by relating potentials and prospects for art teachers to begin their personal work in cross-cultural art education.

Cultural Influences on Children's Drawings A Developmental Perspective*

S. William Ives and Howard Gardner

INTRODUCTION

Consider the following "thought experiment." A collection of hundreds of drawings produced by children from a score of cultures is presented to a group of experts on children's art work. All identifying marks are removed from the drawings and the experts are asked to indicate the cultures from which each of the drawings came. Following this introductory exercise, an even more difficult problem is posed. Now the experts are presented with drawings from the same children, but this time all the youngsters have been instructed to draw precisely the same subject matter: a person standing next to a tree. Once again, our cadre of experts is challenged to designate the cultural source and the age group of each of the collected drawings.

To our knowledge, neither of these thought experiments has ever been conducted. It is simply not known whether some experts, or even any expert, could accurately indicate the age, sex, or ethnic background of the youthful producers of a representative set of drawings. Nor is it known what criteria would be of special help in accomplishing this task: use of color, shape of figures, command of perspective and foreshortening, style of line, or some combinations of these factors.

Whether it is possible to identify the source of children's drawings is more than an interesting puzzle or academic exercise. Indeed, this issue

*Preparation of this chapter was facilitated by grants from the Spencer Foundation and the National Institute of Education (G–78–0031).

touches on crucial aspects of the growth of the child as well as the optimal regime for education in the arts. If it should be the case that children's drawings from disparate regions are easily identified as such, if each culture leaves its traces in a readily recognizable fashion, this set of results suggests that the culture assumes a determinant role in children's artistic growth. Moreover, such a set of findings would provide comfort and support for those art educators who stress the need for exposure to the works of others, to formal instructions, to tasks like copying, and to other intrusions (or stimulations) by the surrounding milieu. If, on the other hand, drawings from various corners of the earth turn out to be quite similar to one another, difficult or impossible to correctly classify, this outcome suggests that the major factors in artistic growth are processes of universal unfolding. Such a set of results would be consistent with the position that artistic growth is a natural evolving process, one which ought to unfold with little interference—be it instruction, modeling, or reinforcement—from the persons and institutions of the surrounding cultures. To be sure, determination of the variety in children's drawings across cultures does not (and should not) in itself constitute a prescription of how education ought to be done. Nonetheless, at the very least, information about the identifiability of diverse children's drawings is powerful data on which any theory—and practice—of aesthetic education ought to be based.

Because the above thought experiments have not been performed, we lack definitive information on the effect of culture on children's drawings. Still, it should be possible to make a preliminary assessment, at least offer a tentative set of hypotheses, about the extent to which and the manner in which the culture affects drawings by children of various ages. Our sources for the inquiry to be undertaken in the pages that follow are twofold. On the one hand, there are scattered studies and even more scattered anecdotes that provide valuable information about the drawings of children from various cultures, their variation from one another, which materials they employ, which objects are represented, and the like. Any inquiry into cultural effects on art logically begins with a review of this wealth of materials. The second, more novel source guiding this inquiry is a framework for understanding children's general growth—the point of view that has come to be known in contemporary psychology as the "developmental approach." A developmental perspective indicates the general course through which all children pass during the opening decades of life; it includes cognitive, social, and affective aspects and indicates the points at which cultural influences can be expected to have the most decisive effect. Taken together, the existing information on children's drawings and the organizational perspective provided by the developmental framework should allow us to offer an initial response to the questions raised above. And even if our own speculations prove to be ill-founded, they can at least provide a point of view which researchers can explore in their efforts to find a more definite answer to the role of culture in the child's production of drawings.

THE DEVELOPMENTAL APPROACH

As framed by Jean Piaget and some of his followers (namely, Elkind and Flavell 1969; Furth 1969; Piaget and Inhelder 1969), the developmental approach invokes a number of assumptions. To begin with, it is assumed that children are not merely miniature adults. Rather, in the course of their growth they pass through a series of qualitatively different stages and during each one they think in a characteristic way about the world of persons and objects. Infants know the world through their sensory systems and their motor behaviors; toddlers can use symbols of various sorts (words, pictures, gestures) to denote and organize the world; and adolescents are able to reason about hypothetical possibilities through the use of verbal or mathematical propositions.

The particular stages through which children pass are genetically determined. Each normal child, living in a reasonable environment, will eventually pass through the same stages in the same order. However, the point of view developed by Piaget and other developmentalists is not nativist, for in no sense is the child born with these various forms of knowledge. Rather, these stages unfold ineluctably as a result of children's interactions with the world around them and particularly their actions upon the world of physical and social objects. Since a significant part of the surrounding world is the culture in which children live (including its institutions and its artifacts), and since all children are acted upon and must in turn act upon the culture in which they live, there is a distinct (though often unappreciated) role within the developmental framework for the effect of the culture on the child.

We will here review three of the principal stages of development. In each case we will offer a general picture of that stage and then consider more specific aspects of drawing at that time. In this way, we will be extrapolating from a general developmental framework to consider an area of growth—that of the graphic arts—about which relatively little has yet been established (cf. Gardner and Wolf 1978). However, two aspects of our analysis go beyond standard developmental treatments and these should be briefly indicated at this point.

First, the developmental framework has been relatively insensitive— or blind—to the particular symbolic medium in which knowledge is captured and conveyed. For the standard Piagetian, it makes no difference whether information is presented in verbal, pictorial, mathematical, or gestural form: so long as the content is basically constant, children's general level of knowledge (their "cognitive stage") will determine their perception of that domain. We believe, however, that, particularly in the arts, specific symbolic media may well influence—or even determine—the nature and level of the child's apprehension. The very child who is linguistically precocious or musically gifted may be apprehending the visual-graphic realm in a much different (and developmentally less sophisticated) manner. As some of the current research and discussion of the cognitive nature of symbolic activity has shown (for example, Gardner 1977; Gardner, Wolf, and Smith 1975; Golomb 1974; Ives 1978; Olson 1970; Smith 1978), the use of different media and their underlying symbol systems involve different mental operations. Therefore, representation in any single medium (that is, paint, clay) or symbol system (verbal language, graphic image making) does not directly capture the extent of a child's understanding; each medium places its own limitations on what can be expressed and tends to pull out different aspects of the child's thought. In what follows, therefore, we will be stressing the nature and "demand characteristics" of graphic media to a greater extent than is traditionally found in developmental treatments.

Our second deviation from the developmental perspective inheres in our consideration of the culture's effect on the child. To the extent that specific aspects of culture are considered in developmental treatments (and they often are not), the culture is assumed to be relatively fixed, to exert much the same influence independent of age, developmental stage, and the like. In our view, however, the culture is a dynamic, ever-changing set of influences; it works its effects in different ways on children of diverse ages and is in turn apprehended in quite different ways, depending upon the sophistication and medium preferences of the young child. Thus, to a much greater extent than is usually the case, we will probe the ways in which specific aspects of cultures may exert their effects at various points in the developmental cycle.

PRINCIPAL STAGES IN THE DEVELOPMENT OF CHILDREN'S DRAWINGS

The Dominance of Universal Patterns (Ages 1 to 5)

One of the greatest contributions of developmental psychology has been to sketch out the patterns that all normal children follow as they first begin to explore the world of objects and persons. Whether they live in an urban industrialized society, a preliterate tribal culture, or a nomadic desert group, youngsters all negotiate the same steps as they come to discover the nature of objects, the actions that can be performed upon them, and the ways that these objects relate to one another. Knowledge of the basic temporal, spatial, and causal relations which govern objects is generally acquired by the age of eighteen months, the conclusion of the so-called sensori-motor stage. In the ensuing years the child comes to know those cultural artifacts—words, pictures, gestures, and numbers—which can denote objects, groups of objects, and their relations. By the age of five or so, children are quite fluent in the use of such symbol systems. They can describe in words their own experiences; can readily understand the sentences, descriptions, and stories of others; and have attained a basic understanding of the number system, the realm of musical patterns, and the way that gestures can be used to express, enhance, or modulate meanings. Again, what has strikingly emerged from studies in many cultures is the remarkably similar way in which children negotiate this pair of milestones: the acquisitions of knowledge of the sensori-motor world and of an initial fluency with the most universal symbol systems.

Nearly all experts who have considered the early evolution of children's drawings find quite striking parallels across the full range of human cultures. (See, for example, Belo 1955; Goodnow 1977; Kellogg 1969; and Lark-Horovitz, Lewis, and Luca 1967). Assuming that they have available the materials with which to make marks, children begin scribbling in the second year of life; start to monitor their scribbles, to place marks near other marks, and to imitate the marks of others by their second birthday; create simple forms, like circles and crosses, in their third year; combine these forms into composites, like mandalas, at about the age of three; and are producing simple but recognizable schemas, like tadpoles and suns, by the age of four. Even after these schemas have evolved, drawing continues to follow a universal pattern for at least another year. And from all over the world, children's houses, dogs, cars, girls, boys, trees, and flowers are astonishingly alike in their visual forms.

It might therefore be concluded that the culture exerts little or no influence on children's drawing during the first five years of life. (And, indeed, as a first approximation, this statement is reasonable.) Nonetheless, inasmuch as all knowledge proceeds from an interaction with the environment, the specific nature of the environment within which the child develops does exert its impact even in these opening "universal" years. As extreme examples, one can consider a culture in which there are neither marking implements nor surfaces on which to make marks, or, alternatively, a culture in which these materials are available but in which exists strong prescriptions against their use by preschoolers. In either case, one can safely assume that none of the children in these cultures would have passed through the allegedly universal scheme described above.

But even in the absence of these extreme cultural interferences, the impacts of the surrounding society on the child's early drawing can be readily identified. One area in which the influence is great is in the media of expression made available for the child. If, for example, as in Taleland (Fortes 1938), there are no markers available but plenty of clay, the child will progress into three-dimensional representation but will have little opportunity to explore two-dimensional media. If within two-dimensional expression children have only fine-haired brushes available, their opportunities to vary lines, to produce thick swatches of color, or to make broad circular forms will be fewer than if they have available a range of markers, pencils, and pens. Evidence of the effects of such availability comes from Bernbaum's (1974) study in Honduras. Unschooled children had difficulty copying geometric forms with a pencil, a medium unfamiliar to them; however, when allowed to copy forms through the familiar practice of finger drawing in the sand, their performances improved greatly.

The kinds of referents available in the culture and the attitudes of adults toward those referents constitute another area in which the culture exerts an early influence on children's drawings. One eighteen-month-old child who had been making circular markings for some weeks switched to a series of lines after being exposed to pieces of notebook paper that were lined in red. Two months later, this same child had evolved a scheme for making a bounded circle as well as one for making vertical lines. As a member of a *Sesame Street* culture, she soon learned to apply labels to these contrasting forms, calling the circular forms "0" and the linear forms "1" or "I." Back and forth lines were called "N." It is quite likely that the child would have produced these same forms even if never exposed to lined paper or to a televised children's program. But the time at which these schemas were developed, and the uses to which they were put in communicating with other individuals, doubtless reflected the occasion of their initial encounters within a given cultural context.

A third area in which the media affect early drawing involves the kinds of referents which the child is likely to depict (Smith 1978). Using paint, children are likely to represent fire, rain, or grass. Using clay, they will designate food, snakes, and balls. Using blocks, they are likely to depict tunnels, things to carry, and buildings. Once again, the general structural principles used for these vehicles are rather similar across instances, and yet, once the child proceeds beyond the most elementary schemas, the particular options available within the medium will exert effects on each representation. Thus, the child depicting a house with blocks is likely to explore arches and staircases; the child working with paint will draw windows, trees, and suns; the youngster modeling a dwelling out of clay is likely to produce a single cube-like mound and then attach to it as separate elements a chimney, an antenna, a mailbox, and other entities that can readily be designated by a single piece of clay.

Thus, even as the availability of media and the naming practices of the culture exert influences at an early age, so, too, the structure of the media per se have their impact during the first years of life. Among others, Golomb (1974) and Olson (1970) have shown that the child's apparent knowledge of a given graphic domain, like the human form or diagonality, will differ dramatically, depending upon the particular medium in which this knowledge is tested. For instance, presented with a set of isolated elements and asked to combine them, children are more able to produce an acceptable diagonal or to produce a human figure with component parts than is likely to occur when they are required to produce these forms "from scratch" or "from scribble." By the same token, the facets of a given referent stressed by children will reflect the nature of the medium with which they are working. For example, consider the works of a three-year-old boy who liked to create "water works." When working with paint, he recorded the flow of water by moving the paint-filled brush over the flat surface of the paper, even as he left out the context within which the water moved. In contrast, when working with clay, he traced with his finger the movement of the water from one bump in the clay to another, but did not leave any record of that movement in the three-dimensional medium. Thus, the clay medium created the context in which the water moved but relied on the young artist's gestural and verbal descriptions to supplement the presentation.

The Flowering of Drawing: A Time of Transition (Ages 5 to 7)

By the age of five or so, young children are already quite competent within their personal milieu. They have consolidated their knowledge of persons and objects; have gained an initial grasp of the dominant symbolic forms of their culture; have established enduring relationships with the individuals around them; and are already able to use language to communicate their basic wants, needs, and experiences. Indeed, this period is a time of symbolic fluency, a time of flowering in the expressive domain. Children can produce lengthy stories, numerous tunes and their variations, charming dances, and gestural sequences. Their "works" already have gone beyond single elements to assume a scene-like quality, and they have inferred the basic grammar governing the various domains with which they are familiar.

A number of important trends also mark this point. Language increasingly controls much of children's behavior, as they become able to plan and then carry out a set of actions. Children's egocentrism declines, as they are able to adopt others' viewpoints, to anticipate how they would conceive of a specific situation, to expect a certain response, and then to react on the basis of that expectation. Children are also coming to know the institutions of their society, the schools, churches, games, and rituals: no longer simply a part of their nuclear family, youngsters are invading the larger community within which that family resides.

These factors and influences leave their imprint on children's graphic activities. Having passed beyond a set of simple though serviceable forms, children can now vary their basic schemas, producing not just a house but a large house, a small house, a red house, a firehouse, and even a scary house and a happy house. Elements can be organized into scenes, so children are now drawing houses on streets and with cars, suns, and flowers properly arrayed around them. They can plan on a drawing, make adjustments so that the plans are faithfully carried out, begin to anticipate what others will think of these drawings, and then make further adjustments accordingly. And they can make (and revise) drawings in such a way that their drawings will be interpretable by others without the need for special instructions (Korzenik 1977).

Such factors have led some authorities to consider the age of five to seven as a time of transition in the child's development (White 1965). At this point the child is seen as moving from behavior patterns that are basically dominated by genetic and universal environmental factors to those that occur largely at the behest of the specific culture in which the child happens to live. In other words, children are seen as poised between capacities that they must develop by virtue of their membership in the normal human species (such as the capacities to draw representationally, to produce simple schemas, and to vary them for specific purposes) and those capacities which are only likely to develop, and to flourish, by dint of their living in a specific cultural surrounding (such as the capacities to render perspective, to make caricatures, and the like).

Possibly because children are at a point of transition in so many areas, the works by children at this age have a very special quality. Their categories and classifications have begun to be formed but have not yet become crystallized, solidified, or rigid. Therefore, their drawings are recognizable and clear without being clichés or stereotypes; they feature invigorating combinations of colors and forms, ones which often possess a special charm and liveliness for adults in our culture, without being so idiosyncratic or wild that we find ourselves unable to relate to them. Indeed, the special flavor of these drawings, their fusion of universal with individualized features, their mixing of reality and fantasy, their blending of canonical and anomalous colors, forms, and patterns, have led us to consider this age as a time of artistic flowering, a time in which the expressiveness of children's art works bears at least a superficial resemblance to some of the most treasured of adult forms, for example, the twentieth-century child-like art of such artists as Klee, Picasso, and Miro.

Whether the drawings of specific children of this age reflect the universal factors of earlier years or the cultural influences of the school years depends on several factors. A first consideration is the extent to which the culture intrudes itself upon children. Those children who live in societies where schooling begins earlier, or where children are from an early age surrounded by peers, are more likely to produce drawings which bear the stamp of that culture than are children in societies in which influences from the surrounding culture are still minimal. A second factor is the rate of development of the specific child. Those children who are progressing more rapidly through the principal stages of development, who have already made the transition to symbolic fluency, are more likely to attend to cultural factors than are those children who are still working out the basic grammar of the medium and who have not yet reached the point where language dominates action. Certainly, the opportunities for copying, and the constraints placed by adults and peers on such mimetic activity, constitute another potent influence upon children's drawings. Thus, those children who arrive at means of depiction primarily through their own explorations—for example, those who fashion x-ray drawings in which the interiors as well as the exteriors of objects are rendered—are less likely to reflect their cultural surroundings than are those children who observe an artist-model on television and then faithfully copy his efforts.

While the factors cited above have a general effect on children's drawing, certain cultural devices can have a more specific and possibly more potent impact. One obviously influential candidate is writing. Children initially view all graphic marks as similar; only with experience do they differentiate writing from drawing (Lurcat 1974). However, this is a gradual process and many young children continue to decorate their letters and write on their drawings.

More specific effects have been noted as well. Whereas preschool children in Israel and America both draw circles clockwise, American school children draw circles counterclockwise in a manner similar to the way in which they pen the letter O (Goodnow, Friedman, Bernbaum, and Lehman 1973). As further examples, Dennis and Raskin (1960) report that in cultures where writing begins on the left, children are likely to place figures on the left side of the page, while Goodnow (1977) indicates that figure drawings of preschool Australian children proceed from right to left whereas older children who have learned to write, draw figures from left to right. The distinction between Hebrew scripts where letters are formed from left to right and Arabic script where both script and individual characters are formed right to left also has its effects upon drawings. Arab-Israeli children generally draw lines from left to right in kindergarten but shift to a right to left drawing direction as they learn to write; Jewish-Israeli children, however, maintain a consistent left to right direction in drawing lines after they have acquired writing skills (Lieblich, Ninio, and Kugelmass 1975). Finally, the overall conceptual organization modeled in school may also have an effect on drawing procedures. Bernbaum (1974) found that unschooled children in Honduras do not exhibit a consistent top to bottom strategy in copying complex forms, whereas schooled children in America and Australia (Ghent 1961; Goodnow 1977; Goodnow and Levine 1973) move reliably from top to bottom in their drawings.

It seems quite clear, then, that certain potent cultural forces, such as the centrality of writing, begin early on to influence the way in which children go about their drawings, both in terms of which lines they are likely to use and the way in which these lines are realized on the paper. It is less clear that these differences are sufficiently substantive to affect the overall impact and character of drawings; and given the numerous ways in which schooled and unschooled societies differ, it would be difficult to attribute overall differences in drawing simply to the presence of literacy. Nonetheless, the studies cited above offer ample evidence that the culture influences drawing in quite specific ways during the period of artistic flowering and developmental transition.

The Height of Cultural Influences (Ages 7 to 12)

Eight- or nine-year-old children are well socialized and enculturated individuals. Secure in the knowledge of their physical world, fluent in symbolic capacities, they now confront head-on a major challenge: to come to know in detail the practices, rules, customs, and mores of their society. This act of familiarization and mastery is essential if they are to become members of their culture in good standing, if they are to know which behaviors, actions, and thoughts are expected of them, as well as which are proscribed by the surrounding culture.

However, learning about the culture is more than a simple cultural imperative. It also appears to be the way in which children naturally proceed. Having worked out, as it were, the universal patterns of growth contained in the genotype, they now appear to require intensive exposure to their culture; they need, in other words, to discover the specific ways in which their specific culture modulates the basic domains of human experience: language, drawing, music, sports, social norms, and the like. Therefore, the children actively turn to others in their surroundings—to elders, peers, teachers, and masters—to observe how they accomplish their daily activities, to attend carefully to the details of their behaviors, and to copy them as faithfully as possible, so that eventually, as young adults, they can produce proper instances of these activities.

In many ways, this is an extremely constructive period for children. They are interested in learning, classifying, categorizing, and mastering modes of knowledge. Whether or not theirs is a "schooled society," they can be avid students. (They may watch the making of canoes, the playing of instruments, the hunting of caribou, even if they do not read history, learn to perform sums, or tinker in the chemistry laboratory.) Yet, in learning how to do things, there is always a cost, for certain activities and practices become taboo—things *not* to do. And because, during a time of learning, one needs to focus on what is *right*, as well as what is wrong, there is a tendency during this period to become extremely literal-minded. Children want games to be played in an absolutist manner, and they brook no tinkering with rules; they want language to be used in a precise manner and show little tolerance for figurative departures; and, in the case of drawing, they become extremely attuned to what seems to be favored and spurned in the society in which they live and look.

The effects of this "literal" or "latency stage" have been widely documented in our own culture. For one thing, children come to draw much less, and many children cease drawing almost completely (Gardner 1973; Lowenfeld 1947; Read 1943). Those that draw do so in a variety of ways and for a variety of purposes, but in general they place a strong premium on visual realism. Children want drawings to look like the things which they designate. This means that they want to draw objects in the real world (not abstract designs) and that they want to draw those objects in such a way that they look as much as possible like photographs and like the objects they designate. They accordingly scorn drawings that are illusionistic or fanciful; they seek realistic models; they solicit help in making accurate renditions; and they become frustrated when their own drawings fall short of these demanding criteria of verisimilitude.

The progress of drawing during the preteen years, then, is dual-edged. On the one hand, children are eager to learn, acquire skills, understand how drawings are rendered, and attain these skills for themselves. They are often ideal students, and certainly this period appears to be an optimal time for classroom instruction, perhaps including exposure to models for copying. On the other hand, however, there is regrettable shrinkage in the kinds of materials and subject matter that children are willing to render and the ways in which they are willing to render them. And, if children's absolutist standards are not met, there is the unpalatable possibility that they will altogether cease their drawing activity.

The sketch of the "latency period" has thus far focused entirely on the child's drawing progress within a Western culture, more specifically, within America and Western Europe. Much less is known about the variety of drawing trajectories in diverse cultures during this period of growth. Nonetheless, the available evidence suggests that at this time children the world over begin to make drawings which at least in some cases clearly bear the stamp of their culture. In those societies that feature strong stylization—for example, in Bali—the drawings of the five-year-olds look little different from those of American five-year-olds; however, drawings by the average Balinese child aged eight, nine, or ten can be readily identified and is readily distinguished from those of American peers (Belo 1955). Other rendering practices are also acquired by youngsters. For example, in adult Chinese art, scenes are usually drawn as if viewed from a small rise above the depicted elements (Goodnow 1977). Interestingly, this same tendency can be observed in the drawings of contemporary Chinese youths (*Pictures by Chinese Children*, 1976) and might even suffice to identify these drawings amongst a larger collection of preteen artistic productions. The relative importance placed upon visual realism should also affect children's drawings. The illusion of photographic accuracy is not a part of the valued art traditions of central and southern Africa (Stevens 1930; Wangboje 1970); consequently, drawings produced by children in these cultures exhibit little concern with issues like linear perspective (Deregowski 1972, 1978; Mundy-Castle 1969).

When a premium is placed within a culture on certain aspects of picturing, then one can expect to find a specific developmental progression for those domains. In Western culture, for example, the acquisition of linear perspective based on Euclidean coordinates is a highly valued achievement. Thus, as early as age eight or nine most children make initial attempts to create drawings from a single perspective and to depict objects in proper proportion (see Freeman and Janikoun 1972; Lewis and Livson 1967). A series of stages is negotiated which culminates in the early teen years in quite accurate renditions of pictorial depth. Another domain of import in Western culture is the ability to map a spatial terrain. During the school years, children often independently attempt to draw maps of their surroundings, and, increasingly, mapping exercises have become part of the standard school curriculum. Thus, by their early teens or sooner most American and Australian youngsters can fashion maps that quite effectively capture spatial and size relationships (Goodnow 1977; Ives, Houseworth, and Pond 1978). In contrast, youngsters of an equivalent age in isolated mountain villages in Nepal, when asked how to get from home to school, generally produce pictures of their surroundings in which little effort is made to capture proper spatial correspondence (Dart and Pradhan 1967).

A number of other influences on children's drawings should also be noted. Quite often members of each sex make characteristic drawings. Thus, at least within our culture, drawings depicting combat and space exploration dominate the works of boys, whereas more pastoral and person-related scenes pervade the output of girls. Even within the area of combat, sex differences can be noted; boys tend to portray fighting in the context of team sports, armies, and other rule-governed activities, whereas girls portray fighting as direct, unstructured conflict between two people, generally friends and relatives (Feinburg 1977). Sex influences have also been noted in drawings from other cultures. Thurber (1976) analyzed the drawings from a group of Navaho kindergarteners and first graders in a community that is rapidly being assimilated into American society. He found fewer sex differences than in traditional Navaho communities, where only males are allowed to engage in artistic activities. By the same token, Laosa, Swartz, and Diaz-Guerrero (1974) found that Mexican children were more likely than American children to differentiate sex in their drawings, quite possibly because of the sharper distinctions among sexes made in Latin cultures.

Attitudes held by members of the culture are also registered in children's drawings. Dennis (1966) documented that the kinds of persons, clothing, and life styles admired in a given culture proliferate in the drawings of children of that culture. Particularly striking is the fact that members of minorities, especially abused minorities, rarely draw themselves or their own customs but instead choose to render representations of the "dominant culture." However, this type of representation may change as children become involved in movements to promote cultural pride and identity, just as recent changes have been reported in the self-identity of black children in the United States and their subsequent choices in symbolic activity (Hraba and Grant 1970; Moore 1976).

Other cultural values are also reflected reliably in drawings from a given culture. For instance, consistent with the premium placed on smiling and friendliness in Thailand, drawings by Thai children feature relatively more smiling (Gardiner 1974); correlatively, the emphasis on cooperation and work in New Zealand and Canada has resulted in a proclivity to depict these themes (Smart and Smart 1975). It is also probable that the general value placed by a society on visual depiction may affect the products of the youngsters. Thus, the high performance of Japanese students on a visual version of an intelligence test (a mean IQ of 138) has been attributed to the overall emphasis within that culture on visual expression (Hilger, Klett, and Watson 1976).

While the culture's influence on children's drawing during the years of schooling has been amply documented, it would be an oversimplification to maintain that the culture becomes wholly determinant. For one thing, many of the factors cited above reflect differences in the content favored across cultures or in the standards invoked in the making and judging of drawings. Much less is known about whether the actual ways in which the same subject matter is rendered differ materially across cultures, and, if it differs, whether it differs on only one or on a variety of dimensions. Furthermore, there are other aspects of drawings—such as the extent to which children can draw objects from a noncanonical point of view— which appear to develop in a similar fashion across a variety of cultures (Ives and Houseworth 1978; Ives and Rovet 1978). In other words, about those topics generally considered most central in drawing—command of the medium; exhibition of aesthetic properties; the ability to use lines, forms, and colors in certain ways—little is known of the degree to which different cultures can (or do) influence the youngsters growing up within their borders. This may be, in part, because these features are less apparent to observers and have been less important to researchers than the most obvious criteria of subject matter, prevalence of drawing, and general cultural attitudes.

Later Drawings: Some Concluding Remarks

Developmental psychologists have found that adolescence is a time of rapid change. The youth becomes able to think on a much more abstract plane, to reason on the level of propositions, to entertain hypothetical possibilities, and even to construct and test theories. There are equally compelling changes in the affective and social realms, as the passage of puberty brings in its wake a heightened interest in sexual matters, a capacity for deep emotional involvements, and a potential for anticipating the feelings, desires, and wants of others. Possibly as a product of these cognitive, social, and affective influences, adolescents become newly concerned with themselves—with the establishment of an identity, or sense of self, with which they are comfortable. However, in a genuine sense, this involvement with self is a cultural phenomenon, too, for the kind of self evolved by a youth must make sense within the cultural milieu in which he or she lives.

Relatively little has been established about the drawing of adolescents in our culture, and there is even less concerning the art works of adolescents in other parts of the world. We do know that the decline in artistry plagues many adolescents, quite possibly because the rise in their critical faculties is sharp: often their own artistic output seems so wanting that children in desperation discontinue their production. We know too of an increasing command of the ability to handle aspects of volume, shape, and other technical facets of artistry, as well as a heightened involvement in exploring the realms of persons and feelings. Whereas the drawings of the pre-teenager tend to highlight external scenes and to avoid psychological issues, the adolescent who draws is likely to create many portraits, self-portraits, depictions of interpersonal situations, and explorations of the depths of emotions and feelings. It must be stressed, however, that the youngsters who go on to draw, and can do so at a high level, constitute a distinct minority in our culture, at least when it comes to any public exhibition of their works. The extent to which adolescents draw solely for their own satisfaction, or to fulfill their own needs, is simply not known.

Given the adolescents' awareness of their culture, as well as their increasing knowledge of artistic practices and standards, one could predict certain outcomes among adolescents who draw. Children now have the option of drawing in a number of styles and rendering techniques: those with necessary skill are likely to become more pluralistic in their values—unlike the pre-teenager who has tolerance only for realism, the adolescent can explore illusionistic, abstract, and other nonrepresentational forms. Art carrying social, political, or historical content now also becomes a possibility, as the child comes to appreciate the fact that art can be used to make statements of this sort. Similarly, aware of the possibility of exploring hypothetical worlds, youths may also invent their own styles of graphic representation, their own notations, decorations, characterizations, stylizations, and the like.

Whether adolescents continue their artistry, and if so, in what way, remains a complicated issue, one intertwined with the personality of the individuals in question. Certainly one would expect the cultural norms to play an important role here. Where the educational system in general and the "art world" in particular are devoted to national art forms that serve social needs, one would expect a lessening of individual differences in favor of a common, popular mode of expression. In contrast, in societies which heighten individualism and cherish originality, a range of adolescent styles can be anticipated. Whether there is a discrepancy between what children do in school and what they do when on their own, and whether the art education community is generally conservative and jealous of traditions or liberal and in search of new forms, will doubtless have an impact on the nature of the youth's work (Hurwitz 1976, 1977). General opportunities for a career in the arts, as well as the culture's attitude toward artistic practice as an avocation, will certainly determine how many individuals eventually become artists, proficient artists, and masters.

The above survey has suggested our lamentable ignorance concerning artistic development across cultures. Much of our survey has had to be speculative and programmatic rather than (as we would have preferred) summary and conclusive. It is clear that we cannot pass the stronger version of the test cited above. Once the obvious identificatory elements were removed we would be unable to identify the sources of most art works, and we are skeptical that a panel of experts would do much better. It seems reasonable to assume that recognition would prove most difficult for the preschool years and that, during the years where training is at its height, one could make shrewd guesses concerning the standards, if not the actual locale, of the culture in which the drawing was made. Making an equivalent determination about adolescent art might well prove more difficult because so little of that art has been collected and because the overall attitudes toward art within given cultures might interact in unpredictable ways with individual proclivities that had developed in earlier years. Nonetheless, we retain a lingering confidence that individual predispositions, genetic potentials, and cultural influences should interact in ways which can in principle be specified, though as scientists we are still far from knowing what these ways will be. Perhaps if a similarly framed review article is written in fifty years, our successors will be able to provide a convincing answer to the puzzle that we have posed.

REFERENCES

Belo, J. "Balinese Children's Drawings." In *Childhood in Contemporary Cultures*, edited by M. Mead and M. Wolfenstein. Chicago: Univ. of Chicago Press, 1955.

Bernbaum, M. "Accuracy in Children's Copying: The Role of Different Stroke Sequences and School Experience." Ph.D. diss., George Washington Univ., 1974.

Dart, F.E., and P.L. Pradhan. "The Cross-Cultural Teaching of Science." *Science* 155 (1967): 649–56.

Dennis, W. *Group Values Through Children's Drawings.* New York: Wiley, 1966.

Dennis, W., and E. Raskin. "Further Evidence Concerning the Effect of Handwriting Habits on the Location of Drawings." *Journal of Consulting Psychology* 24 (1960): 548–49.

Deregowski, J.B. "Drawing Ability of Soli Rural Children: A Note." *Journal of Social Psychology* 86 (1972): 311–12.

———. "Cross-Cultural Studies of Drawing." Paper read at the "What is a Picture?" Conference, April 1978, at Philadelphia.

Elkind, D., and J.H. Flavell, eds. *Studies in Cognitive Development: Essays in Honor of Jean Piaget.* London: Oxford Univ. Press, 1969.

Feinburg, S.G. "Conceptual Content and Spatial Characteristics in Boys' and Girls' Drawings of Fighting and Helping." *Studies in Art Education* 18 (1977): 63–72.

Fortes, M. "Social and Psychological Aspects of Education in Taleland." *Africa* 11 (1938): 1–64.

Freeman, N., and R. Janikoun. "Intellectual Realism in Children's Drawings of a Familiar Object With Distinctive Features." *Child Development* 43 (1972): 1116–21.

Furth, H. *Piaget and Knowledge.* Englewood Cliffs, N.J.: Prentice-Hall, 1969.

Gardiner, H.W. "Human Figure Drawings as Indicators of Value Development Among Thai Children." *Journal of Cross-Cultural Psychology* 5 (1974): 124–30.

Gardner, H. *The Arts and Human Development.* New York: Wiley, 1973.

———. "Senses, Symbols, and Operations: An Organization of Artistry." In *The Arts and Cognition*, edited by D. Perkins and B. Leondar. Baltimore: Johns Hopkins Univ. Press, 1977.

Gardner, H., and D. Wolf. "First Drawings: Notes on the Relationships Between Perception and Production." Paper read at the "What is a Picture?" Conference, April 1978, at Philadelphia.

Gardner, H.; D. Wolf; and A. Smith. "Artistic Symbols in Early Childhood." *New York University Education Quarterly* 6, no. 4 (1975): 13–21.

Ghent, L. "Form and Its Orientation: A Child's Eye View." *American Journal of Psychology* 74 (1961): 177–90.

Golomb, C. *Young Children's Painting and Sculpture.* Cambridge, Mass.: Harvard Univ. Press, 1974.

Goodnow, J.J. *Children's Drawing.* Cambridge, Mass.: Harvard Univ. Press, 1977.

Goodnow, J.J.; S. Friedman; M. Bernbaum; and E.B. Lehman. "Direction and Sequence in Copying: The Effect of Learning to Write in English and Hebrew." *Journal of Cross-Cultural Psychology* 4 (1973): 263–82.

Goodnow, J.J., and R. Levine. "The Grammar of Action: Sequence and Syntax in Children's Copying of Simple Shapes." *Cognitive Psychology* 4 (1973): 82–98.

Hilger, M.I.; W.G. Klett; and C.G. Watson. "Performance of Ainu and Japanese Six-year-olds on the Goodenough-Harris Drawing Test." *Perceptual and Motor Skills* 42 (1976): 435–38.

Hraba, J., and G. Grant. "Black is Beautiful: A Reexamination of Racial Preferences and Identity." *Journal of Personality and Social Psychology* 16 (1970): 398.

Hurwitz, A. "School Art: The Search for an Avante-Garde." In *The Arts, Human Development, and Education*, edited by E.W. Eisner. Berkeley: McCutchan, 1976.

———. "On Advanced Technology-Related Art Teaching at the Primary and Secondary Schools of Newton, Mass., U.S.A." *Leonardo: International Journal of the Contemporary Artist* 10, no. 2 (1977): 101–5.

Ives, S.W. "Children's Ability to Coordinate Spatial Perspectives Through Structural Descriptions." In *Explorations in Inner Space: Aspects of the Nature and Development of Spatial Cognition*, edited by D. Olson and E. Bialystok. Hillsdale, N.J.: Erlbaum, 1978.

Ives, S.W., and M. Houseworth. "The Role of Canonical Orientations in Children's Drawings of Relationships." Unpublished paper, Harvard Univ., 1978.

Ives, S.W.; M. Houseworth; and J. Pond. "The Development of Children's Mapping Abilities Through Drawings and Language: Preliminary Findings." *MAEA Bulletin* (Spring 1978): 4–6.

Ives, S.W., and J. Rovet. "The Role of Graphic Orientations in Children's Drawings of Familiar and Novel Objects in Motion." Unpublished paper, Harvard Univ., 1978.

Kellogg, R. *Analyzing Children's Art.* Palo Alto, Calif.: National Press Books, 1969.

Korzenik, D. "Saying It With Pictures." In *The Arts and Cognition*, edited by D. Perkins and B. Leondar. Baltimore: Johns Hopkins Univ. Press, 1977.

Laosa, L.M.; J.D. Swartz; and R. Diaz-Guerrero. "Perceptual-Cognitive and Personality Development of Mexican and Anglo-American Children as Measured by Human Figure Drawings." *Developmental Psychology* 10 (1974): 131–39.

Lark-Horovitz, B.; H.P. Lewis; and M. Luca. *Understanding Children's Art for Better Teaching.* Columbus, Ohio: Merrill, 1967.

Lewis, H.P., and N. Livson. "Correlates of Developmental Level of Spatial Representation in Children's Drawings." *Studies in Art Education* 8, no. 2 (1967): 46–57.

Lieblich, A.; A. Ninio; and S. Kugelmass. "Developmental Trends in Directionality of Drawing in Jewish and Arab Israeli Children." *Journal of Cross-Cultural Psychology* 6 (1975): 504–11.

Lowenfeld, V. *Creative and Mental Growth*. New York: Macmillan, 1947.

Lurcat, L. *Etudes de l'acte graphique*. Paris: Mounton, 1974.

Moore, C.L. "The Racial Preference and Attitude of Preschool Black Children." *Journal of Genetic Psychology* 129 (1976): 37–44.

Mundy-Castle, A. Unpublished data, Harvard Univ., 1969.

Olson, D. *Cognitive Development: The Child's Acquisition of Diagonality*. New York: Academic Press, 1970.

Piaget, J., and B. Inhelder. *The Psychology of the Child*. New York: Basic Books, 1969.

Pictures by Chinese Children. Peking: Foreign Language Press, 1976.

Read, H. *Education Through Art*. London: Faber and Faber, 1943.

Smart, R.C., and M.S. Smart. "Group Values Shown in Preadolescents' Drawings in Five English-Speaking Countries." *Journal of Social Psychology* 97 (1975): 23–37.

Smith, N.R. "Developmental Origins of Structure and Variation in Symbol Form." In *Symbolic Functioning in Childhood*, edited by N.R. Smith and M.B. Franklin. Hillsdale, N.J.: Erlbaum, 1978.

Stevens, G.A. "The Future of African Art." *Africa* 3 (1930): 150–60.

Thurber, S. "Changes in Navajo Responses to the Draw-A-Man Test." *Journal of Social Psychology* 99 (1976): 139–40.

Wangboje, S.I. "Some Issues on Art Education in Africa: The Nigerian Experience." In *Education Through Art: Humanism in a Technological Age*, edited by B.J. Davis. Washington: National Art Education Association, 1970.

White, S. "Evidence for a Hierarchical Arrangement of Learning Processes." In *Advances in Child Development and Behavior*, edited by L.P. Lipsitt and C.C. Spiker. Vol. 2. New York: Academic Press, 1965.

The Themes of Children's Story Drawings   A Tale of Four Cultures

Brent Wilson and Marjorie Wilson*

> The many stuffs—matter, energy, waves, phenomena—that worlds are made of are made along with the worlds. But made from what? Not from nothing, after all, but *from other worlds*. Worldmaking as we know it always starts from worlds already on hand; the making is a re-making (Goodman 1978, 6).

Art is a means by which versions of the world or models of reality, of the self, and of the universe are made. As Nelson Goodman (1978, 102) says, these are "versions that are visions, depictions rather than descriptions." Through the graphic and plastic arts, humans recall their collective past, record their present, reflect upon possible futures, and contemplate their conceptions of good and bad.

In the history of art—whether it has taken the form of biblical stories arranged sequentially on the walls of a church (for example, Michelangelo's *Creation* on the ceiling of the Sistine Chapel), of myths of the gods on red and black Greek pottery, of the life of Krishna in painted miniatures, of the "Harlot's Progress" in six engravings by Hogarth, of Wilhelm Busch's "Max und Moritz," of McKay's "Little Nemo," of Walt Disney's "Mickey Mouse," of the superheroes of Marvel Comics' Stan Lee, or of a plethora of television and cinematic narratives—the narrative vision has been the most pervasive. The narrative, executed with characters, setting, and action and including a sequence of events and a conclusion, presents a relatively complete "as-if" working model of the

*We are indebted to Dr. Nabil El Husseini and Dr. Heta Kauppenin for the collection of the Egyptian and Finnish drawings, respectively, and for assistance in the analysis process, and to Bonnie Deutsch, who also assisted with the analysis.

world in which Erikson (1977, 44) calls "the human propensity to create model situations in which aspects of the past are re-lived, the present represented and renewed, and the future anticipated." Erikson notes that dramatic play in childhood "provides the infantile form" of this propensity. In an examination of the sometimes vast spontaneous production of children who frequently draw daily, we have found that for an overwhelming number of these children, drawings also provide a format for creating just such model situations. We have seen, in fact, that the desire to produce these complex narratives serves as the impetus for the drawing activity of these unusual children (Wilson and Wilson 1976, 432). As our interest in this narrative dimension of children's drawings grew, we began to provide children with large sheets of paper divided into six printed frames and to ask them to tell stories through the pictures they drew. In spite of our extensive study of children's spontaneous story drawings, we could not have anticipated the depth, richness, variety, or profound nature of these narratives.

In the first narrative drawings, collected from children in the United States, we were able to observe how pervasively the contemporary culture of the United States was reflected—the superheroes, space creatures, anthropomorphized animals, and, perhaps too often, the view of the world as a threatening and violent place in which difficulties are to be overcome by more violence. Indeed, it was not surprising that the worlds drawn by children and the "many stuffs" of those worlds were created from worlds "already on hand," from familiar worlds, worlds that necessarily reflected the culture in which the children were ensconced.

Because, as Piaget (1972, 27) has said, "In order for a child to understand something, he must construct it himself, he must reinvent it," the process by which children learn about the culturally unique world in which they must live is a process of reinvention, wherein the symbolic artifacts provided by the culture are received and recycled in the children's own play, dramas, and drawings. The questions that thus presented themselves were: Just how idiosyncratic are the graphic narratives of American children? Do children in other cultures produce story drawings with the same themes as those found in the American children's drawings? Are there some themes that are universal? Are there themes that are characteristic to particular cultures? In order to answer these and other related questions, we set out to collect story drawings from other countries.

In addition to the 93 sequential story drawings by nine- and twelve-year-old children from Boston, Massachusetts in the United States, we collected 100 drawings from children of the same ages in Adelaide and Canberra, Australia; 69 drawings from children in Cairo, Egypt; and 58 drawings from children in Helsinki, Finland. (Since this initial collection of story drawings, thousands more have been gathered from children in New Guinea, Brazil, Nigeria, Greece, and Hungary and from Australian Aboriginal and American Navajo, Pueblo, and Zuni Indian children.) In each of these four groups, drawings were collected from middle-class urban children. This sample was not assumed to represent all of the children in the country but was thought to be somewhat typical of advantaged children in each of these large cities.

For the analysis of the story drawings we have developed a complex system including over 200 classifications, some of which deal with themes, with subthematic and plot elements, and with the basic organization of graphic narratives. What we found when we analyzed these narratives was that the four groups generally employed the same themes and structures, but these elements were frequently found in significantly different proportions. It is the differences rather than the similarities with which we are concerned because it is the differences that provide us with insights about the diverse worlds into which the children are enculturating themselves through their drawings.

From Propp's "Morphology of the Folktale" (1968) we have excerpted two basic underlying principal structures: 1. *lack* (where a character either lacks something or desires to have something)/*lack liquidated* (wherein the lack is dissolved by some means); and 2. *villainy/villainy* nullified. Tolkein's prescription for a good fairy tale includes, in addition to fantasy, "recovery, escape, and consolation—recovery from deep despair [Propp's lack liquidated], escape from some great danger [Propp's villainy nullified], but, most of all, consolation"—a happy ending (Bettelheim 1975, 143). To these Bettelheim adds the element of threat (Propp's lack or villainy, p. 144). These are the elements from which, it seems, all good fairy tales are made. Therefore, it should not seem unusual that children's stories should have at their base these same elements.

To growing children, the world-now and the world-to-be may present an awesome and threatening aspect of trials, of lack, and of difficulties to be overcome. Perhaps that is why, when children draw stories, disequilibrating elements appear in great numbers, some as dramatic as those of the Brothers Grimm, others as basic as a little girl lost or another without playmates. Through the creation of these situations in the graphic symbolic mode and the subsequent solution or lack of resolution, children are able to explore and to rehearse a variety of means for surmounting problems or to comprehend more fully the consequences of failure.

In our analysis of the story drawings of the four groups, we saw that the American and Australian children produced over twice the number of lack/excess disequilibrating elements than either the Egyptian or the

American story drawing

Australian story drawing

Egyptian story drawing

Finnish story drawing

Finnish children. Although the second disequilibrium-producing element, villainy, was shown less often than the lack element by children in all four groups, each of the groups showed villainy with the same frequency. As one might expect, the American and Australian children also used the classification of disequilibrium overcome (lack liquidated) more frequently than either of the other groups. This can undoubtedly be explained by the more regular occurrence in the stories of the American and Australian children of the initial lack category.

The reason for these differences is not so easily explained. Why, in fact, is the view of the world of the American and Australian children such a stressful one, filled as it is with difficulties and lack? The world "on hand" of these children is probably not less fulfilling or more difficult than that of the Egyptian or Finnish children. Although our investigation cannot answer our questions, it is possible to speculate that the view of the world presented through the medium of television commercials—our culture's modern myths whereby a magical agent (be it detergent or deodorant or toothpaste) transforms the hero—fulfills all desires and liquidates all lack, and other such stock television formulas are presented as models from which American and Australian children work.

Two other themes provide us with interesting insights into the very different worlds that children are in the process of symbolically constructing. The theme *contest/combat* deals with situations in which individuals or groups of individuals engage in a fight or a contest. The theme *destruction* deals with demise—being swallowed up, eaten, burned to the ground, shot dead, and so on. The American children were more competitive; they drew contest/combat themes approximately 40% more frequently than the Australian and Finnish children and 72% more frequently than the Egyptian children. The American and Australian children depict stories of destruction 60% more frequently than Finnish children and 80% more frequently than the Egyptian children. We may decry the destructive themes in the stories of American and Australian children, but the model presented by the mass media is a world of violence—whether it is in the nightly news or the action shows or the soap operas—and, although the world may be a much more benign place than that depicted in the media, children have had little firsthand experience of the world. They seem only to be in the process of cognitively manipulating and reinventing one of the more troublesome aspects of what they perceive in the culture, the world "on hand."

Success is a theme that classifies triumphs, rewards, achievements, and recognition of the protagonists in children's stories; it also relates to Tolkein's *consolation*, or happily-ever-after, theme. There is often a wish-fulfilling element here, as when the protagonist becomes the hero. In this category the Australian children were overwhelmingly ahead of the children in the other three groups. They employed the success theme 30% more frequently than Finnish children, 60% more frequently than American children, and over 90% more frequently than the Egyptian children. We will have to leave it to the Australians to explain why their children seem so preoccupied with success—perhaps it is that they still believe in fairy tales—and to the Egyptians to explain why they apparently have almost no concern for it, or we will have to look into the worldviews held by these two cultures to discover why children use these themes in such different proportions. One finding is certain: the worlds of the Australian child and of the Egyptian child are indisputably a great distance apart.

Of these four groups, in fact, the Egyptian children stood apart. The theme of *natural rhythm* was not employed once by Egyptian children but was used extensively by the Finnish group. This category classifies depictions of the forces of nature or the change from one state to another—winter to spring, night to day, storm to calm, sunshine to gloom. Moreover, the Finnish children depicted natural rhythm approximately 66% more frequently than the Australian and American groups. One might speculate that, because the Finnish children are continually exposed to extremes of weather and to acute changes from long, almost endless days of sunshine in the summer to short days and longer nights of darkness in the winter, their lives are inextricably linked to natural phenomena; on the other hand, weather in the Middle East is somewhat constant. And although environmental factors surely contribute to a child's conception of the world and could account for some of the differences we saw in the stories, we think that more emphasis must be placed on explanations based on cultural worldviews. The data we collected may not yield explanations; it does, however, help us to formulate the questions for subsequent research.

The classification *everyday rhythm* deals with depictions of the common or ordinary activities in which individuals customarily engage—waking, going to school, returning home, going to bed; baking a cake; washing one's hair; going to the park; playing in the playground. As with natural rhythm, the Finnish children depicted the everyday elements far more frequently than the Egyptian, American, and Australian groups—70% more frequently than the American and Australian children and 56% more frequently than the Egyptian children. It appears that the use of commonplace subject matter is higher when the use of stories with plot or disequilibrating elements is lower. Although the precise nature of narrative models remains to be studied, it appears that the reason for the paucity of stories with plot elements produced by Egyptian and Finnish children surely related to the presence or absence of particular narrative models within the culture.

Any cross-cultural study is necessarily limited by the cultural blind spots of the investigators. Although it was easy to classify the stories of all of the Finnish children and most of the Australian children—surprisingly, the investigators had some difficulty in classifying or, more accurately, in finding themes in approximately 13% of the narratives of American children—it was not surprising that over 40% of the drawings by Egyptian children either failed to fit into the usual classifications or they were nonsequential in nature and thus contained no single major theme, imbedded subtheme, or plot element. When the latter was not the case, many of the themes with which the Egyptian children dealt were ideas quite remote from any entertained by Western children in their story drawings. The Egyptian children often depicted stories that created models for a caring, sympathetic, and empathizing world, where sacrifices are made on behalf of another—a world diametrically opposed to the more competitive and success-oriented world of the Americans and Australians.

One frequently hears art educators say that children's art is the same all over the world, that it is, in fact, a universal language. Our data present quite another picture—one in which children from diverse cultures draw with distinct cultural styles in order to depict particular symbolic versions of vastly different worlds. We agree that it is appropriate that art educators look for the attributes in children's art that show that all children belong to "the family of man," but we also think that it is essential to be sensitive to the features that set each group of children apart. If we believe that all children are the same, then we are in danger of being lulled into believing that there is little to be learned from others. That would be unfortunate.

REFERENCES

Bettelheim, B. *The Uses of Enchantment*. New York: Knopf, 1976.

Erikson, E. *Toys and Reasons*. New York: Norton, 1977.

Goodman, N. *Ways of Worldmaking*. Cambridge: Hackett, 1978.

Piaget, J. "Some Aspects of Operations." In *Play and Development*, edited by M. Piers. New York: Norton, 1972, pp. 15–27.

Propp, V. *Morphology of the Folktale*. Austin: Univ. of Texas Press, 1968.

Wilson, B., and M. Wilson. "Visual Narrative and the Artistically Gifted." *The Gifted Child Quarterly* 20, no. 4 (Winter 1976): 432–47.

Cross-Cultural Research in Arts Education: Problems, Issues, and Prospects*

Elliot W. Eisner

In this paper I shall address five questions that I believe to be important for the development of cross-cultural research in arts education. First, what is the state of cross-cultural research in arts education? Second, what are the potential utilities of such research? Third, what kinds of problems might be studied? Fourth, what are the possible problems in conceptualizing, implementing, and interpreting cross-cultural research in arts education? Fifth, what are the prospects for cross-cultural research in arts education?

WHAT IS THE STATE OF CROSS-CULTURAL RESEARCH IN ARTS EDUCATION?

Perhaps the best place to begin with this question is to clarify the meaning of *research*. Although the term typically conjures up images of statistical analysis and complex probability tables, research activity need not be either empirical or quantitative. If we conceive of research as any systematic, careful inquiry designed to further our understanding of the

*A modified version of this paper was presented at the research conference held immediately prior to the 23rd World Congress of the International Society for Education Through Art, Adelaide, Australia. This article was previously printed in *Studies in Art Education*, volume 21, number 1 (1979), pages 27–35. *Studies in Art Education* is a publication of the National Art Education Association, 1916 Association Drive, Reston, Virginia 22091.—ED.

way the world is, the way it can become, or the way it ought to be, then research activity is wider than quantification or empiricism. From my viewpoint, research includes the theoretical activities of scholars attempting to develop concepts, models, or paradigms that explain or in other ways foster our understanding of the world. Examples of such research are the developmental theories produced by Erik Erikson (1950), Abraham Maslow (1954), and Sigmund Freud (1962), as well as the models and concepts of perception developed by Rudolf Arnheim (1964), Herman Witkin (1962), and Viktor Lowenfeld (1947). Within the theoretical arena I would also include not only descriptive or scientifically oriented theory but normative or value theory as well. Thus, the work of John Dewey (1934) in the United States and R.S. Peters (1966) in England would count, in my view, as systematic and useful efforts to develop ideas that can help us understand the world or enable us to improve some aspect of it. While the theoretical work I have mentioned is empirical in the sense that it is referenced to the world, it is not empirical in the sense that the data it uses were intentionally collected and systematically analyzed in order to create or verify theory. The theories that these individuals have created are attractive maps; their function is to guide perception and to direct inquiry; it is not necessarily to explain specific experimental results.

A second species of research is directly empirical. It is activity, generated by theory, that tests theory and expands and refines it through the investigation of specific empirical phenomena. Studies of the relationship between forms of socialization and aesthetic attitude; studies of the characteristics of children's visual images as a result of different forms of motivation; studies of classroom teaching practices in the arts and their effects upon children are all examples of empirical inquiries guided by theory of some kind, but directly related to specific populations and particular contexts. Note also that although all of such research is empirical, not all empirical research is quantitative. Empirical research also includes systematic inquiry that is qualitative in character. By qualitative research I refer to investigations reported in terms that are verbally descriptive, expressive, and even metaphorical. Historical and ethnographic studies of schools and classrooms are examples of what I am referring to. In England the work of Rob Walker (no date), in Scotland the work of David Hamilton (1977), and in the United States my own work (1977) and that of my students (Greer 1973; Vallance 1975; McCutcheon 1976; Davidman 1976; Alexander 1977; Sternberg 1977; Berk 1977) are examples of qualitative empirical research.

The last distinction I wish to make is between descriptive as contrasted to experimental research. In doing descriptive research, whether quantitative or qualitative, the investigator makes no attempt at intervention.

The investigator's role is to describe, interpret, and appraise; it is not to intervene in the setting being studied. In experimental research this is not the case. In experimental studies variables are manipulated in order to determine their effects on students and teachers. The end-in-view is to identify those experimental treatments that are both sufficiently robust and reliable that they will enable others to replicate those results under the same or similar conditions.

In making the distinction between experimental and nonexperimental (or, as I have called it, descriptive) research, one final important caveat should be entered. Nonexperimental research studies can be undertaken in school or classroom settings that are themselves "natural" examples of pedagogical variation, the effects of which can be related to the differences between treatments in different classrooms. That is, one can secure experimental-like conclusions doing studies that require no experimental intervention by the investigator.

I have discussed the meaning of the term *research* because unless we have a shared view of its characteristics, we are likely to have significant problems in communication. I have pointed out that research includes both theoretical and empirical investigations, that in the theoretical domain research can be normative as well as descriptive, and that in the empirical domain research can be qualitative as well as quantitative. Finally, I have pointed out that research can be nonexperimental as well as experimental in nature and that experimental-like results can be obtained from nonexperimental studies.

Compared to what was available a quarter century ago, a great deal of cross-cultural research in arts education is currently being published in the United States. Still, there are very few studies that are cross-cultural in character. By "cross-cultural research" I mean efforts made by the investigator to compare or contrast ideas or practices in more than one culture; I do not mean that an investigator from one culture simply goes to another culture to collect his or her data. An American going to Japan to study the influence of Japanese culture on the attitudes of Japanese adolescents toward traditional and contemporary art in Japan would not be engaged in cross-cultural research unless explicit efforts were made to draw parallels or contrasts between Japanese and, say, American cultures. Using this criterion, in the American research journal *Studies in Art Education*, only one study (Anderson 1976) that might be legitimately referred to as cross-cultural has appeared since the journal was started in 1959. The availability of cross-cultural research in the field of music education, while somewhat greater, is also very limited. The reasons are not difficult to discern. When it comes to cross-cultural empirical research, whether quantitative or qualitative, investigators must have access to a culture other than their own. This requires either the resources to travel or a communication network with scholars in other cultures who would be willing to collect the necessary data or provide the resources for the study to go forward. In arts education research funds have been scarce, and although international communication with scholars in the field of arts education has increased notably during the last decade, it is still limited as compared to what takes place in the scientific community.

The scarcity of fiscal resources and the tenuousness of communication networks are only two of the factors that have militated against cross-cultural research in arts education. Perhaps the most significant factor is the fact that systematic disciplined inquiry in arts education is scarce in general, whether cross-cultural or introcultural. I believe it is accurate to say that the United States has the most extensive training programs for the preparation of educational researchers in the world. In the United States, in the field of visual arts education alone there are numerous universities that have programs leading to the doctoral degree in art education and an equally large number in music education. Most of these degree programs are designed to train individuals to do research. Almost all programs require a doctoral thesis which entails the conceptualization and completion of a substantial piece of research, whether theoretical or empirical, qualitative or quantitative, experimental or descriptive. Yet only a few of those who receive doctorates in arts education each year do research after completing their degrees. The paucity of active, research-oriented scholars increases the difficulty of securing cross-cultural research in arts education, a kind of research that is even more demanding than the conduct of a research study in one's own community. I am suggesting here that the paucity of cross-cultural research in arts education is related not only to the scarcity of funds and the limited forms of communication across cultures, but to the shortage of researchers in arts education as well.

Surely the most extensive cross-cultural research studies that have been undertaken in the context of education are the International Studies of Educational Achievement (IEA) (*International* 1962). This research program, involving over thirteen countries, was initiated in 1967 and is still under way. Its major aims are to determine the level of achievement in a variety of academic subjects by students in the countries that participated in the study. It has also attempted to measure the students' attitudes toward the subject and the amount of time allocated to it, and to identify other variables related to achievement in order to explain why a nation's young perform as they do. Some individuals associated with the study in Europe have expressed the hope that through the IEA studies it may be possible to develop a common, unified, and coherent curriculum for European schools. In the curriculum areas in which students have been examined, the visual arts and music are nowhere to be found. Unlike many other areas of school achievement, the arts tend to frighten non-arts researchers and evaluators because of the formidable problems they pose in judging the quality of performance. Mathematics achievement presents no comparable difficulty.

I mention the IEA studies because they represent the most ambitious effort ever undertaken to assess academic achievement cross-culturally. We need not, in arts education, emulate either its design features or its aims, but it does provide one model of the kind of collaboration that is possible.

There have been cross-cultural studies undertaken specifically in the arts. Irvin Child's work in the United States is one of the most impressive examples of such research (Child and Siroto 1965). However, Child's research was undertaken largely to determine the extent to which aesthetic values were common across cultures and to identify the relationship between the perceived aesthetic value of art forms and the kinds of training and experience individuals have within their respective cultures. His research was not conceptualized for purposes related to arts education. Indeed, as I have suggested, although the potential for such research is great, it largely remains to be done.

WHAT ARE THE POTENTIAL UTILITIES OF CROSS-CULTURAL RESEARCH IN ARTS EDUCATION?

The major assets that flow from the conduct of cross-cultural research emanate from the fact that the contexts in which problems are studied differ so radically, thus making it possible to regard the differences in settings as natural laboratories whose experimental treatments cause the differences found. If two countries were culturally identical but politically distinct, studies across such nations would not be examples of cross-cultural research. What makes cross-cultural research cross-cultural are the differences among the cultures studied. This means, of course, that cross-cultural research can, in principle, be pursued within a single country if the differences between one cultural group and another are sufficiently great. In Australia, for example, studies of the arts education received by Australian Aborigines in the bush and the arts education received by Australian Anglo children living in Sydney or Adelaide would constitute as radical a cultural difference as any to be found between countries anywhere on earth. More often, however, studies must be undertaken across national boundaries to secure the cultural differences that make it possible to achieve the aims of cross-cultural research. What are those aims, and what are the utilities of such research?

Perhaps the most significant utility is the generation and refinement of theory. By having access to different settings, research on such matters as the character of children's artistic development, their perception of expressive qualities, their aesthetic preferences at different levels of development can be undertaken that are theory-generative. Assuming one has some firm sense of what the cultural variables are, differences in levels and types of performance in these and other areas can be generative of theory or can be used to refine and verify theory. There are many ideas and benefits that are held by arts educators almost as dogma—the virtue of nonintervention in the artistic activity of primary-age children, for example—that could be tested and possibly altered with theory that cross-cultural research might generate. Similarly, the relationship between the status hierarchy among subjects with the school curriculum and the values students believe the arts to have in their own lives in general and in school in particular could be made possible through such work. Because all of us operate with certain beliefs about the role of the arts in education, and because we conceive of the child's optimum development in certain ways, we are all guided by theoretical ideas. Within a culture these ideas or theories often become so ubiquitous and widely accepted that we lose the distance needed to criticize them adequately. Cross-cultural research has a potential contribution to make by taking us out of our familiar context and by showing us settings that differ from our own: settings guided by other ideas, practices based upon other assumptions. Such a view has the potential of providing another platform from which to view the theories we hold and with which to reconsider our own practices. Thus, the potential utility of cross-cultural research is that it affords us an excellent opportunity to test and refine our theoretical beliefs by checking them against the performances of individuals functioning within different cultures. It does this by bringing us face-to-face with different theories and different pedagogical practices and in this way gives us another vantage point from which to examine our own assumptions. I believe it was Goethe who said, "A man who knows only one language does not know his own."

In discussing the potential utilities of cross-cultural research in arts education I have used examples that are primarily empirical and to some extent quantitative. I have not discussed value theory explicitly, but this is not because the parallels in this area cannot be made. Historical and normative cross-cultural research can be justified on grounds comparable to those I have used to discuss the more traditional social science research.

WHAT KINDS OF PROBLEMS MIGHT BE STUDIED?

I have already suggested some of the problems that might be formulated for cross-cultural research. To reiterate, cross-cultural research problems can be formulated that are theoretical as well as empirical, qualitative as well as quantitative, experimental as well as nonexperimental. I will now briefly provide one example for each of these types of research.

With respect to theoretical research, consider the following question: What accounts for the fact that in industrial societies school structures develop that assign artistic learning to a low status while in nonindustrialized societies the status of the arts in schools tends to be significantly higher? Theory that could adequately account for such a set of facts would at once be sociological and political in character and would, in principle, help educators understand the factors that relegate the arts to marginal positions within a school curriculum. Presumably, with more adequate understanding of these factors, arts educators would be in a better position to alter them.

The creation of such theory—theory that would require empirical data—might alter our view of what we consider appropriate content for arts curricula. The use of such theory would require familiarity with different cultures, and it would find support to the extent to which it made the facts intelligible or brought new considerations to our attention. An example of such theory is found in Herbert Marcuse's *Essay on Liberation* (1969).

In the realm of cross-cultural quantitative empirical research one could ask: What are the effects of different rewards systems within schooling on the content and form of teaching in the visual arts at the secondary level? This question could be treated either quantitatively or qualitatively, or both. It is based on the assumption that the reward system within a school—an examination system, for example—influences the ways in which teaching occurs. By locating cultures with substantially different reward systems (assuming other significant variables are taken into account) one could begin to secure data on the ways in which such influences emerge. Sufficiently understood, it would make it possible, in principle, to create school structures that supported the educational ends one embraced in the arts instead of sustaining school structures that often militate against the achievement of those ends.

In the qualitative domain one could ask: In what ways do the styles of teaching used in different cultures reflect the values of these cultures and what influence do such teaching styles have upon the content and form of children's artistic performance? Such a study could, like the previous one, be handled quantitatively or qualitatively. However, if one were doing it in a qualitative mode, the format or approach one might use is what is called "educational criticism" (Eisner 1976, 1977, 1979). This approach is in some ways analogous to what literary and film critics do with literature and film. The task of the critic is to illuminate through description, interpretation, and evaluation what he or she attends to. Criticism is, as Dewey said, aimed at "the reeducation of perception of works of art" (1933, 324). The critic's function, as it were, is to serve as a facilitator of perception by describing vividly and by intelligently interpreting what his or her connoisseurship allows him or her to perceive.

To carry out such a research project one would, of course, need to be able to recognize the subtle but pervasive values of two or more cultures. One would then need to perceive teaching in such a way that made it possible to locate expressions of those cultures (if they manifest themselves) in the practice of teaching. Once having located those cultural expressions in teaching, one would then examine children's artistic activity and their art products to find manifestations of the culture's values in them. Thus, in such an investigation three levels of phenomena would be identified: those within the cultures at large, those within teaching, and those within the student's work. All of this could be done using qualitative methods of research, of which educational criticism is an example.

Regarding descriptive or nonexperimental research, one could ask: What relationships exist between artistic performance and aesthetic preference among children in different cultures? Such an investigation would be aimed at finding correlates of what children and adolescents prefer and the kinds of images they create. Put another way, it is a way of asking whether preferences for particular styles or forms of art have any bearing upon the kinds of images children create when they have the opportunity to choose. Such an investigation could shed some light on the discrepancies within and between cultures on perceptual preference and artistic performance. From such data one could begin to investigate the satisfactions and dissatisfactions students have with their own artistic activity in light of the images of artistic virtue they hold. One might hypothesize that the larger the discrepancy between the child's preference and his or her performance, the greater the likelihood of antagonistic feelings toward art and the lower the child's estimate of his or her ability as an artist.

Finally, regarding experimental studies, one might ask: Given the same three forms of motivation for children of the same age and social class living in different cultures, what is the degree of variability that results in the kinds of artistic images those children create? To conduct an investigation would require, of course, a rather elaborate research design. One might, for example, use stories that elicit imaginative processes, emotionally loaded experiences secured from the "real world," or simple still life set-ups that children might be asked to draw or paint. Whether these specific methods are used is not the point. The point is that it is possible to create forms of motivation designed to elicit different kinds of experience and thinking. Research on the kinds of artistic variability that different forms of motivation generate could begin to provide some clues as to the ways in which cultures influence children's cognition. One might speculate that the wider the variability, the greater the latitude the culture provides for children to exercise their imaginative capacities. From such data one could move to an analysis of the macrostructures that might account for such variability.

I have not, in the examples I have provided, attempted to be detailed or exhaustive, simply illustrative of the kinds of research questions that could be raised within each of the types of research I have identified. Obviously, the adequate execution of such research would take considerably more specification regarding both the questions themselves and the methods that might be used to deal with them.

WHAT ARE THE PROBLEMS OF CONCEPTUALIZATION, IMPLEMENTATION, AND INTERPRETATION IN CROSS-CULTURAL RESEARCH IN ARTS EDUCATION?

The problems of conceptualization in cross-cultural research when such research is a collaborative venture of scholars in different countries center upon the questions and phenomena worth attending to in the first place and the meaning of the concepts and theories being employed. While such problems are present in collaborative efforts within one's own culture, the problems are exacerbated when collaboration is cross-cultural. The intellectual contexts within which individuals operate, particularly in a field such as ours, are diverse and difficult to operationalize. Thus, the meanings we confer upon ideas, not only those we choose to work with but the meanings we extract from the data we interpret, are fraught with a great many potential difficulties. In order to minimize such difficulties, shared frames of reference are necessary, and the wider the differences among cultures studied, the greater the likelihood that differences in meaning will occur. Americans and Japanese, Armenians and Brazilians do not necessarily view the world in similar ways. Although such differences can become strengths in cross-cultural research, they can become formidable obstacles as well. At the very least, communication must be good enough to know when there is a lack of communication. Commenting on some of the problems in cross-cultural research, Ray Birdwhistle (1977, 107) writes:

For more than fifty years ethnologists and social and cultural anthropologists have sought to develop and try out carefully ordered cross-societal and cross-cultural methodologies that could secure data that would become evidence about the extent of human social malleability. An essential question for most anthropologists has been whether it is even possible to develop methods that would make cross-cultural comparisons feasible and reliable. It has been an essential doctrine of anthropology that no comparisons can be any more reliable than the ethnographies upon which the comparisons are based. Any investigatory technique which cheapens the data enervates cross-cultural comparison. The establishment of either ranges of cross-cultural variation or human universals requires the most rigorous caution in establishing the comparability of data. One of the most serious developments in recent years has been the resurgence of the version of universalism that maintains that since any human is so similar to all other humans physiologically there is a reduced need for the development of safeguards that would enable us to detect and comprehend the social significance of seemingly identical acts. Theory and training in cross-cultural investigation give way before the destructive assumption that however noncomparable the data, it can always be generalized significantly by statistical procedures or computer. It requires very little training to count: a very intensive training is required to develop significant units for the counting.

Other difficulties, especially in research done in school settings, are in determining the comparability of the major variables studied. Seventh graders in one country may be the equivalent of fourth graders in another. Two years of instruction in one nation may be the equivalent of five years in another. Indeed, one of the difficulties with the IEA studies of education achievement in mathematics is their failure to recognize the extensive array of "after-school" schools which many Japanese children attend in order to increase their skills in mathematics. Without an understanding of the context, not only in the school but in the culture, the probability of misinterpretation is great. Furthermore, the meaning of events and activities within cultural settings such as schools can differ radically from the meaning they hold for individuals in one's own culture. The emic and etic perspectives described in anthropological literature provide a reminder to cross-cultural investigators that both the participant's view and a spectator's view are needed to understand what has been experienced and what it signifies within a cultural system. Cross-cultural research in arts education calls for no less.

If one does not collaborate with others in cross-cultural research but uses others to secure data only, such as to find a suitable population, to secure permission to do the study, and to administer instruments and so forth, one places oneself in the vulnerable position of not knowing exactly how the populations were selected, how permission was secured, and how the tests were administered. Furthermore, one does not have the opportunity to secure the context cues that can enable one to make the data intelligible. In short, such a procedure leaves one somewhat in the dark, and what one has not seen, one is not likely to know. In such cases the investigator suffers from the worst kind of ignorance: secondary ignorance—not knowing that one does not know.

These are not the only problems of doing cross-cultural research, whether in arts education or in other fields. But in arts education the problems are particularly difficult because we do not have a body of experience to help us anticipate and correct our problems and because criterion problems are more difficult in the arts than they are in fields where unambiguous standards can be applied. It was not for nothing that the International Study of Educational Achievement started its cross-cultural research with the study of achievement in mathematics. Who could imagine investigators starting such an enterprise by examining the performance of students in the visual arts, dance, drama, or music?

WHAT ARE THE PROSPECTS FOR CROSS-CULTURAL RESEARCH IN ARTS EDUCATION?

Perhaps by now you are prepared to give up the idea of doing cross-cultural research in arts education. That is not what I intended. I believe that it is far more promising in the long run to appreciate the complexity and the sources of error in doing cross-cultural research than to spend time and effort in naive attempts that result in shoddy work. The agenda of difficulties that I have identified simply reminds us of what to look out for. It is not intended to present detours or roadblocks.

Besides the problems I have identified, there are practical problems that need attention if cross-cultural research is to flourish. Without extensive elaboration I would like to conclude by identifying three of them.

First is the problem of money. It is not a theoretical, lofty consideration but nevertheless has significant practical consequences. To do research that requires the collection and analysis of data requires also the availability of funds. One cannot rely upon one's own resources or the resources of friends to do what needs to be done to produce useful educational research. There might be some exceptional cases, but these exceptions demonstrate the truth of the rule. Money is important, and money for research in arts education in the United States, at least, is scarce, even for problems that pertain directly to national interest. Yet, without funding, the likelihood of being able to do such research is small.

To say this is not to say that the necessary funds could not be secured. It is to say that research is dependent upon them. It might very well be the case that with attractive conceptions and problems some international agencies might be willing to support some initial efforts.

Second is the problem of communication through publication. Arts educators do not have an internationally read journal. Although the National Art Education Association's journal, *Art Education*, has a circulation of about 11,000 for each of eight issues, and *Studies in Art Education* has a subscription list of about 3,500 for each of three issues per year, the readership of these journals is largely American. What is needed is a journal that would publish the fruits of our intellectual efforts on an international scale. Publication in obscure or professionally remote journals limits the very benefits we seek to provide.

Third, a communication network among scholars interested in cross-cultural research in arts education needs to be established. One such network occurs at international research conferences. Such conferences provide contact, facilitate communication, and, not least, cultivate professional friendships. While these conditions do not guarantee that cross-cultural research will be undertaken, they do at least contribute to its beginning. I, for one, believe that the field of arts education is ready to make a start.

REFERENCES

Alexander, R. "Educational Criticism of Three Art History Classes." Ph.D. diss., Stanford Univ., 1977. *Dissertation Abstracts International*, 1978, 0212.

Anderson, F. "Esthetic Evaluations and Art Involvement in Australia, Pakistan and Thailand." *Studies in Art Education* 17, no. 3 (1976): 33–44.

Arnheim, R. *Art and Visual Perception: The Psychology of the Creative Eye*. Berkeley: Univ. of California Press, 1964.

Berk, L.M. "Education in Lives: An Application of Biographic Narrative to the Study of Educational Outcomes." Ph.D. diss., Stanford Univ., 1977. *Dissertation Abstracts International*, 1978, 02132.

Birdwhistle, R.J. "Some Discussions of Ethnography, Theory and Method." In *About Bateson*, edited by John Brockman. New York: E.P. Dutton, 1977, pp. 102–44.

Child, I., and L. Siroto. "Ba Kwele and American Aesthetic Education Compared." *Ethnology* 5, no. 4 (1965): 349–60.

Davidman, L. "A Formative Evaluation of the Unified Science and Mathematics in the Elementary Schools Curriculum." Ph.D. diss., Stanford Univ., 1976. *Dissertation Abstracts International*, 1976, 25987.

Dewey, J. *Art as Experience*. New York: Minton, Balch and Co., 1934.

Eisner, E. "Educational Connoisseurship and Educational Criticism: Their Forms and

Functions in Educational Evaluation." *Journal of Aesthetic Education*, Bicentennial Issue, 1976.

————. "On the Use of Educational Connoisseurship and Educational Criticism for Evaluating Classroom Life." *Teachers College Record* 78, no. 3 (1977).

————. *The Educational Imagination: The Design and Evaluation of School Programs.* New York: Macmillan, 1979.

Erikson, E. *Childhood and Society.* New York: Norton, 1950.

Freud, S. *The Ego and the Id.* New York: Norton, 1962.

Greer, W.D. "The Criticism of Teaching." Ph.D. diss., Stanford Univ., 1973. *Dissertation Abstracts International*, 1974, 13632.

Hamilton, D. et al. *Beyond the Numbers Game.* London: Macmillan Education, Ltd., 1977.

International Studies in Education, Hamburg UNESCO Institute fur Padagogik. Educational Achievements of 13-year-olds in 12 countries; results of an instructional research project, 1959–61–72 (34 reports). Reported by Arthur W. Foshay and others, Hamburg, 1962.

Lowenfeld, V. *Creative and Mental Growth.* New York: Macmillan, 1974.

McCutcheon, G. "The Disclosure of Classroom Life." Ph.D. diss., Stanford Univ., 1976. *Dissertation Abstracts International*, 1976, 26037.

Marcuse, H. *An Essay on Liberation.* Boston: Beacon Press, 1969.

Maslow, A. *Motivation and Personality.* New York: Harper, 1954.

Peters, R.S. *Ethics and Education.* London: Allen & Unwin, 1966.

Sternberg, B.J. "What Do Tokens and Trophies Teach?" Ph.D. diss., Stanford Univ., 1977. *Dissertation Abstracts International*, 1978, 08851.

Vallance, E.J. "Aesthetic Criticism and Curriculum Description." Ph.D. diss., Stanford Univ., 1977. *Dissertation Abstracts International*, 1976, 5820.

Walker, R. "The Conduct of Educational Case Study: Ethics, Theory and Procedures." In *SAFARI Innovation, Evaluation, Research and the Problem of Control*, edited by B. MacDonald and R. Walker. Some Interim Papers, Norwich: Center for Applied Research for Education, no date.

Witkin, H. *Psychological Differentiation: Studies in Development.* New York: Wiley, 1962.

II
The National Profiles in Art Education

The chapters that follow attempt to provide a framework for the art teacher's search for answers to issues in art education. Such a framework, formed by the National Profiles in this book, are the contributions of practicing art teachers from a variety of countries and indicate that teachers of art in various countries conduct their programs in order to develop the creative and artistic abilities of their students towards the betterment of human life in their particular culture and country.

Even though no single publication could answer all of the questions that come to the minds of art teachers upon reading these accounts, nor could a single book attempt to relate all of the various practices in existence throughout the world, the National Profiles present one of the first meaningful collections of such accounts to be found within any single text. (Another available record of programs and issues can be found in the "INSEA Report on the 19th World Congress," NAEA pub. 1968.) The chapters that follow could only be written by art teachers who know what art teaching is actually like in their particular country.

Each contributor has been carefully selected for his or her individual leadership in among and knowledge about the conditions and practices of one country. These art teachers indicate that art education must extend beyond the four walls of the studio art classroom and must utilize the resources of museums, parks, homes, and community institutions in order to fully benefit education in their nations. This point of view, as well as the valuable information about art teaching found in the National Profiles, is of particular importance to the art teacher who is concerned with art education goals, objectives, and curriculum issues, and is involved in the search for solutions to questions that arise over meeting the needs of students in multiple-art learning environments. No single solution to problems and issues exists; rather, it is the differences within the art teaching in various countries as well as the commonalities which provide the richness of information for insights into art education issues.

One important distinction to the historical, political, and practical formations of current art education is the trend to merge modern art teaching with instruction on the artistic heritage. In Poland this is accomplished through a synthesis of the pupil's individual expression by acquainting him or her with the artistic culture while teaching the perception of works of art. In Germany the natures of contemporary and traditional art forms are the reference points for teaching art in the schools, while in Finland four areas of art education—the expressive, the perceptual, the analytical/critical, and the historical/cultural—provide the basis for conceptualizing the content of art education in the school curriculum by pervading the entire learning process.

The traditions of art teaching and art works in the collections of various cultural institutions are not ignored in the National Profiles. In these various chapters—and especially for those countries rich in traditions such as Egypt, some African countries, India, China, and the USSR—references are made to relating these forms of artistic heritages to contemporary art teaching. In India, for example, we are reminded that for thousands of years the artistic heritage has been handed down from generation to generation, assuring a place for art education in the Indian society. Egypt's cultural heritage of more than 7,000 years is part of a child's art education, as the child is taught to develop cultural and aesthetic knowledge in contemporary society through the practice of art. In the Afghanistan chapter we learn that in planning art curricula consideration is given to the country's ancient artistic heritage as well as to the arts of nearby cultures which interact and affect traditions. Ghanaians recognize that traditional arts and crafts are important elements in school programs and that art teachers have to prove themselves as cultural catalysts. Even in England, despite the richness of the cultural heritage and the English traditions, there remains a need for teachers to know more about art as a basis for adding to their knowledge of designing and making art and craft objects.

These perspectives are just a few of those found in the National Profiles which help to develop the theme of teaching artistic heritages in art education. In the Israeli chapter a formal approach that solves the need for bringing the artistic and cultural heritage to the people through the art curriculum is shown in an account of the Youth Wing of the Israel Museum in Jerusalem. Tamsma's description of support in the Netherlands for the study of art history at all levels and the uses of museums shows that country's determination to include the total school population in learning about the artistic and cultural heritage. In Part III of this book additional formats in teaching the artistic and cultural heritage as reflected in Jerusalem and the Netherlands are presented in other European and international art education programs.

The term *aesthetic education* reflects still another related format for teaching the cultural heritage in art education that many countries are now incorporating into their programs. Soviet author Yusov admits to the direct influence on the USSR of the CEMREL model (Central Midwestern Education Laboratory in the United States), and Wojnar, Poland's leading philosopher in Marxist aesthetics, describes the Polish interpretation of the concept, which in all countries calls for a concern for all of the arts with attention paid to responding to and understanding the special natures of the visual, aural, and performing arts. The ends of aesthetic education, however, have greater political implications in Poland and the USSR than in the United States, and the means of achieving goals obviously differ widely.

Yusov's paper was prepared especially for one of the first groups of U.S. art educators to officially visit Soviet colleagues. Hurwitz's chapter, however, reflects several visits to the Soviet Union and numerous discussions on the ways in which the USSR pays special attention to visual education. His work with teachers in Soviet schools, art centers, and Youth Palaces, as well as his study of the professional literature in aesthetic education presently existing in translations, provide insights into art teaching there. Although Szekacs does not mention aesthetic education as such, the Hungarians are also clearly interested in relating visual art to other art forms, particularly literature and music. Like her Soviet, Polish, and American counterparts, Szekacs sees art education as instrumental in developing the total personality of the child and in facilitating cognitive development through the power of sensory and affective experiences. She takes readers into the school rooms of Hungary to provide specific examples of classroom application and presents us with an image of a system that allows for exceptional diversity and experimentation; in so doing, she puts into question the preconceptions about the monolithic character of education in the Eastern European countries.

Both Dutch author Tamsma and Klager of Germany review contending art education systems in their countries and use single subjects to dramatize differences between these systems. "Free expression," as Tamsma describes it, is still the most pervasive philosophy in the Netherlands, with "phenomenological" didactics residing at the farther end of his analysis of art education. The "visual communication" system of art education in Holland is shared by many German art teachers and is equally a part of some American thinking, although it surfaces under other wording. An example of studying international art education in the manner Tamsma presents would be to look at the art activity first and then study its context. Art teachers in three countries engaging in the same art learning experience through a community mural project may find differing results. Such an activity might be classified as "pure" or "fine art" in the United States or as a political education experience in a socialist country. The same project in Egypt or Israel would be seen as a socially effective means of bringing diverse groups closer through an art project that shares ideas, processes, and materials.

All of the National Profile authors enjoy a position of professional eminence in the countries where they teach art. The degree to which each chapter and account of art teaching responds to the initial format mentioned in the Introduction varies, however, as these authors have adjusted editorial changes to their own agendas. What remains are the opinions and responses of each of these authors and not those of the editors. In some cases language has proved to be a problem for these authors or their translators, and some chapters have required careful editing. Indeed, editing original writings from art teachers from many countries has been a difficult and sensitive problem. The editors have attempted to clarify phrases and words while taking great care not to destroy the individual tone of the words. The most painful task was the elimination of statements because of space limitations, which is a realistic condition for this book. In the cases when a native art teacher or professional was unavailable for a statement, a sensitive and knowledgeable foreign observer was entrusted to convey the information for a particular article on a more personal level. Such contributions have, in these cases, clearly stated the nature of their perspectives.

Although contributors were asked to be clear and specific, a certain degree of ambiguity became inevitable. A term with a clear meaning in one country often has different connotations in another. One example of this problem is the term *free expression*, which means a laissez-faire approach to art teaching in the Netherlands, but suggests a "related arts" approach with overtones of art therapy to many Finnish art teachers. In the United States *free expression* is often considered outdated as both term and concept, having expired with the demise of the progressive education movement. The reader must always be open-minded and willing to respond to the context of these writings through inquiry, inference, and interpretation. Above all, it is important to accept the contexts for what they are by attempting to hold back personal judgments and biases. This action will permit more open-mindedness in the inquiry.

It is difficult not to be judgmental, especially when one has been teaching art successfully for some time. It is also difficult to be confronted with ways of thinking that appear to contradict one's accustomed way of resolving an art teaching problem. Yet to be truly open-minded means to give the context or article a chance. Each National Profile contains possibly useful information, as insights are revealed by these authors concerning international art instruction.

Japan is often cited as a country in which art education is a successful melding of a centralization policy of cultural traditions, foreign influences, and a supportive culture regarding the arts. Wachowiak introduces the system in which art education functions in Japan and, as a long-time advocate and observer of the Japanese scene, describes more specifically what are exemplary practices in Japanese art education. Japan, however, continues to undergo transitions that effect the purposes of art education. Western influences, particularly from professional artists, are significant in determining new directions.

Kauppinen exposes Finland's problem of being a country not large enough to justify adequate translations of foreign texts. She has co-authored a book with a U.S. art educator, which serves to strengthen cross-cultural relations between Finland and the United States. Finland's impressive history in the area of architectural and applied design, however, has not penetrated the curriculum as have other classical subjects. Finland's current interest in the mass media and in environmental and interdisciplinary education does place Finland at the forefront of much of U.S. thinking and moves the center of art education away from the sole activity of picture making, which dominates most of the world's art programs.

Klager makes some careful distinctions between the ideas behind art education in the Federal Republic of Germany and those in the German Democratic Republic (the DDR). His interpretation of the new-Marxist, anticapitalistic view is radically different from the Soviet identification with Marxist art education. Although Russia and the DDR might concur on ultimate goals, the means of achieving these goals differ markedly. Klager details the sharp departure of those countries which have formerly looked to the United States for guidance from a much wider range of disciplines. The relationship of a regional model (for example, Bavaria) to national trends is also worth noting. Germany shares with Hungary a general feeling of ferment because of its interest in new contexts for art experiences. In Hungary new ideas come from the arts themselves; in Germany, from philosophy and politics.

Bradley's chapter on the United States reminds us that we live in a world in which dialogues and familiarity among various countries are continually increasing. Looking specifically at the nonindigenous influences on North American art education, he challenges art teachers to question their backgrounds and philosophies of art education, thereby learning more from each other through inquiry and research in cross-cultural education. This could serve to create a new consciousness for art education. One such country from which more could be learned is the People's Republic of China. Cultural exchange is new; the range of professional visitations is just beginning to include art teachers. Visitors often cannot establish contacts on their own or visit art academies at random, and there is little professional literature available for study other than that which exists from a few exhibition catalogues. Any attempts to compare this culture to others with common racial roots (such as Japan, Taiwan, or South Korea) or to similar political structures (as in the USSR) would be unrealistic. China developed without the Western tradition of painting that is so closely allied to Soviet art and art education, and, unlike Japan, bears no debt to Western influence in art education. It has its own rich artistic traditions, although it does understand and utilize some Western concepts of space, and its school art is far more committed than is the Soviets' to socialist content in student work. The Chinese acceptance of copying and tracing signifies a dramatic departure from mainstream thought in other countries and sets the country's school art programs truly apart. Because of their unique history, the Chinese have yet to develop a coherent theoretical basis for their style of instruction—at least no such record exists in this country as of this writing.

The relative effects and merits of Western influence on cultures is often the basis for many questions among art educators. Cultural conflicts can exist because of the influence brought about by foreign students who attend U.S. graduate schools and return to their own countries, eager to put theory into practice. China has not been faced with this problem, but with the easing of international relations between China and the United States, student exchange programs will begin as a result of cultural exchange. It is likely that the art curricula of Chinese schools will eventually begin to reflect the U.S. influence and that art education in China will inevitably undergo changes not unlike those that occurred in Japan, where Western ideas were blended with oriental traditions.

This should be a particularly interesting phase for future scholars to study, since the names of Lowenfeld, Dewey, and Read by then will have diminished in stature as major sources of theory building. One can only speculate about the content of graduate work that awaits the Chinese graduate student of the future.

Omabegho and Nyarkoh, in telling about present-day art education in Nigeria and Ghana, respectively, describe situations typical of African nations that are moving from primitive/agrarian societies to some stage of industrial civilization. Neither country is going to cast off traditional art forms because in many cases these are still bound up with local life styles and with nonvisual art forms, yet both countries look to the West for guidance in planning curricula. When Omabegho was asked to direct teacher training at the University of Lagos, she faced the same problem Lederman confronted in serving the University of Kabul in Afghanistan. Neither could, nor intended to, cast off the past, and both were faced with severe economic strictures. Both had to ask: how does one institutionalize forces that have been accepted as a way of life? and, how does one preserve art forms that are linked to customs that are the casualties of progress? (This latter question is particularly pertinent with the Zulu and Bantu in South Africa.) In Omabegho's article on Nigeria one can identify parallel issues with Ghana and Afghanistan.

Lederman and Grossert, authors of, respectively, the chapters on Afghanistan and South Africa, were faced with similar situations—that is, planning art programs for cultures to which they are outsiders. Although Lederman created training programs for art teachers in Afghanistan, and Grossert, as art inspector for Natal in South Africa, was concerned with the education of Zulu children, both had to be sensitive to the specific cultural character of their clients. The respect and care with which both approached their tasks is impressive and proves that a sensitive outsider can contribute as much as someone working from within the group in question. Both writers have managed to integrate local craft forms into their curricula while incorporating relevant ideas from Western thinking. In so doing they have closed the gap between vernacular or folk art and the art of the schools. In Iran, for example, the child who observes potting, metal forming, or weaving in his rural village is not likely to engage in such activities in his school and will have less chance of practicing such skills in an urban school. Iranian students are also less likely to opt for crafts training in higher education because of the association that crafts has with rural life, poverty, and outmoded life styles. It is this attitude that Lederman, Grossert, and Omabegho are attempting to change.

Because of its size, its former cultural dependence upon Britain, and its difficulties in synthesizing its many streams of thought into some unified body, India poses a particularly complex problem for review. Sen has attempted to see some order in a country with areas of poverty and an overwhelming population problem. The Indian society accepts both transcendental meditation *(yogin)* and hedonism *(bhogin)* as a way of existence and has not completely relinquished its ties to the British raj for its models of governance and education. It is a country where ancient epics such as the *Ramayana* and *Mahabharata* still live through public festivals, with villages which practice highly individual styles of painting and with settlements where only women engage in art *(Mithila)*. Figures such as Tagore and Shankar are still revered as great individualists who served art education outside of the established institutions. For the most part, India is a country of independent operators, where coalitions form and dissolve and where colleges and universities can still become rallying points for the testing of new ideas. Although this chapter was based upon the author's expertise, it continues to raise issues on the subject that demand further inquiry.

Goitein points to the distinction between the religious and the public schools in Israel and reminds us that the Jews and the Moslems share a tradition that discourages figurative imagery, thus creating a crafts rather than a fine arts emphasis in the religious schools. The problem of assimilation of cultures, the nature of the kibbutz, the special role of group art, and the role of the museum all set Israel apart from other countries in the Mid-East. Bassiouny, on the other hand, identifies increased foreign influences on the Israeli curricula that have been added to ideas peculiar to Egypt, such as a reverence for its architectural past, a reputation for weaving that has created a world market for at least one village, and one of the largest teacher education programs now in existence (at Helwan University). Egyptians and Israelis alike feel that group art processes have special value for their children, and a careful reading of Bassiouny's goals in art education will show that the two countries are close neighbors in the aesthetic if not in the political arena. Considering their severe economic and political problems, Egypt and Israel place art education at a commendably high position on the scale of educational priorities.

The chapter on Brazil shows a clear example of a country struggling for identity when local conditions are determined by colonial imposition (Spain and Portugal in this instance) and when indigenous traditions (specifically Indian and Mestizo) are further complicated by European and American philosophy, logical positivism from France, the Bauhaus from Germany, John Dewey from the United States, and other influences. It also points to one of the most effective grass roots movements of independent art schools for children and for teacher training—the forty-odd "Eschohlinas" begun by poet-painter Augusto Rodriguez. This chapter alerts art teachers to be more aware both of the past and of art education theory because a lack of historical artistic knowledge is presently responsible for the Brazilian art teachers' enslavement by the new. The historical conditions that precede the current movement toward strengthening cultural identity through the redirection of educational policy are outlined by Barbosa.

WESTERN EUROPE

England Old Stability, New Ferment

Brian Allison

CULTURE AND SOCIETY

Popular education in England has developed in an aesthetically rich world, the results of which to some degree—if not at a conscious level then at a subconscious or unconscious level—may be expected to have been impressive. One of the curious outcomes of this situation, certainly as far as art education is concerned, is that it would seem to be either all too familiar to be regarded as important or not important enough to be regarded as a matter deserving particular concern.

A further matter which is important in setting the scene for a discussion and description of art education in England lies in the way the country has developed historically in a more or less continuous way over almost 2,000 years. There certainly have been many disturbances to continuous development which contemporaneously were of enormous and often blood-thirsty proportions, yet the perspectives of time smooth these out considerably. Changes and developments have arisen and occurred more often than not from small beginnings and a kind of evolution rather than by dramatic revolution. Until fairly recently there has been a very evident stability, and this stability can be regarded as being characteristically English. The Donald Schon epithet of "dynamic conservatism," which he described as "fighting like mad to stay the same," might have some applicability in this regard.[1]

Based on a historically long, hierarchical class structure, popular education in England is relatively recent and owes much in terms of structure as well as content to that of the elitist classical education. Following a pattern of private or local initiatives preceding government intercession, popular education in England had its origins in individual philanthropic ventures or those of religious groupings.[2] Whilst the government has taken an increasingly active role in education in the last 140 years, the system has retained much of that kind of diversity which inevitably arises from local developments. Within certain constraints tenuously determined by central government political philosophy, the local education authorities have great degrees of freedom for interpretation. Within the local education authorities, the schools themselves have an even greater degree of autonomy, which is cautiously cherished by all, including the central government. Within each classroom, as a further point, the teacher could be considered a more or less free agent in terms of both teaching method and content, and any matters that would appear to impinge on this individual autonomy and authority are readily challenged. As may be expected, there are a variety of ways by which teachers are guided in what they do despite this apparent freedom, and there is little of what might be described as educational anarchy.

Expectations of what should go on in classrooms are made apparent in all kinds of ways; certain teaching methods are advocated; graded text books are available; and the peculiar external examination system, applying at the end of mandatory schooling, tends to dictate subject syllabuses in a variety of different ways.[3] Some of the matters that influence art teachers in particular will be referred to later.

STRUCTURE OF BRITISH EDUCATION

The educational system in England can, for convenience, be divided into two levels—general education and further/higher education. General education is mandatory for all children between the ages of five and sixteen years and optional for those up to eighteen or nineteen years. Further and higher education is also optional and, all other matters being equal, eligibility for continuing into these levels is mainly dependent upon accepted evidence of ability and aptitude.[4] Except for some independent schools, all general education is the responsibility of the local education authorities, as is a large section of further and higher education. The universities have autonomy, although funded for the most part directly from central government.

The local education authorities have devised a number of ways of structuring general education, but in the main it is divided between primary and secondary education. Primary education is frequently further divided into infants schools (5 to 7 years) and junior schools (7 to 11 years). Secondary education (11 to 16 or 18 years) is generally either continuous

Tempera painting of
teacher by English child,
age 9

in single schools or divided in a number of ways such as high schools (11 to 14 years) and upper schools (14 years and older). Some local education authorities are now developing what are termed "middle schools" for the 9 to 14 years age group, as well as Sixth Form colleges and community colleges for the 16 to 19 years age group.

Teachers in primary schools, although frequently specialising in a main subject study during training, generally teach all subjects in the curriculum, whilst teachers in secondary schools are mainly teachers of the single subject or two subjects in which they specialised during a three- or four-year teacher training course or of the single subject which they studied as a first degree prior to a one-year postgraduate course of teacher training. Art in the primary school, therefore, happens to be only one of the subjects the teacher is required to teach, so it is rare to find, for instance, an art specialist in a primary school.

In the secondary schools most art teaching is the responsibility of specialist art teachers, many of whom, as indicated above, have graduated in a particular art or design specialism. In addition to the teachers in the schools, many local education authorities employ specialist art advisers to give support and guidance to the teachers. As a further contributor, an independent but government-related group of Her Majesty's Inspectors have subject specialist responsibilities and are able to give guidance and advice.

There is a wide variety of art, craft, and design provision in the post-general education sector. Colleges of further education provide many vocational courses either preparing students specifically for art, craft, or design jobs in industry or commerce, or as part of a "liberal study" or "supporting study" element in other courses. Some colleges provide foundation courses as a preparation for students intending to enter degree courses in art and design. A small number of universities provide degree courses in art and design, but the majority of such courses are provided in polytechnics and colleges of art and design. Degree courses are usually of three or four years in duration, and postgraduate courses in art and design leading to higher degrees are provided in a number of institutions, including the Royal College of Art. Students are eligible for maintenance grants, and costs of fees and grants for postgraduate teacher training students are mandatory.

STATUS OF ART EDUCATION

Despite the fact that art has had a place in almost all popular education since its beginnings[5] and that it has had a variety of values and purposes attributed to it at one time or another, it still occupies a more or less peripheral role in most schools. This is partly because art is considered a "practical" subject as against an "academic" subject, and it is traditional as well as in many ways realistic to value "academic" subjects, particularly by career-conscious parents. Underlying these notions of a "practical" subject is the widely held conviction by the majority of art teachers as well as by others outside of the field that art education is primarily, if not solely, concerned with making art and "behaving as an artist." Few intellectual demands have been made on pupils,[6] and this affects not only the attitudes of the pupils to their art activities but also those of head teachers and other teachers as well as the parents of the children.

A pattern of art teaching in England has developed in which it is believed that the circumstances necessary for art activity are dependent upon (a) the promotion of a "creative" atmosphere in the classroom (not unlike that in an art college); (b) the ready supply of a wide variety of materials and equipment; (c) the encouragement that anyone can be successful in art; and often (d) the teacher acting as an exemplar of an artist. The result has been "tons of child art." In point of fact, some excellent pieces of art work have been produced as a consequence of this approach, as exhibitions at the national and local levels show, but teachers are now beginning to ask what it is the children actually do or can learn by producing art work. Of course, it is asked what the art teachers ought to teach. Very few art teachers ever claim that they are intending to produce "artists," yet almost all their activities would seem to suggest that this is what they are designed to do. There is little need to describe what all of these activities consist of, as they are so well known, except to point out that they are largely oriented toward technique, process, materials, and product, and cover almost anything that can be remotely considered as art and craft. There is considerable dependence upon the attractiveness of new materials and techniques. Projects and work based on the seasons and festivities such as Easter and Christmas are almost universally commonplace, particularly in the primary schools. In the secondary schools, the particular specialism, interests, or even idiosyncrasies of the art teachers and the ways they have equipped their art rooms determine to a great extent which particular art activities will be undertaken.

Because of this dominance of art-making activities, there has been relatively little attention given in schools to the development of aesthetic sensibility other than that which it has often been assumed arises simply out of making art. Despite the richness of the cultural heritage, the study of the history of art, or "art appreciation," has received very little attention and even then it has mainly been with the older age group levels. Interestingly enough, the history or appreciation of art is generally taught as virtually a different subject to "art" and for the most part is not related to any concurrent art-making activities.[7]

DESIGN EDUCATION

Even within this generalised concept of art education there is diversity and a number of variations have been developed with lesser and greater degrees of success. One such variation which has gained support in some areas is that generally referred to as "design education." Design education has been developed partly in an attempt to include the traditional "heavy crafts" in schools—that is, woodwork and metalwork—into a more broadly based structure and partly to respond to what have been felt as the needs of a technologically orientated society. Underlying this variation also is the notion that "design" permeates all man-made phenomena along with a subscription to the "problem-solving" approach which presently curries much favour in educational thinking. One of the interesting outcomes has been the development of some open-plan work-shop/studio complexes around which the children rotate on what is de-scribed as the "materials circus" and spend a little time in each area, one of which may happen to be "art." The theory underlying this variation has been much stronger than its application in practice, but, even so, it has been strongly criticised for attending to certain matters at the expense of many others of equal, if not more important, value.[8]

CULTURAL DIVERSITY

One of the most important factors affecting the stability of the "long English tradition" referred to earlier is that England is rapidly becoming a multiracial, multiethnic society. There is an increasing number of first and second generation immigrants in England, mainly from the Indian subcontinent, the West Indies, and East Africa, and in schools in some of the urban areas, immigrants constitute up to ninety percent of the pupils. As against the characteristic of early English colonialism, which imposed or attempted to impose English cultural values and practices, it is now being seen by many as becoming necessary to recognise cultural plu-ralism as a fact of life, and this is profoundly affecting educational prac-tices. Differences in cultural backgrounds are probably more evident in relation to pupils' art behaviours than any others, and whilst this brings a rich variety of responses in the classroom and a considerable challenge to the teacher, perhaps more importantly, it is bringing into sharp focus questions regarding the very nature of the cultural determinants of learn-ing in art as well as a valuing of the art of other cultures.[9] As yet there is little coordination of effort or substantial material regarding this impor-tant area, but it is clear that the diverse cultural richness of the country's heritage will be invaluable as a resource for curriculum content and de-velopment.

The curriculum problem is now beginning to loom large and there is a clear concern in many art teachers to clarify aims and intentions, as may be evidenced by a proliferation of local art teachers' associations being formed in many different areas of the country. Coupled with this is a growing recognition of a need for the sequential structuring of the art curriculum[10] and a need to relate art activities in the primary school, for instance, to those in the secondary school. The singular "artist in the classroom" role of the art teacher is slowly giving way to a recognition of a collective and therefore collaborative responsibility. A number of agencies are encouraging this attitude, not the least important being the essential participation by teachers in secondary schools in some of the examining of pupils' work at the end of mandatory formal schooling.[11]

Another important contribution to art teachers becoming more professionally conscious has been through courses for teachers which in some cases have been specifically concerned with curriculum development. These have been particularly successful when attended by both primary and secondary school teachers and when related to the teachers' concurrent work in schools. One of the most notable outcomes of these courses has been the identification by teachers of a need to *know* more about art as a basis for determining curriculum content rather than, for instance, simply adding to their repertoire of skills in making art and craft objects.

At a national level, attention to giving breadth to the art education curriculum has been promoted by the Art Committee of the Schools Council. The Schools Council, which is a national, government-funded body charted with the responsibility for advising on a wide variety of educational issues, has promoted a few projects in the field of art education in recent years, and their publications have a widespread distribution throughout the whole educational system. One completed project, "The Arts and the Adolescent," which covered a broad range of issues, has been well received. A project recently undertaken, entitled "Art and the Built Environment," considers ways in which visual aesthetic literacy with regard to the man-made environment can be enhanced as a valid and worthwhile aim in itself as against, for instance, the environment merely being used as yet another stimulus for producing art work. This project may very well make an important contribution to the cultivation of response to a major part of that cultural heritage referred to at the beginning of this chapter.

EXAMINATIONS

The complicated English system of external examinations is being studied by the Schools Council in order to consider the development of a common system of examinations as a possible replacement for the present multiplicity of examination boards.[12] Although it will be some time before the influence of this project is fully realised, it is important to note that as far as the examinations in art and design were concerned, art in schools was clearly seen as having a much broader frame of reference than that of the prevalent "behaving as an artist" concept. The report of one of the groups commissioned by the Schools Council Art Committee identified (probably for the first time in the literature on English art education) clearly and explicitly defined goals for art education with attention being given to the perceptual, analytical and critical, and historical and cultural domains of art activity as well as that described as the expressive and productive domain.[13] Although it is still accepted that appropriate opportunity must always be provided for the infinitesimally small number who will become the artists and designers of the future, the proposals do put forward a framework for art education that can be considered as being realistic and a relevant aesthetic preparation for people in all walks of life.

TEACHER EDUCATION

Many of the developments in prospect will be realised through art teacher education programmes, and there have been some very real advances in this area in recent years. It would be fair to say that some of the one-year postgraduate specialist art and design teacher training courses are more advanced both conceptually and in practice than similar training courses for teachers in other subjects. This is partly due to such courses being almost unique in having large numbers of student teachers of a single specialist subject area and allowing for a concentration of concerns within a "centre of excellence" concept. Much of the underpinning of these developments springs from an increasing amount of research in the field of art education, which has arisen mainly as a consequence of advanced courses for serving teachers. There is a continuing increase in the number of such courses leading to higher qualifications as well as in registrations for higher degrees by research. As may be expected, there has been a considerable influence from the research carried out in the United States, but it is becoming manifestly clear that the uniquenesses characteristic of English art education require a research and study base that addresses itself directly to the problem of diversity. This is an emerging situation, and it is interesting to note that, whilst English art education is still very much dependent upon and appreciative of the literature produced by art educators in the United States, there is an increasing amount of literature being produced in England.[14]

It is generally recognised that art education bridges many national and international boundaries and certainly makes a greater contribution to international understanding than many other aspects of educational endeavours. Nevertheless, there is a commendable variety of approaches and attitudes to art education between countries and cultures. Art itself, despite many claims to the contrary, is not an international language, and the cultural differences in art often are as distinctive as in oral language and ideologies. The value of attempting to understand and appreciate the qualities, characteristics, and uniquenesses of art education in other countries is important not only for its own sake but also because such an understanding can contribute greatly to the recognition and development of art education in one's own country.

NOTES

1. Donald Schon gave the BBC Reigh Lectures in 1970 under the title "Change and Industrial Society." See *The Listener* 84, nos. 2173–78.

2. For an excellent history of English education, see S.J. Curtis and M.E.A. Boultwood, *A Short History of Educational Ideas* (London: Univ. Tutorial Press, 1953).

3. See B. Allison, "Problems and Recent Developments in Art and Design Examinations in England," *Art Education* 30, no. 8 (1977): 1–12.

4. Ibid.

5. See G. Sutton, *Artisan or Artist?* (London: Pergamon Press, 1967) and S. Macdonald, *The History and Philosophy of Art Education* (London: Univ of London Press, 1970).

6. "Pupils" refers to learners in general education, whilst "students" refers to learners in further and higher education.

7. B. Allison, "'Either-Or' and Its Effects on Education" (1978) to be published in the *Journal of Aesthetic Education*.

8. H. Cameron, "Design and Creative Studies Departments—Have We Gone Too Far?" *Studies in Design Education and Craft* 9, no. 2 (1977): 247–51.

9. See B. Allison, *Art Education and the Teaching About the Art of Africa, Asia and Latin America* (London: V.C.O.A.D., 1972).

10. B. Allison, "Sequential Programming in Art Education: A Revaluation of Objectives," in *Readings in Art and Design Education. Vol. 1. After Hornsey*, ed. D.W. Piper (London: Davis-Poynter, 1973), pp. 59–68.

11. See B. Allison, "Problems and Recent Developments in Art and Design Examinations in England," *Art Education* 30, no. 8 (1977): 9–12.

12. Ibid.

13. Schools Council, *18+ Research Programme Report* of the Craft Commissioned group, based on the National Society for Art Education (1976).

14. This development is more fully discussed in B. Allison, "From the Periphery to the Core," *Times Educational Supplement*, 19 May 1978.

Finland Emphasis on the Individual

Heta Kauppinen

The development and character of art education in Finland is determined by three factors: the uniform general curriculum in the country, the position of art education in the general curriculum, and the general goals set for art education. Art education has traditionally had a position as a discipline common to all students in the general curriculum throughout the comprehensive as well as high-school level. This position has served to develop the goals of general culture in art education. Generally, cultivating art education for every citizen is more prominent in Finnish art education than schooling artistically talented individuals or training merely a student's artistic aptitude.

HISTORICAL CHANGES IN ART EDUCATION

Art education first appeared in Finnish schools in 1833 as a voluntary subject. In early years Pestalozzi's educational philosophy was of great importance. Uuno Cygnaeus, who is said to be "father of public education in Finland," also established, in 1860, the ideological basis of art education. In the educational plan of the public school system Cygnaeus mentioned that art education has significance in formal education and is practically beneficial. He said that in schools drawing and modeling were to be practices because of the generally cultivating effects and because even a farmer can get practical benefit from them. The task of the teacher was strictly to prevent copying and schematic reproduction and to organize teaching to develop accurate perception and a pupil's sense of form and beauty. It is noteworthy that in an agricultural society, which Finland was in those days, art education had a more secure position than, for example, crafts, although Cygnaeus created pioneering ideas in crafts which became known worldwide.

In practice the recommendations of Cygnaeus lost their influence, and calligraphy and technical skill in drawing were stressed. The international congresses of art teachers (1904 in Bern and 1908 in London) brought new ideas into art education.

Drawing exercises depending on a student's memory were practiced to develop visual memory. Greater freedom to permit a student's personal expression was also embraced. The Finnish department in the international exposition in London was praised by the presses in many countries. The works of several students showed methods of using natural forms for design based upon Art Nouveau ideas and applied to the style of nationalistic romanticism. In 1905 statutes governing compulsory education in Finland were given and art education was included.

Art education in the late 1930s was influenced by the Bauhaus ideology, which integrated technology into art and preferred to replace teaching by individual experimentation with different kinds of materials. Although many authorities of art education in Finland thought that activities with materials belonged rather to crafts, the use of materials spread in schools and turned into empty, meaningless manual activity taught without deep awareness of the Bauhaus ideology. The ideas of neoplasticism and constructivism in art within Bauhaus also had negative effects. Designing with simple basic forms or copying a figure on the set of squares or points pressed art education into strict formalism for many years. It may be necessary to note here that the Bauhaus ideology had no significant effect on the development of Finnish design, which derives its origins more from folk art and craft with its appreciation of the interaction of material, form, and function. In the 1950s and 1960s the influence of Herbert Read and Viktor Lowenfeld spread in art education. This meant a greater understanding of child art and helped teachers to understand a child's individual emotional growth through art. Unfortunately, these ideas which can improve teachers' attitudes and empathy towards children too often served as a refuge to avoid teaching for those teachers with poor teaching ability and a weak mastery of the subject matter.

During the renovation of the school system in 1970 and the introduction of the comprehensive schools, the renovation of art education took place as well. The readiness of teachers to realize a new curriculum was not at its best in surges of creativity, and this demanded curriculum guides and effective in-service training programs in recent years to carry on the curriculum.

A special factor in the development of Finnish art education is the barrier of language. Nuances of meaning have always suffered in the process of translation. None of the well-known foreign books in art education are translated into Finnish. That partly explains the originality and self-sufficiency of Finnish art education.

THE STRUCTURE OF CURRENT FINNISH ART EDUCATION

The structure of the curriculum in Finnish art education contains the following divisions: domains, objectives, subject matter, planning, individualized learning, integration, forms of teaching, and evaluation. Each of these will be described briefly.

The four domains are Expressive, Perceptual, Analytical/Critical, and Historical/Cultural.[1] These provide a basis for conceptualizing the content of art education and pervade the learning process. The four domains are stressed with increasing complexity as the capacities of the learner develop.

Objectives contain the general educational goals of art education. They include objectives related to the four domains as well as basic (core) objectives. Goals also deal with the capacity to work together, developing responsibility for work and environment and engendering aesthetic attitudes.

The objectives of the four domains are composed on the basis of the generally cultivating effects of art education as well as the states of readiness of expression. Basic objectives describe minimum achievements on a particular school state and try to avoid unnecessary heterogeneity.

Subject matter is structured in visual means, mass media, and environment. Visual refers to visual elements and their use: colour, plastic arts, graphics, and technical drawing. Mass media deals with analysis and interpretation of pictures, graphic design, photography, film, and television. Environment means education in planning and protection of environment, including landscape, architecture, and design. The fields of art history, history of styles, and pictorial art are integrated in this area.

In application of the curriculum, the four domains penetrate every field of subject matter, engaging activities in all four domains. This structure facilitates the integration of subject matter within itself and with other disciplines. Every field of subject matter can form a unit having several lessons, and students move through these lessons sequentially. A unit on mass media may first contain pictures from the mass media that are explored through analysis and interpretation realized both visually with pictures and by discussion. When students have learned to understand and use the language of mass media images, they can move to more demanding activities such as film. Within a school year every field of subject matter is dealt with to some extent.

In planning instructional content and activities, educators arrange students for sequential learning within the instructional units of the school year. Motivated and purposeful learning implies that students participate in planning. Instructional objectives are reviewed at the beginning of every unit and lesson to activate learning and to correct the plan when needed. Effective planning helps both teachers and students to evaluate learning and to better understand assessment.

Individualized learning reduces learning difficulties and raises the level of students' achievements by diversification of activities and instruction. Individual instruction has an important place in teaching art because it is important to observe the performer and because processes and products are appreciated. Individual instruction allows for differences in readiness and ability and for diversification of objectives, instruction, activities, and evaluation.

Abilities, achievements, personality, motivation, temporary moods, differences in development and in social background: these all require individualized learning.

Students are encouraged in a special area, but, to avoid one-sidedness, performances in other areas are also encouraged.

Teachers find means for individualizing instinctively through empathy in the various everyday situations and by studying the personality of the student and characteristics of behavior that appear in expression and activities, and by noting temporary moods of the student which may arise from sorrow, illness, tiredness, depression, or from events at home such as death or conflicts. Teachers must be capable of empathy.

Differences in development often call for remedial work. Defects in seeing shapes and forms may be diminished when students use large, uncomplicated figures, limited hues, and even lines in two-dimensional works. Students with motor defects may use rulers, templates, and stencils or can be helped by rhythmical exercises, printing, or repeating figures. There is an increasing need to develop remedial means in art education, especially for the general student in the comprehensive school system where many negative differences in development, such as emotional disturbances, seem to grow.

Differentiated activities make teaching easier in some ways, since they result in greater interest and fewer problems in discipline. The low-ability students can be helped independently; the advanced students can move ahead and progress more rapidly.

Forms of teaching (teaching methods) serve as functional models for activities during lessons. Teachers must know many forms of instruction to be able to select a relevant method for the performance of a task.

Four main forms of teaching can be observed and classified: the preparatory method, the problem-solving method, the exercising method, and free expression.

The preparatory method contains three phases, instructional, expressive, and evaluative. In the instructional phase the teacher introduces the task and objectives, and gives the necessary knowledge of the area to be learned. During the class, the teacher observes the student and advises when needed. In evaluation, learned things are recalled to mind with activities and products evaluated on the basis of objectives. The preparatory method is the most common method and usually gives good results, but the influence of the teacher may sometimes become too dominant and too structured.

The problem-solving method is a product of theories of creativity. The task is presented as a problem to be solved, and brainstorming in groups usually follows. The actual teaching takes place in evaluation. The problem-solving method has advantages in learning new tasks and new frames of reference. In a typical situation, a student must give a clear visual answer to a posed problem—he must express a pictorial message that is understood by other people. Problems to be solved visually may be posed as follows: "The Greatest," "A barrier," "Too little," "Near to fall," "Too many in a small room," "Transformation," "Here is safe," "Coexistence," or "The Circle of Nations."

The exercising method refers to a renewed version of the early methods in art education. Students develop skills and technique by studying values, colours, lights, and shadows or other elemental design. This method can considerably raise the level of expression of students and lends itself to sequential learning.

Free expression as a form of teaching implies expression inspired by music, sounds, movements, poems, moods, or feelings. It is also sometimes used therapeutically. The teacher is responsible for avoiding learning situations that deteriorate into aimless, empty activities which erroneously are sometimes considered creative.

In actual practice the forms of teaching are varied according to the situation and task. One empirical study proved that, when only one method of the four was used, the preparatory method led to the best results.[2] By varying the four methods, achievements improved the most.

Evaluation implies both evaluation of the teaching-learning process and assessment of the product as well as the stage of development of the student. Evaluation and assessment are based on the assigned topics.

Poster by Finnish
child, grade 6

Therefore, it is necessary that the objects are familiar both to teacher and students. In meaningful and motivated learning, when a unit or lesson is planned, the students have the opportunity to plan the criteria of assessment together with the teacher and to participate in its evaluation and assessment.

Therefore the significance of the content of objectives and learning activities are evaluated by the extent to which the student achieves goals such as visual and aesthetic readiness for everyday life, readiness in expression (including art appreciation), and the states of readiness for continued studies. Evaluation and assessment serve to plan further studies and are linked to the circle of education—planning—learning—evaluation.

FIELDS OF INTEREST IN THE PRESENT ART EDUCATION

The structure of subject matter consists of three main fields: visual means, mass media, and environment. The area of visual means has the longest tradition in art education as a basis for all activities. The mass media took a major position in the late 1960s. It then became apparent that, although people were big consumers of all kinds of images from the mass media, the schools ignored this essential part of contemporary life. Art education assumed the responsibility of educating students into becoming more critical and conscious consumers of pictures. To carry out this task, art education had to develop a whole field of visual and pictorial pedagogy of analysis, interpretation, and classification of mass media pictures. The mass media brought new, purposeful content into art education and expanded expression to areas of photography, film, and television.

INTERDISCIPLINARY APPROACHES

In recent years, problems of planning and protection of the environment have been evident everywhere and have again brought a new duty to art education, being the only discipline in the schools which considers problems of man-made environment—landscape, architecture, and design.

Environmental studies penetrate disciplines such as biology, geography, history, and art education, which involve both interdisciplinary and discipline-centered curriculum planning. A curriculum structure that gives the necessary links to interdisciplinary studies and a valid basis for environmental studies in every subject involves the following:

PHYSICAL ENVIRONMENT	Natural Environment Man-made Environment
PSYCHO-SOCIAL ENVIRONMENT	Social Environment Psychological Environment

History, planning, and protection provide a basis for the studies of the four fields of environment, which are considered to work as an interactive, ever-changing whole, the character of which is affected by man.

Art education is predominantly responsible for the studies of man-made environment, but it has activities as well in each field—to a certain extent. For teaching practice in art education, the man-made environment is structured into landscape, architecture, and design. The way of approach is aesthetic and functional, and the main field of knowledge is art history, especially the history of styles and folk art.

Interdisciplinary studies may be centered about a common project, a weekly theme, or a theme for a year, and every participating discipline brings its contribution to the topic. Studies overlap also in disciplinary studies. Natural environment is mainly studied in the natural sciences, but the aesthetic properties belong to art education. Man-made environment's beautiful incorporation with nature; perceiving, understanding, and visual description of characteristic features of a landscape or parts and particles of it; learning the aesthetic meaning of nature to man—all are included in art activities. Another field of environment, the psychosocial, needs the contribution of art education since social and psychic problems may arise from the poor aesthetic quality of the environment.

Studies usually start from the nearest surrounds of student and expand with increasing depth and complexity as the student acquires cultural, aesthetic, and functional awareness of the environment and its development, as he learns to analyze and judge the environment, and as he explores ways of changing, preserving, and improving his surrounds.

Environmental studies in art education emphasize visual and pictorial activities that enable the student to apply and plan visual solutions. The environment provides a natural basis for learning in art education and affects natural connections with other branches of study.

NOTES

1. B. Allison, "Sequential Programming in Art Education," in *Readings in Art Education*, ed. D.W. Piper (London: Davis-Poynter, 1972).

2. B. Karlavaris, "Die Methodologie bei der Objektivierung von Bewertung von Kinderzeichnungen in der wissenschaftlichen Forschung" (Zagreb: INSEA Regional Conference, 1972).

Germany Decentralization in the Federal Republic

Max Klager

THE STRUCTURE OF ART FOR SCHOOLS

The situation of art education in Germany is characterized by the division of prewar Germany into two parts: a larger part in the west and south called the Federal Republic of Germany (BRD) and a smaller eastern and northeastern part called the German Democratic Republic (DDR). The two states developed radically different political, social, and economic systems. Germany has a parliamentary democracy and a market economy. The DDR has a communist-style system with a socialist, state-controlled economy. The DDR school system is strictly centralized, whereas the German one is decentralized. The West German *Länder* (states) enjoy a constitutionally guaranteed cultural autonomy. The Federal Office of Education, located in the capital city of Bonn, functions in a consultative capacity only. Traditionally, German schools are organized in a dual system, with the four-year elementary school as its basis. There is a general stream, *Hauptschule* (grades 5 to 9) and *Realschule* (grades 5 to 10), and a college preparatory stream, *Gymnasium* (grades 5 to 13). In recent years this system has been supplemented in some German states by *Gesamtschule* (comprehensive school), which integrates both streams (grades 5 to 13). The introduction of this type of school (in the 1920s advocated as *Einheits-Schule*) is largely dependent on the political situation in the various states. Social Democratic governments favor the comprehensive school; Christian Democratic governments want to maintain the traditional dual system.

German art education dogma, since the beginning of the art education movement at the turn of the century, maintains art education as an obligatory general education subject for all the pupils in the schools. This tradition has continued up to the present, with some minor deviations regarding the amount of time per week and the introduction of alternative choices at some grade levels.

Art teacher education in Germany has also developed along a kind of dual system within the last fifteen years. In the past, academies of fine arts trained the only full-fledged art teachers, who taught at the *Gymnasium* level. Their preparation included two years of internship after graduation from art school. They consider themselves as artist-teachers.

Teachers with a major or minor in art education, who are employed in the elementary and general secondary schools *(Hauptschulen* and *Realschulen)*, are educated at colleges and universities. There the art experiences of the students are strongly supplemented with education courses. Student teaching and internships are included as part of the course of study. A two- or three-year probation period, with full teaching load and additional courses and supervision, conclude the professional education of this second type of art teacher, who consider themselves as teacher-artists. Both are state civil servants with life tenure.

COMPETING CONCEPTS OF ART TEACHING

During the 1950s theory and practice in the elementary and general secondary schools were strongly influenced by the Britsch-Kornmann ideas.[1] The followers of Britsch contended that art practice, called pictorial perceiving, is ruled by certain laws of perception. The concomitant pictorial expression occurs in distinct phases. In actual teaching these educators emphasized form to the detriment of color. Art production was considered largely a result of natural growth rather than of systematic instruction. In the United States, Henry Schaefer-Simmern represented this point of view in his *Unfolding of Artistic Activity* (1948).

On the *Gymnasium* level, art teaching was shaped by Bauhaus ideas. Very popular during the 1950s was the "playing with pictorial means," that is, with lines, form, volume, various materials, etc. At the same time traces of *Musische Erziehung* ("musical" in the sense of integrated aesthetic education, aiming at individual fulfillment and personal happiness) could be observed. The ideological tendency discernible in *Musische Erziehung* was a stance against civilization, against the machine age and rational thinking. Feeling, *Erlebnis*, direct sensual experience were emphasized. All three positions, Britsch-Kornmann, Bauhaus, and *Musische Erziehung*, took little notice of contemporary art and design appreciation.

This situation was profoundly changed by Reinhard Pfennig's *Presence of the Fine Arts—Educating Pictorial Thinking* in 1959 (this 340-page volume had four editions in eleven years), which marked a turning point in German art educational thinking and practice.[2] Pfennig postulated that the elements of contemporary art as well as those of the past are the reference points of teaching art in the schools. Pfennig's spiritual source is Paul Klee, who had formulated the concept of pictorial thinking in the 1920s. In his book Pfennig presented a consistent, streamlined course of study, divided into three levels of experience. These interrelated instructional sequences are characterized by the integration of "seeing," "doing," and "saying." The first level, roughly corresponding to the primary grades, includes figures and ground problems, articulation of signs, establishment of relational structures, usage of the form qualities of processes, experimentation with methods of grouping and with various materials. The second level, corresponding to the lower secondary grades, deals with "syntactical structure," posing problems in space, form, color, and movement. These experiences are then combined and treated in greater depth at the third level of experience. Art teaching here deals with structures and patterns, with formation and transformation, and with the process of making. This integrative program documented in Pfennig's book has had a pervasive influence on art instruction.

Five years later, in 1964, another publication signaled a new trend. In Gunter Otto's *Art as Process in Teaching*[3] an attempt was made to base art teaching on a strong scientific-empirical orientation. Neither modern art nor the art of the past but the life experiences of pupils in a contemporary, technological society were to be the basis of theory and practice. In concrete art educational terms, this means: creating a complementary situation between producing and reflecting, between rational thinking and an experimental approach towards art production. In the wake of the antiart tendencies of the late 1960s, Otto changed his emphasis in later publications more towards the critical and verbal aspects of art teaching. He succeeded in giving the term "art instruction" a definite meaning. Thus, art instruction concerned itself primarily with those aspects that can be evaluated as the result of planned and purposeful teaching.

This change of emphasis from the more intuitive to the more rational coincided with the introduction of "operationalization" into German curriculum making. Otto's scientific approach, together with the impact of information theory, linguistics, semiology, and sociologies of various kinds, took German art education curricula as well as the publications in professional magazines and books to a high level of abstraction. The practitioners in the field, however, had difficulties in adjusting to the new theoretical approaches. Art educational jargon, sometimes with a new-Marxist flavor, impeded the necessary communication between the theorists in the colleges and the teachers in the schools.

In this situation many of the frustrated teachers turned to a new publication, *The Didactics of the Fine Arts*, written by Hans Daucher and Rudolf Seitz.[4] Didactics offered guidance in art teaching on a scientific basis and presented perceptual psychology and creativity theory with a compendium of practical recommendations. Theory was emphasised, but not to the detriment of artistic practice. The visual thinking aspects elaborated in the book justified the continued practical work in the art room. Daucher and Seitz combined in their approach the emotional, perceptual, and critical functions of art teaching in such a way that the necessary transfer into actual teaching situations was facilitated.

The most controversial single event in the history of German art education during the period between 1965 and 1975 was the emergence of a concept called "visual communication."[5] The theoretical background for the proponents of this new school subject meant to replace art education was largely influenced by the writings of Theodor Adorno *(Frankfurter Schule)*, Walter Benjamin, and Herbert Marcuse. Roughly speaking, the label "visual communication" was used by two groups of educators called here Group A and Group B.

Group A wanted to make art teaching more relevant in terms of society and mass communication. The subjects of reference were the mass media such as television, movies, comics, and advertising. Emphasis was placed on scientific thinking, rational assessment, and analytical critique. Since art—with the exception of a small segment of political art—may not be very helpful in questioning society, it is of little significance for teaching, yet it may still be useful in a hedonistic way.

Group B consists of new-Marxist, anticapitalistic educators who want to see art education have its share in bringing about political change in Germany. Such change would eventually lead the nation into a new socialist society of a utopian kind (the socialism of the DDR is not necessarily a valid model for this new social order). In this view the teacher must be partial to this overriding aim of changing the consciousness of the pupils in favor of the new society. He should expose the machinations of the capitalist exploiters and uncover the function of art and advertisement as a means of maximizing profits and of perpetuating the economic and political power of the few. For these educators, the function of art practice in the schools lies primarily in its emancipatory potential within the framework of the ongoing class struggle.

The direct influence of the visual communicators in schools depends on the political situation in the various states. The curriculum directives in the state of Hessen marked the first and lasting success of the proponents of the new subject. Speaking of the whole of Germany, however, it seems that a pluralistic and eclectic attitude prevails, with art, design, and the individual pupil as the main reference points for art teaching in the schools.[6]

PROBLEMS AND NEW DEVELOPMENTS

One specific problem that can illustrate the impact of the controversies of the late 1960s on the art room teacher is the problem of art analysis and appreciation. This trend was marked by a strong emphasis on verbalization and by the concomitant neglect of art practice in the new study courses for art teachers. This generalization probably applies more to the college and university departments of art education than to the art schools. The rise of criticism and "debunking" with a political intention which influenced the graduates of these institutions had paradoxical results. On the one hand, it contributed to the widening gap between theory and practice in actual teaching, for it tended to alienate pupils who were unwilling to give up art work, treasured as "recreational," "doing things with your own hands," and "having fun." They often called the new art education, alias visual communication, "another type of social studies." Yet the new trend also alienated many teachers, who came to doubt the feasibility of teaching strategies depending primarily on verbal responses.

Thus it happened that the new emphasis which could have contributed to a necessary and legitimate strengthening of art and design analysis, had the opposite effect. Teachers retreated to the sanctuary of practical art studies and neglected to treat the creative interpreting and handling of art and aesthetic objects in the art room. To confound the situation further, the artistic sensibilities of some teachers appeared to be insufficient in motivating and guiding pupils to meaningful artistic skills and understandings. Thus, it was not surprising that in the mid-1970s, analogous to certain trends in the United States, the German Federal Office of Education together with the Federation of German Artists started a pilot program for "artists in residence," especially for the general secondary school *(Hauptschule)*, grades 5 to 9.

In later developments of art education several new promising trends can be discerned. One such trend refers to the primary level, where programs are tested in which the conventional artistic subjects, such as art, music, poetry, crafts, and dance, are integrated into an "aesthetic

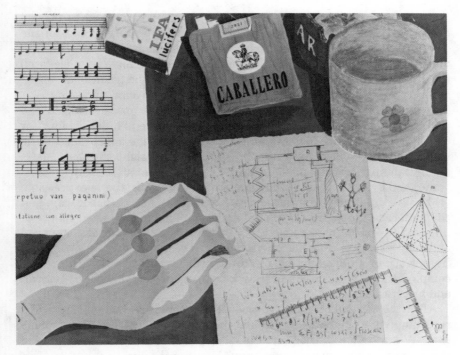

Ink and wash drawing by West German child, age 13

field." The other interesting and important development—which has already come into effect by mutual agreement in all German states, with certain variations in content—is the *Reformierte Oberstufe*, "reformed upper level," in the *Gymnasium*. This signifies a fundamental change in general and specifically in the role of the arts, and represents the final and logical conclusion of the German art educational dictum, mentioned at the beginning of this article, which is that art education should be taught as an obligatory subject in all grades in all schools regardless of talent or future occupation.[7]

In the reformed upper level, comprising the twelfth and thirteenth grades, the last two years of the *Gymnasium* and the college preparatory stream of the comprehensive school are divided into semester courses. There are four major learning areas: mathematics/natural sciences; German/foreign languages/the arts; social sciences (social science, geography, history, and religion); and physical education/sports. The pupil must choose two of these subjects as "achievement-courses" (five lesson hours a week for each) and a specified number of basic courses as well. A complicated credit-point system plus the written and oral exam at the end of the fourth term (thirteenth grade) constitute the final grades of the diploma *(Abitur)*. The revolutionary aspect from an art education point of view is that the arts (art education and music as well) have been elevated to a full-fledged *Abitur* subject with equal status to the traditional *Abitur* subjects such as mathematics, English, German, Physics, and so on.

A model for art education in Germany has been operationalized and postulates the following aims in the art field. There is a desirability for capability and readiness to (1) perceive sensitively the appearance of the visual and tactile environment; (2) use scientific insight and methods in understanding artistic phenomena; (3) experience affectively, understand, and evaluate works of art and other items of aesthetic expression; (4) behave creatively, express oneself artistically in a personal way, and communicate and strive for mutual understanding in the visual sphere of life; and (5) participate responsibly in preserving the cultural heritage and help create a humane environment. The pupil studies within the framework of a delicately balanced program, which tries to achieve the complementary integration of practical art work and analytical, critical, and historical aspects.

After the turmoil of the last decade, such models are hopeful signs of a returning vigor and self-assertion in the teaching of art. Fiedler's aphorism, "A world view without art is incomplete,"[8] may again be reflected in the eminently humanistic tradition of German art education.

NOTES

1. G. Britsch, *Theorie der bildenden Kunst* (Munich, 1926).
2. R. Pfennig, *Gegenward der bildenden Kunst-Erziehung zum bildnerischen Denken* (Oldenburg, 1970).
3. G. Otto, *Kunst als Prozess im Unterrict* (Brunswick, 1964).
4. H. Daucher and R. Seitz, *Didaktik der bildenden Kunst* (Munich, 1971).
5. Der Hessische Kultusminister, Rahmenrichtlinien Primarstufe, *Kunst/Visuelle Kommunikation*, 1972.
6. P. Heinig, *Kunstunterricht* (Heilbronn, 1976).
7. Staatsinstitut für Schulpadagogik, *Curricularer Lehrplan fur Kunsterziehung in der Kollegstufe* (Donauwörth, 1976).
8. K. Fiedler, *Schriften uber Kunst* (Hrsg.v.H.Marbach: Leipzig, 1896).

The Netherlands Tradition and Advanced Ideas

Maarten Tamsma

The great majority of world art is within the reach of every Dutchman. The budget for art in the Netherlands is considerable, so that, on paper, conditions for art education in Holland are attractive.

THE EDUCATIONAL SYSTEM

A relatively accurate but general view of art education within the Dutch educational system can be provided. At this time, however, plans for a total renewal of the educational system in the Netherlands have been designed. Presently, after kindergarten and primary school, a Dutch twelve-year-old enters the "bridge year" of a high school. During that year a decision is made as to the type of high school the student will enter; based mainly on the academic achievement of the student, the decision is the consensus of the parents, the student, and the school system.

A thirteen-year-old student has the opportunity to enter a lower high school, or a two- to three-year vocational school, or a middle high school, which is a three-year, nonacademic high school. The high school may also be a choice, but this school prepares the student in four years for higher vocational education such as teacher training. Still another choice, the university preparing high school is five years in duration after the bridge year.

Only ten percent of the student population in any one year enter a university in the Netherlands. Art schools and teacher training centers in Holland are considered high vocational education. Large comprehensive high schools exist which include vocational and middle high school education and enroll 1,000 to 2,000 students. Students in these schools may, after completing the comprehensive high school program, continue into the high high school and finish a four-year program, then enter the university preparation high school. In all programs during the first years, students take Dutch, English, German, French, mathematics, physics, chemistry, biology, geography, history, art, crafts, textile design, music, economics, and physical education. In the last years before graduation, students select up to seven subjects. Seven subjects are, in fact, required in the university preparing high school. One of these subjects may be an art-related subject such as art, crafts, textiles, or music. Federal graduation examinations are given in art and are nationwide and federally controlled.

ART TEACHER TRAINING

Severe entrance requirements exist for Dutch educators to teacher training institutions, and various levels exist. Lower and middle high schools are third-level education and employ primary school teachers who have taken one or two years of additional art courses, usually in evening sessions, and have successfully completed the federal examination. Second-level art teachers, working in the high high schools, have completed a three-year program at an art academy. First-level degrees are obtained by adding two more years and completing the federal examination, thus qualifying that educator to teach in a university preparing high school, a teacher training center, or an art school. Programs for all levels of degrees do not vary but are government controlled. Those typical for the second-level art teacher include courses in portrait and figure drawing, still life composition, two- and three-dimensional design, fantasy drawing, line drawing, lettering, watercolor, art history, perspective, psychological and pedagogical methods of art education, and explanatory sketching on the blackboard. Each subject requires a federal examination. Programs of further education leading to the first-level degree also include anatomy, figure drawing, still life oils and watercolors, etching, lithography, advanced art history, museum guiding, art education methods, cultural history, student teaching, and art historical sketching on the blackboard.

Opportunities for a Ph.D. in art education do not exist in Holland; therefore, university faculty are not engaging in the philosophical concepts underlying art education. Rather, the first-level degree is the highest degree available to Dutch art educators. In Dutch teacher centers only part-time faculty teach the philosophy of art education, and such faculty are usually high school art teachers with a personal interest in the theory of art education. Such limited attention to philosophical concepts of art education causes Dutch art education to reflect a practical approach to art in schools.

The Dutch Art Education Association, however, attempts to fill this void. This agency produces a monthly publication that traces the development of Dutch art education by documenting that system's characteristics, which range from the traditional free expression approaches to the Bauhaus, phenomenological, and visual communication approaches. The Dutch art educator who is versed in English, French, and German also has many international art education publications at his or her disposal.

THE EDUCATION BUDGET

Art is a federal responsibility in the Netherlands. Art education courses inside and outside of the schools are federally funded, as are museums, orchestras, dance ensembles, and theatres. Ninety-nine percent of the arts in the Netherlands are federally funded and, although there are admission fees, this federal policy has obvious financial advantages for the arts. Art educators are responsible to the ministry of culture and the ministry of education for their budgets.

ART IN DUTCH SCHOOLS

Primary school teachers are prepared to teach art after a limited background. Dutch law required that art be taught in schools each week. Because of a lack of training and understanding, however, many schools replace art with other activities. Art teachers are hired by some city schools, but the professional art teachers are generally employed on the secondary level. The higher the category of a high school, the better educated the art teacher will be. Depending on the program in a high school, the students will follow two, three, or four hours of required art, crafts, or music per week. On the college level there is no art outside the

Woodcut of hospital scene by Dutch child, age 13

art academics and the art teacher training centers. Art departments in universities do not exist because art belongs to the high vocational section.

OUTSIDE ART ACTIVITIES

Towns with more than 50,000 inhabitants have creativity centers in which art courses are provided on day and evening schedules. Thousands of Dutch citizens enroll in these courses, which range from filmmaking, silkscreening, etching, dance, and jewelry making. As are all forms of

Woodcut of car ferry by Dutch child, age 17

education (including private schools) in the Netherlands, these courses are federally supported and compose twenty-four percent of the national budget.

VARIATIONS IN DUTCH ART EDUCATION

After the Second World War, art education for high school students in Holland was concerned with still life drawings in pencil or with studies from plaster casts of portraits from wall plates in plaster. Viktor Lowenfeld, whom the Dutch considered in the Austrian School along with Franz Cizek and Richard Roth, influenced a group of nine art teachers from The Hague in the mid-1930s who were known as the "H9." Their work was interrupted by World War II.

Herbert Read's *Education Through Art* had the most influence upon art education in Holland after 1945, becoming the "Bible of Free Expression" of the Laissez-Faire movement in Dutch art education. The free expression movement categorized the visual aspects in children's art work and pledged more schematic teaching. By the 1960s, however, over forty percent of the required art hours were taken away from the educational system.

The Bauhaus had a great impact on Dutch art education. Holland had its own Stijl Group with Mondriaan, but this movement was not so much involved in the educational process as was the German Bauhaus. Paul Citroen, a Dutch artist from the Bauhaus, wrote *The Art Lesson* and *The Dot*, which outlined a step-by-step training method for art teaching. This curriculum prescribed line and tone studies, followed by a concentration of line, tone, and material studies, with free work to occur only during vacations. Tone studies were much favored for teaching, with exercises of forty little squares starting with white, adding more blue, until all forty squares were filled to pure blue. Many art teachers were attracted by a combination of the child-directed theories of Read and the discipline-directed theories of the Bauhaus. The child-directed theories seemed to give art teachers a means of doing something pedagogical while the Bauhaus provided a more scientific rationale.

Phenomenological studies in Dutch art education were based upon the philosophies of Merleau Ponty, Heidegger, and Wouter van Ringelestein. Van Ringelestein, a Dutch art educator, developed a theory in which art education was considered a tool for the visual relations between the object and the subject, and was known as a dialectical method. This method is a dialogue between the free expression of the child and the Bauhaus concept stressing the object as the ensuing learning process. In this method, belief is in the artists' ability to open perceptions. The artist's way of looking at and interpreting the visual world has become the model for the way that others should perceive the world. The quality of the looking-working dialogue is expressed in the level of "reality" that can be found in the art work. "Through images, the world becomes reality" is a central philosophy to the phenomenological art educators. Toon Geritse expanded the philosophical base of Van Ringelestein's theories and published a book with practical examples of this variation of Dutch art education.

In the 1960s a new concept of art education from the Frankfurt School was introduced into Dutch art education. Reflecting the general emancipation of students and emphasizing the preparation of the student as an active and critical citizen, this concept exposed students to visual commercials and the *Visuelle Kommunikation*, techniques of visual communication. Dutch art teachers using this approach teach students to be aware of their dependencies on the capitalistic system and critical of the visual temptations and manipulations of contemporary society. This visual communication system has not yet achieved a full Dutch identity, being based upon translated German textbooks and articles. Rob Blume and Brian Oostra are the main standard bearers for this movement in Holland.

Dutch art education does not today reflect these variations in pure form, but the phenomenological method enjoys the most support. This method appeals best to the conventional Dutch art teacher by giving to the teaching of art a solid philosophical basis. It does, however, negate efforts toward integrating art with nonvisual art activities and other disciplines. Those first-degree teachers with the most thorough art backgrounds are the chief supporters. On lower levels it is often blended with other variations of art education.

REFERENCES

Contourennota. *Nieuwe Uitleg*. The Hague: Ministry of Education. (English version of educational plans for Dutch education system.)

Gerritse, Elzinga, and Engbersen Gerritse. "Tekenles in de praktijk." Postbus 24, de Bilt, The Netherlands: Uitgeverij Cantecleer. (Practical suggestions for art teaching with pictures of student work.)

Gerritse. "De geschiedenis van het tekenonderwijs." Postbus 24, de Bilt, The Netherlands: Uitgeverij Cantecleer. (The history of Dutch and European art education.)

Lesson Letters. Oudegracht 27, Utrecht, The Netherlands: L.S.B.V. Office. (Dialogical viewpoints and visual communications ideas.)

Tamsma, Maarten. *Zienswijzer*. Postbus 100, Amsterdam: Uitgeverij Meulenhoff Educatief. (International reader for art education day-to-day practice in schools.)

Van Ringelestein. *Art Education*. Journal of the National Art Education Association. June 1969.

EASTERN EUROPE

Hungary Developing Visual Culture

Maria Vida-Szekacs

The art critic Károly Lyka from the first years of the century fought for public education in Hungary through perpetuating a combination of the analysis of art products with intensive sketching and drawing for thirteen- to eighteen-year-old students in schools. By 1911 such exponents of Hungarian intellectual life as the painters József Rippl Rónai, Károly Kernstock, and Mark Verdes, as well as the aestheticians Lajos Fülep, György Lukács, and Bela Balazs continued to expound on the need for art education in schools by addressing numerous educational conferences and through emphasizing this need in their writings. According to György Bölöni, a contemporary of Rodin and Brancusi, children in the lower grades should be introduced to "why a picture is a picture" and its colors, lines, and harmony, not just the value of the picture's subject matter. Bölöni suggested that the comprehension of art products should be taken out of the hands of pedagogues and entrusted to artists, but this stance has been attacked as being unrelated to the elements of education. Such controversy continued for a long time in Hungary, with the dominating conservative pedagogy holding their ground.

During the 1919 Revolution, the School Reform Committee of the Hungarian Republic of Councils began a drawing program in the new eighth grade public elementary schools. The program was designed by Moholy-Nagy, an original member of the Bauhaus and a pioneer in the study of children's drawings. Moholy-Nagy had presented the works of Hungarian village children at the first Berlin conference on children's drawings and, as early as 1905, had authored a text on the development of children through drawing. Three objectives were developed in Moholy-Nagy's programs: (1) the communication-centered approach, in which drawing was considered an ally of language and writing in the communication of thoughts; (2) the aesthetic development approach, in which students are active participants in the cognition and production of objects of beauty; and (3) the harmonious development of a child's spiritual powers, in which a pedagogical approach in art was intended to develop the personality of the child. The new eighth grade schools of the School Reform Committee failed to materialize, however, because of the collapse of the revolution, and the Moholy-Nagy project was never realized.

Moholy-Nagy's work on the significance of the development of visual culture, the influence of the Bauhaus school, and recognition of pictorial illiteracy influenced the continuing struggle for art education in the state-controlled schools of Hungary. Agost Reiter established a large scale reproduction exchange center in Hungary. Here ten- to fourteen-year-old boys could acquaint themselves with the art works, models of buildings, and reproductions in the center by arranging them in an individual fashion and according to various viewpoints, thus expressing their value systems through art history by means of a playful method. The students were given the opportunity to evolve their own museums as they learned about beauty in objects and developed their tastes and discriminations.

Kálmán Szabó and his colleagues built upon Nagy's legacy as well as American and modern European art education practices, but instruction in the sciences during the 1950s pushed art education to the background. Art was abolished in the first grade, while the number of lessons in the higher grades was reduced. Despite these restrictions, experimentation continued as teachers sought new ways of using the drawing of forms and solids, of making pictorial combinations, and of developing both space perception and fantasy.

THE CONTEMPORARY CURRICULUM

After considerable preparation, a new plan for grade school education, including the first to eighth grade instructional program in drawing, reached completion. The plan states some of the goals of the new program:

> The object of instruction in drawing is to develop the visual culture of the students by inducing them to consciously observe, and pictorially represent, reality, thereby guiding them towards an ever more complete cognition of nature and society. It should educate reflective people bent on making discoveries and capable of creating, who can interpret phenomena by visually analysing them, can investigate their relationships, and are properly oriented in the flood of pictorial information.

In visual culture education, children's visual expressions of space, form, and color are enriched and their conceptions of visual phenomena

are made more exact by means of visual, tactile, and kinaesthetic observations. A permanent outcome of the visual art programs is the improvement of the children's visual memory, fantasy, and sense of form.
This latter is effected by recalling form and function, as well as by leading
children to discover and represent beauty. One such a basic premise is
realized with the level of children's ability to identify colors that has been
brought from their families. Teachers recognize these premises while
developing the children's familiarity with colors towards more sensitive
and conscious observation and systematization of color. The practice of
the expression of emotions, thoughts, and visual experiences, as well as
the practice of the ability to compose, is cultivated. Attention is given to
the teaching of the explanatory drawing, furnishing information with
industrial drawing as it incorporates elements of the international system
of notations.

Familiarizing students with art works linked with our age is another
important element in visual cultural education in Hungary. During the
fifth grade, children often study cave drawings and the manner in which
the Egyptians represented space, ancient architecture, and staturary. In
the sixth and seventh grades children analyze Romanesque, Gothic, Renaissance, and Baroque art works located in Hungary and in other countries. Study of the work of the most significant foreign and Hungarian
exponents of nineteenth- and twentieth-century art completes the process by the eighth grade, with the choice of foreign masters left to the
teacher's discretion.

RELATING THE ARTS: INSTRUCTIONAL FORMATS

For the primary grades in Hungary, a lesson format was evolved which
combined singing and traditional children's games with improvisation
dramatics, painting, and modeling.[1]

Hungarian schools have been afforded the opportunity to experiment
in grade schools, amongst children living in families. In these classes,
which are democratic in atmosphere, new mathematics as well as native-
language education and singing, movement, creative dramatics, and
painting have become part and parcel of the children's experiences in
these classes. During the fourth grade, one half of a year is often spent
intensively studying a nineteenth-century tale, such as "Rose and Violet"
by János Arany, which is written in verse. A project of a class might also
be, for example, a forty-page, large-sized picture book that has led to the
preliminary stages of dramatics, a phase-by-phase acting out of the
scenes, with illustration done in various techniques such as the making of
large puppets, paintings of these as models, and movement sketches.

Woodcut by Hungarian child, age 9

Drawing from nature is often oriented to the senses of children nine or ten years old and relates to isolated and uninteresting objects. If the motivation derived from the permanent unit of experience is strong, the children paint attentively, concentrating while observing the model and recreating figures meaningful to them that are expressive and humorous. Movement sketches drawn from a model in pen and ink have also worked well. Such sketching impels the students to be prompt in observation, for their hands are moved by the direction which the scanning of their eyes follows. The kinetic culture has also contributed to enabling children to express, through quick record, the movement of their companions. The alternation of completely contrasted tasks has also stood the test of painting a picture of the motionless puppet followed by a movement sketch. Observation of reality is usually followed by free composition.[2]

Art education in Hungary includes all branches of art; it also is a *relationship between the adult and the child.* In early childhood the arts still coexist, inseparably merging into one another. Later on they must separate. Children should familiarize themselves with the special nature of musical, literary, pictorial, and kinetic expression. That is, they should find in music an atmosphere not to be expressed either by language or by pictorial means. They should perceive the linguistic beauties of literature and the independent laws of the pictorial world. The life and development of children involve tasks that in certain periods make it possible for them to form some synthesis. Around the age of ten the segregation and polarization of various branches of art is natural if the whole is synthesized by movement and dramatics.

In the subsequent phases from the first grade onwards, good cooperation between the persons of colleges exists. Class work finds variety in sensory exercises and the recognition of materials; the making of puppets out of corncobs and potatoes, the making of masks and carnival costumes, weaving, and spinning are linked with the games of folk festivals. An example is found when the children perform and chant, in self-designed and self-prepared carnival costumes, a self-created play that is both original and traditional.

The National Institute for Pedagogy organizes seasonal games in the primary grades of the village schools in a course entitled "Aesthetic Lessons." Seasonal games, for example, use bird games often related to the migration of birds. Included would be observations of nature and games involving movement combined with representation and puppetry. The viewing of folk art works and art products, as well as literary discussions, are incorporated into seasonal games.[3]

In Budapest an aesthetic education program is taught which is fairly successful with first to fourth graders. This program is characterized by complete intensity; a workshop atmosphere evolves in which everybody works with a will. The making of animated cartoons, wall paintings, the various graphical procedures, and the modelling and house building are exciting activities assigned during a school term. In another Budapest school the teacher incorporates dramatics by representing space kinetically into the pattern of the traditional drawing lesson. While learning the convex and concave spatial forms, children reproduce and represent these with their own movements. The children show solutions through paper and pasteboard models and finally by drawing and painting them.

Furthermore, study by the Váli Street School's fifth graders of Paul Klee's painting *Fuga in Rosso* illustrates a novel method of development of understanding and appreciation of the art product. The children listen to a passage of Chromatic Fantasia and Fuge by Bach. Some of them move in time to the music, intent on collectively expressing the characteristics of the individual melodic lines. They then form a collage of this experience by superimposing on a blue pasteboard field shreds of paper of bluish, grayish, and purplish shades. During the following week slides of their work are prepared. The children receive them with surprise, and, under the impact of the enlarged versions of their own pictures, they discover certain pictorial laws. They articulate ideas which attest the sensitivity balance, the struggle of colors and forms, and so on. Only after a good discussion is Klee's beautiful painting presented to them.

The following week the work—both that of the children and the artist—is examined once again. Through their own work, the children feel Klee's work kindred to them and near to them; they admire it and view it with pleasure. The sequence ends with them swinging their arms and hands in the air to feel certain of Klee's motifs and afterwards giving a collective "performance in dance of the picture."[4]

In other workshops the assumption has never been confirmed that it is in connection with their own activity that the children can best familiarize themselves with works of art. An example of this principle was found in the learning activity in which the class walks around an African Makonde sculpture. The children sketch the sculpture from several views, and thus discover that the main structural line of the statue is the spiral. One student who served as an assistant (art historian Andrea Kárpáti) is now continuing this experiment in a Budapest school and is working in several country schools, in conjunction with other colleagues, on her own program entitled "The Language of the Visual Arts."

Another Budapest school has for several years been working on aesthetic educational programs. These programs, in addition to literature and the visual arts, include eurythmics and yoga. In another school in a village, teachers have been working for ten years to develop an alliance between scientific and aesthetic education and to demonstrate the community-shaping and personality-developing effect of the new program.

The possibility of visual arts culture is alive in Hungary. The curriculum is open; it ensures freedom; and the young people's passion for experimentation is on the increase. This topic is kept on the agenda of the Visual Culture Research Commission of the Hungarian Academy of Sciences by a supportive team of architects, art historians, photographers and visual artists, filmmakers, linguists, semioticians, sociologists, and drawing teachers.

NOTES

1. Maria Vida-Szekacs, *On an Experiment in Art Education* (Keckemet: Kodaly Seminar, 1970).
2. Maria Vida-Szekacs, "Intensive Study with Fourth-Grade Children of 'Rose and Violet,'" *Magyar Pedagogia* 1–2 (1976).
3. Granasztoi, Szilvia, "The Role of Puppetry and Traditional Children's Games Accompanied by Singing in Drawing Teaching," *Rajztanitas* 5 (1975).
4. Maria Vida-Szekacs, *A muveszeti neveles hatasrendszere* (The system of influences of art education) (Publishing House of the Hungarian Academy of Sciences in the press).

Poland Aesthetic Education

Irena Wojnar

The general system of schooling in Poland plays a particularly important role, as it is the schools that make content of the culture and become the mutual language of each generation. A long and consequent goal of the schools (at present, primary schools, but in the near future, general secondary schools) is bound to bring culture "inside." No "outside" action will be adequate because it is not enough to publish a number of books, to organize concerts and exhibitions, and to build cinemas. It is the educational process in Poland that will turn these potentialities into experience. To fully accomplish aesthetic education in Poland, a material base for culture and an active participation of people in it must be provided. What I refer to here are attitudes which enrich our inner lives with new values, and not merely their objective forms. Having in mind the interrelation of these two aspects, one may use the term "participation in culture."

Aesthetic education that determines a more personal and genuine form of aesthetic experience is interpreted in a dual way because of the duality of art: its educational role can be noticed in our personal contact with works of art as well as in an act of creation or expression. Depending on a concrete branch of art, these two aspects can be intermingled. The essence of aesthetic experience evoked by music or theater will be different from that inspired by the fine arts.

Conditions existing in a Poland in the process of shaping a socialist culture threw aside the narrow and exclusive concept of aesthetic education and "cultural affranchisement," or "aesthetic affranchisement." The specific character of cultural development is going to distinguish the socialist countries from the other countries. Culture on a high aesthetic level has a great chance under socialism. The general opinion is that within the next thirty years "the competition between the socialist and capitalist system will slowly be moving . . . in the realm of culture that is in ways of living." Economic stability provides good foundations for the popularization of culture and for deeper involvement within it.

We are now entering into a cultural phase; directly preceding this was the political phase (a revolutionary transformations period) and an economic phase. "Mass aesthetic education resulting from a greater number of cultural sources" is to be accomplished in the cultural phase. The relationship between cultural and educational policy is developing; the entire educational system will realize a new and enlarged form of aesthetic education. These goals are contained within the forecast for the Polish culture until the year 1990, worked out by the Forecasting Committee of the ministry of culture and art. This forecast reminds us that it is first of all the schools that shape our cultural needs, patterns, and ways of living and our sensitive attitudes towards artistic phenomena and moral and social problems. Thus, aesthetic education is moving towards the shaping of the cultural involvement.

Problems connected with the essence and structure of this education are still to be theoretically and practically solved. As to the essence, we have to deal with more general problems linked with the situation in the world's "stock exchange of aesthetic values." The question concerning the ratios, within the essence of aesthetic culture, between the traditional and the contemporary, full of complexities and values, still remains unanswered. Those who plan curricula prefer tradition, but their work is hampered by young people's interests and preferences. The issue is how to prepare a program which would be genuinely good from the educational point of view and which would meet the requirements of young people. A few years ago a certain novelty was introduced in the curriculum of the upper grades in the secondary schools. This novelty was both a series of specialized classes covering the problems of contemporary art and an addition to Polish classes called "Modern Literary Life."

For many years in Poland the relationship between "the classical" and "the contemporary" on the compulsory reading list (Polish literature) has been discussed. The argument started some fifty years ago between those who are for teaching the history of literature in schools and those who suggest that it should be replaced by freely selected great literary works. This discussion is still in progress. Information or experience—this is the problem concerning the essence of aesthetic culture. The essence of intentional aesthetic education should embrace various artistic phenomena and different branches of art. This opinion seems to be commonly shared because it is seen in the broadened program of traditional artistic subjects. The introduction of music and fine arts lessons into the schools some fifteen years ago was a very essential move, since this was the educational counterpart of the dual character of these two branches of art. One-sided singing and drawing lessons were replaced with a synthesis of expressive classes and a shaping of aesthetic culture within proper limits. At present, we are more and more apt to use the terms theatrical

Woodcut by Polish child,
age 9

and film training or literary training, the latter covering in part the Polish language curriculum and dealing with literary culture. Instrumental and expressive language skills belong to a nonaesthetic form of education.

Since art is present in all spheres of life, it should dominate all the aspects of aesthetic education. It is accepted that this kind of education includes all the specialized branches of art (for example, music, literature, painting, and sculpture) and must be their synthesis, but, in fact, this problem is rather controversial and often misunderstood. Stressing the necessity of forming aesthetic culture of an integral character, we are reminded that there exist new foundations of modern integration of arts and that they should operate synthetically in the social and individual consciousness. All this does not reject the autonomy of individual branches of art or the need for existing specialized subjects.

The present situation of aesthetic education in our system of schooling follows in a general education but with emphasis laid on matters of particular importance.

Nursery Schools

A considerable number of children attend the nursery schools, the tendency being to include all the children in this system, both in towns and in the country. Nursery schools are especially operative in the field of aesthetic education since they integrate expressive types of classes, such as fine arts, drama, music, and dancing, with classes of cognitive character and with the complete range of emotional experiences of the child. A free division of time helps create the best educational atmosphere, stimulating interests, imaginations, creative attitudes, and the organization of attractive and various activities.

Primary Schools

The school reform of 1961 introduced essential changes in aesthetic education in the primary schools; the curricula put into effect in 1963 determined a new position for the fine arts and music, resulting in the substitution of drawing and singing lessons by music and fine arts classes. This provided a synthesis of the pupils' individual expressions through an acquaintance with artistic culture and by teaching perception of works of art. It is the essence and character of teaching the native tongue, though, that fully corresponds to broadly understood educational postulates of aesthetic culture.

A Polish language teacher is the one who most often stimulates the pupil's involvement in literary, theatrical, and film culture.

Secondary Grammar Schools

Aesthetic culture at the level of the secondary grammar schools is included in the program of Polish language and literature and is one of the two freely chosen, but compulsory, artistic subjects: training in the fine arts or training in music. The program of specialized subjects covers culture-oriented elements for young people who already have various, firmly developed interests. We face a necessity, so far at the secondary level, of abolishing required subjects; several branches of art must be integrated into a class. In the secondary schools this process has already been started. Humanities-oriented groups of pupils are being prepared for active involvement in social and cultural life, reflected by the introduction of problems concerning modern literature, music, theater, film, painting, and sculpture and the interrelation between them all.

The currently implemented school reform, voted into being by the

Seym of Polish People's Republic in October of 1973, aims at organizing a general, ten-year school of secondary education. As to aesthetic culture, the new curricula comprise three stages of education: elementary teaching (forms I–III), subject systematic teaching (forms IV–VIII), and subjects integrating teaching (forms IX–X). Greater stress is put on developing tendencies into creative attitudes, on forming and improving intellectual skills, on developing emotional life, on nurturing interests, and on encouraging intellectual, social, and cultural activities. Subjects contributing to the aesthetic formation process are supposed to be separated in forms 4 to 8, whereas in the final forms their mutual relationships are to be brought out. Of particular importance here is cultural education as an essential part of the Polish language and literature program. In the future, cultural education will be a separate subject.

Since aesthetic education cannot be fully realized inside the schools, requiring attendance at exhibitions, spectacles, concerts, etc., it is essential that secondary schools cooperate with museums, philharmonics, and theaters as well as with such institutions as the Committee for the Radio and TV Affairs. We do have a certain experience in this field—musical culture movements such as Pro sinfonica, theatrical societies, museumgoers' societies, to mention only a few. The ongoing cooperation between schools and the Committee for the Radio and TV Affairs is reflected in specially prepared radio and television programs for schools.

Centers for out-of-school education make up a separate area within the system of national schooling. These are various kinds of young people's social clubs where classes in the fine arts, music, drama, choreography, and so on, are conducted. Young people attend these classes on their own accord, urged by their own needs and interests. The way these centers develop shows that this method is useful and is a good argument for the effectiveness of education through art. Cooperation between such clubs and schools will be more and more effective and a greater number of children and teenagers will be encouraged to become involved in these activities. The Polish Scouts Association, a powerful group, has long been organizing many interesting forms of aesthetic education for its members.

A difficult problem is presented by aesthetic education on the level of secondary professional (technical) schools and in the universities. Some of the school reform recommendations propose ten-year professional schools—the term *professional* covering not only technical schools but also all kinds of schools that prepare young people for various jobs and professions which will meet the requirements of aesthetic and cultural education. What remains is the problem of cultural education for students who study in technical and medical universities, agricultural colleges, and like institutions. In a socialist society there exists a need for popularizing general culture among the circles of the so-called technical intelligentsia in order to shape attitudes and interests and to evoke a conviction that life has sense and real values.

Therefore, the curriculum of the above-mentioned students presently covers a new subject: selected problems of modern culture. This curriculum is fully justified as Poland is entering the phase of a highly developed socialist society, which has an accompanying need for a radical improvement in the quality of work and for a raise in the standard of living. All this makes it necessary to enrich studies with some humanistic aspects. Evoking cultural needs and teaching how to assess people and social phenomena requires an innovative attitude. Such a new subject encourages students to become involved in the cultural life of their country through active reception of works of art and cultural products as well as through their own creative efforts. Active participation in culture helps the students formulate a more personal and sensitive approach to the phenomena of the surrounding world, gain knowledge and better self-recognition, and establish relations with other people and with their own work as part of the process of building an objective reality.

Admittedly, aesthetic education as a new element in educational activity can threaten traditional concepts of schooling as it questions many fixed patterns, such as the division between teaching and child rearing, school and outside-of-school activities, as well as activities within lessons and education going beyond the school. Aesthetic education requires the close collaboration of schools with museums, philharmonics, theaters, etc.; it breaks down the long-existing barriers that separate schools from cultural life and traditions. The division into education and self-education is no longer adequate because art requires personal experiences and interests on the part of teachers to encourage better contacts with pupils, which, in turn, creates new foundations of educational situations.

That is why we regard art education in schools as a very important element in shaping aesthetic attitudes. This education is not confined to the schools as the only place or period in a person's life. Experiencing art is an open process, valuable at every stage of personality development. It can never be said with certainty that a given person has already been educated by art, because the wealth of art steadily broadens the range of one's experiences throughout life. This begins at the preschool period—prevailed by free expression and a set of integrated experiences of emotional, transformational, and cognitive character—and ends in old age, when art provides some new satisfaction in one's difficult life. Aesthetic education understood as a process that is integrated socially and individually may be considered as a peculiar kind of the permanent, life-long educational model—that is, self-education throughout life. This sort of education, some time ago regarded only as professional training, is

clearly becoming "a new educational concept" and is linked, in B. Sucho-
dolski's words, with "a new concept of man, who is educating himself and
developing himself, and who in the course of this development goes beyond the limits of his own achievements and the examples he has been
following."

Our present concept of aesthetic education also covers the nature of
processes which also take place outside of the schools, namely, in various
educational centers for children and teenagers, in cultural institutions for
adults, and in all kinds of social situations of an informal character where
"a cultural personality" is being shaped. Each nation comes to participate
in art by following a different path. Polish art has always determined the
continuity of national values, which somehow intensified the common
feeling of experiences, passing it on to following generations. Art was a
source of patriotic hopes and expectations even when reality was cruel.
Polish art preserved and strengthened the beauty of the Polish language
when it was systematically persecuted. Paintings reflected the glorious
past of the nation and stimulated national imagination. Polish music
helped to create the moments of exaltation and the patriotic feelings that
are so necessary in difficult times. National pride was founded on the
works by great Polish artists; moreover, it was a source of national self-
recognition. Because of this kind of art, aesthetic education was based on
patriotic grounds and encouraged the people to be faithful to traditions.
The transformations of the past thirty years have made art a common
possession of the nation. Great art of the past interwoven in the process
of changes deepened cultural integration.

The question is whether this kind of tradition can influence current
concepts of aesthetic education and whether it can exist along with the
life and needs of a socialist nation in the period of a scientific and technological revolution. As opposed to some theories of aesthetic education
in western countries, an aesthetic education model, which would include
permanent values of man and culture, values of a universal and national
character, is preferred. Our country's past makes it clear that we once
knew how to defend such values as freedom and tolerance, loyalty to
accepted ideals, honor, and patriotism. Our history makes us notice new
values that stimulate our present and outline our future. We fully realize
that it is only the continuity of tradition that can secure our existence as a
separate nation, and we accept this tradition through experiences of the
present. Chopin and Matejko, Mickiewicz and Wyspianski, Norwid and
Malczewski are "our contemporaries" because they represent permanent
symbols of social consciousness and national memory. To this consciousness we add cherished current values along with those which originated
in the past in Polish culture. Our theoretical concept of aesthetic education makes it possible to enrich this consciousness eternally, assuming,

though, that its solid foundations remain untouched. New ideas concerning creation and expression cannot cross out the loyalty to tradition and the links with its foundations. What we need is imagination, sensitivity, and open minds.

While working out a Polish theory of aesthetic education, one must again refer to Norwid, as his ideas, expressed poetically, still provide a source of inspiration; song and practicality are the two widely accepted aspects of art since both express and shape man's consciousness, man's world, the unity of the beautiful and the useful, and the unity of beauty and truth.

Aesthetic education is, finally, an educational activity that may be accomplished by means of the educational potentialities of art. A close look at the directions of this kind of aesthetic education convinces us that the basic contents are contained in closely related processes of man's self-recognition and self-realization—Man as an individual and unrepeatable being, and Man as a social collectivity linked by mutual inner bonds. Self-recognition gained through aesthetic experience leads to the intensification of moral sensitivity and also to better communication with people because it helps one to understand the world and human relations. Self-realization is possible thanks to the dialectical affinity with the social, human dimension of the world. Objective reality, when alienated, may threaten man and his social needs and make his self-realization impossible. Self-realization of individual and social man may be accomplished only when his creative and personal attitude towards the world helps him to accept it.

Soviet Union Input and Output Objectives*

Boris Yusov

"The content and the teaching methods for art education is a large problem within the five Soviet educational systems" where there are very few elective classes and no open education schools like there are in the United States.

ART EDUCATION ESTABLISHMENTS

The first system, or the kindergarten, is a separate educational unit that includes a specially designed art curriculum developed for the age level of 6 years and under; however, the content of this program is directly linked to the primary educational level of the ten grade level general schools that follow kindergarten.

The next level of education that provides art education programs is the general schools. This level has a ten-year program, with grades one through ten, and is divided into three parts, making it a "3," "5," "2" educational system. The first three years are for children in the elementary part of the system and include 7-, 8-, and 9-year-old boys and girls. The "5" year, or middle, section of the system is the junior high level and includes children who are 10, 11, 12, 13, and 14 years of age. During this five-year period the children are taught by specialists, and at the beginning of this program (the 10 year age, or the first year of junior high

*This article is reprinted from *Art Education*, volume 31, number 2 (1978). *Art Education* is the Journal of the National Art Education Association, 1916 Association Drive, Reston, Virginia 22091.—ED.

level), teaching specialists in all fields—art, physics, mathematics, etc.—become an important part of the educational system. The "2" year third level is the senior high group that provides education for the 15- and 16-year-old children.

Within the first six grade levels of this ten-year system, the children have at least one 45-minute art lesson each week. At the 7 to 10 grade levels, art classes are elective or optional courses that are scheduled for two or three hours per week.

A similar system of education that is directly related to the same levels of the general educational school system is the "Program for Talented Students." These programs are developed in special schools that are located only in the capital cities of the different Soviet republics. Boarding programs are provided in this system for the 10- to 15-year-old talented children, who usually live in outlying sections of the republics. Children who attend these "Pioneer Schools" are offered special classes in art, music, dance, sports, etc., six days a week. They are admitted to these schools according to test results or on recommendation of boards of education or the Union of Soviet Artists, or the parents can bring their children in if they show "good work."

The "Pioneer Palace" located in Moscow has a central program plan so that selected talented children go to general school from 9:00 to 12:30 each morning and then return at 2:00 and stay until 5:00 P.M. to take part in special talent classes for art, music, dance, sports, and so on. This modern school can accommodate 15,000 children and offers 120 different interest subjects. The art and aesthetic education program offers graphics, sculpture, and ceramic classes. There are 4,000 children taking part in this art and aesthetic program area. The children are divided into smaller groups of 15 or 20 and can work in the fine arts or take classes that work with fabrics, embroidery, hand crafts, films, and photography. Studios are provided for all the various activities. Some of the promising students go abroad to learn or just go on special field trips in the Soviet Union as part of their learning experiences. The budget for this program is maintained by the "Moscow Government," and there is no expense to the parents. The children range from ages 7 to 17, but the majority of them are in the 9- to 14-year-old age group.

There are also 17 secondary district art schools in the Moscow area, as well as secondary ballet schools, secondary music schools, etc. Following is a description of one of the Moscow district art schools available to children ranging in age from 7 to 17 years: The building has 34 rooms for classes and accommodates about 600 children. The children come for the three-hour art classes twice a week, and there is no charge for this type of art training. All materials like brushes and paints are free for the children

Woodcut by Russian
child, age 14

to use. The curriculum includes graphics, painting, applied art, and sculpture. In the final year, or the tenth grade level, the students are required to do diploma work concentrating on one or two of the above areas and doing extensive work and study in that concentration.

The teachers for these classes are artists, painters, sculptors, etc., and most of them are working artists and have to have both art training and pedagogy training. Slide files of children's art are maintained and constantly developed to include past and present works of art done by the children in all of the grades one through ten. Children's art exhibitions are on display all year long, with titles like "Summer Impressions" and "My Moscow." These exhibits include work done in several kinds of art media: tempera, pencil, watercolor, pen, and ink. This district art school has been in existence for more than 21 years. The children come here for art training from 3:00 to 6:00, after they have finished at their general school in the morning. In addition to the studio activities, the seventh- to tenth-grade children are allowed one hour per week of art history and also make periodic visits to museums and galleries.

The adults come to the school for art classes in the evening after 6:00. There are six of these district art schools in the Moscow area where adults can attend art classes, and they include more than 70 separate art groups. These district art schools are in addition to the art groups that are meeting at the pioneer palaces. Since 1963 this one particular secondary art school has exhibited student works of art in 36 countries, including the United States. In the past, some art work from American children has been exhibited in the Soviet Union through the efforts of the Friendship House in Moscow. Private lessons or small classes in art are also offered to children in their own neighborhoods in an unofficial way. These classes are usually held in one or two rooms of an older building that is no longer used for apartments.

Another type of established system that provides art education to the Soviet people is the museum school, or "the educational department of the art museum." This system is similar to the museum program being offered in America and in Budapest at the Buda Castle.

In addition to the museum programs, there are the "houses of the amateur artists." This is a system of "hobby centers" that has developed within the trade union organizations and could be adopted in America. This system is organized for the working people, the general public, teachers, or for any adult, and it may also include school children. It is a form of adult education, and there are no age limits for admission, no professional limits, and anyone can go there to work with art materials. Sometimes there is a small payment for the use of some of the materials or for renting tools or equipment, but tuition is free for everyone in the Soviet Union. The majority of the trade union students that are admitted to the art classes are given everything free because the trade unions cover all of their expenses. In the children's art classes all art materials used, such as brushes and paints, are free; however, when the adults attend these schools, they have to buy their own art supplies.

The hobby centers for amateur artists have "all union exhibits for their art work in Exhibition Hall in Moscow near Red Square." With all of these established programs being offered, none of them are for the professional artist. The previously mentioned established art programs are designed only for the preprofessional or the nonprofessional person and offer only that type of training. The main aim of these organizations is to develop the general interest in the arts. There is a special system for those who are specifically suited for the professional schools. It is another type of school, and the Institute of Fine Arts is the professional school located in Moscow.

PROFESSIONAL ART TRAINING

The Institute of Fine Arts of Moscow trains the professional artist and includes the principles of education adhered to in the training of the art student. This school was started in the mid-nineteenth century. In 1832 a new style of art was beginning to emerge in Moscow. Artists left their studios and went into the streets to paint from nature. This action of going out into the environment started a movement that led to the organization of the art school. In the early part of the twentieth century, the great art revolution started in the Soviet Union with a group of five Russian art teachers. The present school and its program are about forty years old now.

Today, this training is for painters, sculptors, and graphic artists and has "a high quality of training and work compared with other Russian art schools that only train art teachers or artists for industry." Those students that finish their art training at one of the 17 higher art schools have the right to apply to the institute for further study. However, there has to be a selection process because there is not enough room for everyone in the institute. There is a competition for 60 Moscow students to enter each year, and these are selected from a total of 1,500 applicants. The selection process for the final 250 choices includes competitive examination and the screening of the applicants and their work. All of the Pioneer School students and the 17 area higher art school students apply for admission.

There are presently 400 students enrolled, and only 100 of these are Moscovites; 36 are from other countries (none are from America); and the rest are from the different republics in the Soviet Union. Foreign students like to come here because this art school gives a very good professional training.

The institute's teachers try to keep a natural approach within the professional training of the students. With this approach the students keep their natural feeling in art. This technique is very successful. There are three kinds of faculties on the institute staff. The first is a painting faculty for 250 students—the largest enrollment. The curriculum includes easel painting, decorative painting for the theatre, and monumental painting (frescos, etc.). The second faculty group is for the graphic arts and includes easel graphics, illustration, and poster painting. The third area, with the smallest number of students, is the sculpture area; here the students' good health is needed because they have to compete with the plastic of stone.

The students have to study at the institute for six years and in the sixth year do their diploma work. They study at the institute for eight months of the year, and then for two summer months they go to summer creative practice to increase their knowledge and perceptions. The study period is from 9 A.M. to 7 P.M. at the institute, and the first six hours of the day are spent engaged in specialized studio subjects such as painting, graphics, or sculpture. The students are taught to work with a variety of materials in the studio classes. Evening hours are reserved for the study of art history and the social sciences, and include one course in anatomy.

After graduation the students are channeled into their work. This is very important in a state system where you have workshops for artists for natural work. Their future work is based on agreements to do a certain job for the state. Some go into the teaching field. The artists have two ways of working: they paint according to their wish or paint to the order of the state.

HISTORICAL CHANGES IN ART EDUCATION

There are four basic periods in the development of art education in the Soviet Union. The first period begins just after the great October Revolution in 1917 and continues up to the Stalinist purge. During that revolutionary period in the history of the country and also in the history of the Soviet schools, there was a search for a free school, a free society, and an education for a free man. Spiritually those times were very high, and naturally the tendency for a free education and an art education was very strong. In these years, 1917 to the early 1930s, there were many kinds of education being used for art and for free education. A lot of tendencies were being used to teach art, but there were no systematic or scientific or pedagogical conceptions.

The second period of historical change started in 1933 to 1935–36 and was the turning point in the direction of art education. The stresses in that case were very severe, and the pressures were hard in making a very distinct outline of what amount of knowledge should be given to children, what kinds of lessons and topics, etc. The next period then, 1933 to 1960, was a time of very strong structuring of the curriculum in all of the subject areas, not only in art but in mathematics, chemistry, and the other education subjects. There was no use of project methods, but this period of time did have two advantages, one being that it initiated a search for an educational program where there could be a systematic education for everybody. Previously, in the 1920s, a lot of the hobby clubs and the teachers' tendencies were so different in scope and direction that it was impossible to develop a single direction in general education that could be used by everyone. During this period every child in the Soviet

Union was given at least a minimal amount of artistic preparation while in school. The 1930s, then, was a good time to search for a new system of education and art education. These actions were too severe from my point of view as an art educator. We can see from contemporary reports that it lacked the intellectual and the behavioral approach to art training. This was quite evident in that there was just a small amount of time for art in the schools and the approaches used were rather technical and lacking in visual literacy.

The second advantage at that time was that two systems of art education were differentiated. One was the general education system used in the public schools, where one weekly general art lesson was given, a compulsory lesson that was very strict in content and methods. The second art education system that developed was the "house of schools—houses of young students." These Pioneer studios were organized on a very free basis, where professional artists were invited to teach the children. These artists did not have any strict curriculum to follow, and every artist-teacher chose his own methods and content direction. These two quite different systems functioned at the same time, one compulsory and very strict, the other a freer program for the students who wished to choose their own content and methods and still get an artistic training.

The third important turning point in the development of art education in the USSR came in 1964. This was after the Second World War and was "another tough period in the history of the Soviet Union." Difficulties existed for many years after the end of the war. New tendencies in art education started to take a direction near the end of the 1950s and the "official change" happened in 1964. At that time quite a new curriculum was approved for the schools by the Soviet ministry of education, a curriculum that turned its face to aesthetic values in art education. Quite naturally, this tendency appeared to unite the two directions that art education had developed over the past thirty years, those two directions or systems that were separate systems since the early 1930s. This meant that there were two influences in the art lessons of these schools: (1) the free artistic approach and the use of the aesthetic imagination, which was characteristic of the extracurricular studio circles that functioned in the popular "hobby groups," and (2) the strict formal art lesson that was given in the general public schools. Under this "Curriculum of 1964," new ideas started to flourish in the schools.

Different materials, methods, topics, and themes and approaches were used. A "wave of liberation" for the arts in the general public schools continued on until the 1970s, and this was the fourth turning point in the development of art education in the Soviet Union. This new 1970 situation would be a very big decision for the future of art education in the USSR. During this fourth period several experimental projects started, being initiated by the ministry of education, the research institutes, and the Union of Soviet Artists. This is why we have professional artists teaching in our schools. In the early 1970s professional artists were limited in taking an active part in this new movement, but later they moved into the schools and started to take a very active leadership part in forming the curriculum and the main aims in the art education program. There was also a demand from the general public education teachers, those specialists in different fields (especially those in the behavioral sciences) who mentioned that artistic and aesthetic education should be a very important element in all education. Those advocates of artistic and aesthetic development in the general public schools started a campaign for new experimental projects, which are now being supervised by the Institute of Artistic Education.

ART EDUCATION RESEARCH

The following scientific and research ideas were part of these new concerns of the 1970s. Research in art and aesthetic education is now provided by many kinds of establishments in the Soviet Union, but the main one is the Academy of Pedagogical Sciences that "consists of a complicated research mechanism which consists of a set of Institutes."

As for research in art education or aesthetic education, "the main kind of research is fulfilled by the Institute of Artistic Education." There are departments for all of "the Arts" within the Institute of Artistic Education. To some extent, some of the different facets of art and aesthetics are developed in the Institute of Working Education. This institute deals with the aesthetics of crafts and general environment and with design problems in connection with making something in technology design and technology.

A second academy concerned with research in art education and aesthetic education is the same type of academy as the Academy of Pedagogy but differs in that it deals directly with the fifteen national republics of the USSR. The institutes within this academy are located out in the republics. The Institute of Schools of the Russian Federation and the Republican Educational Research Institute both develop educational courses that correspond with the national culture and traditions because there are quite different nations within the USSR. Each of the nations speaks a different language, and in the Soviet Union elementary education is provided for everyone and requires the use of a total of fifty-four languages. In all, there are over 100 nationalities and ethnic groups in the

USSR, so, of course, there are some problems in the national republics. The Baltic republics compared with the middle nations republics are quite different in nature, origin, and traditions. Some of these republics are Christian or Catholic in origin. There also are Muslim republics, which had zero percent literacy in the early 1930s.

AESTHETIC EDUCATION

In the essence of education, all instruction should have some of the elements of aesthetic value, including an approach to the structuring of mathematical or physical phenomena, biological process, etc. Artistic educational development by means of the arts is only a part of this development. Of course, our art education theorists say that it is the main part, the main means of aesthetic development, because art is a condensed, concentrated expression of aesthetic values, and therefore it is the main means of aesthetic development. If it is not *the* main means, then it has to be one of them or the term *aesthetic education* does not have any meaning. The USSR's definition of aesthetic education is a much wider one than just the development of the individual by means of art only. Within the structure of artistic development, we consider that the artistic education consists of development through channels of different arts such as dance, music, visual arts, literature, and so on, and that within our theory there are some periods when one of the arts is more important than any of the others. In the age sequence, for example, dramatization (drama or theater) is very important for small children at the elementary and preschool levels up to the age of 7 or 8. After this age level is a level of extreme importance, the visual arts level for children from 8 to 12 or 13 years. Following this age level of early adolescence, literature will become one of the main arts, one of the main ways of creative expression (maybe prose, poetry, etc.). Then, around the age of 15 years it may be the theater, movies, television, or great literature of the world. This may take the form of art appreciation, reading, listening, seeing (some kind of television, movies, theater, etc.), so there are periods when one of the arts is the main art.

This does not mean, however, that the other arts should be neglected at this time or that no other arts should be suggested to the child. The results of a recent sociological study showed that all of the arts should be given to the child all of the time and that none of the arts should be overlooked or missed by the child at any age level. Of course, there are some opponents of this point of view, but the position, as it seems, is that at least one of the arts should always be emphasized for a child. A recent comparative study where all the arts were given the same amount of importance to groups of children of the same age or school level indicated that there was a much lower level of artistic preference by the child for all of the arts. They tended to like everything—music, movies, painting— and nothing special. Among those children who were involved with just one of the arts at a time (music, visual arts, literature, etc.), and who at the same time received some information about a neighboring art, the results showed that the major art had a very good level of taste artistically when it was compared with those who could not differentiate and compare things.

ART EDUCATION TODAY

The three aims in the present structure of Soviet art education are as follows: (1) The student, as a result of the art education course, should be able to draw something from nature or from memory. Everyone needs this kind of skill in any profession; everyone needs to draw something from memory or by way of seeing or looking at something. Viktor Lowenfeld stated that everyone knows how to draw: it's just a matter of how well they express their ideas. (2) Every educated person should be able to generate an image, a desired image, and to make and find an artistic form for it and then practically express it on a sheet of paper or in a sculpture. They should know how to make an image visible and how to generate images. This indicates that "we have two kinds of channels, channel in (input) and channel out (output)." Both of these channels are very important, especially the output channel, which is used to generate images and the ability to make images visible by using paper, pencils, crayons, etc. These are the two main channels. (3) Appreciation. Appreciation is the ability to understand, respond, and see aesthetic and artistic qualities in the world around you and in the works of art yet to come, in man-made things, and in the natural surroundings. These are the three main directions of art education in the Soviet Union. The main question, as far as I know, rotates around an isle—an isle with two ends—Practical and Perception. Around the outside of this isle are all of the problems of modern aesthetic communication. This shows that we have two groups that stand on the isle, each group at a different pole. I can say that in this country (USSR) we have two types of experimental curriculum. One is developed by the Institute of Artistic Education, and the other is developed by professional people in professions like music, education, and the Union of Soviet Arts.

The Soviet art education curricula basically consist of two kinds of concepts. The first is a concept of terms, those main terms and the three elements of the initial terms; *perception* is the term that includes the elements of perception, process, and response. Experience, practical activity, product, and creative expression (in the form of a product) are the elements of the second concept, *practical*. In these two concepts are perception-process-reaction and practical work-product-creative expression. (There is a discussion about these present differences.)

The main idea now in art education in the USSR is that the general aesthetic and artistic development of every child is a necessary part of his or her spiritual, moral, and intellectual development. We seek now to put this idea into the general schoolwide practice for every teacher in the school: the idea of the importance of aesthetic education.

Now we are attacking the schools from the outside and trying to implant those ideas into the general public school in an attempt to overcome the general tendencies of school administrators to not take art and aesthetic education seriously as a means of developing a child's personality. The professional artists also do a very important job in the communities to assist with the development of this new art education curriculum. Their work is all voluntary.

We have one more launching site, the kindergartens, because in preschool establishments art and music have already developed a system of aesthetic education and it is the best system that exists. We are now intending to continue with this kind of aesthetic education program at the primary school in the elementary grades.

An Outsider Looks at Soviet Art Education

Al Hurwitz

Boris Yusov's article, "Art Education in the Union of Soviet Socialist Republics," was delivered as a formal address to a seminar of U.S. and Soviet art educators conducted by the writer in Moscow in the winter of 1975. Held under the joint sponsorship of the Artists Union and the Citizen's Exchange Corps, the seminars were conducted for the purpose of allowing U.S. art educators to share ideas, information, and problems with Soviet colleagues. Dr. Yusov's statement was an attempt to set his country's art program into perspective. It is an admirable example of a careful ordering of pertinent, little-known information, but there are certain kinds of information that were not covered and that may also be of interest to non-Soviet readers. The following comments will try to draw a clearer relationship between the art of the schools, as derived from a close examination of students' works, and the Soviet view of the professional artist working within the framework of socialist realism.

As Dr. Yusov has noted, art education in Russia is mandated at the elementary level, yet it also provides opportunities outside of the schools for the child with special ability. A secondary center, which concentrates upon art, thus opens the door to the fine arts and other kinds of academies for the training of professionals. Graduates who are accepted into the artists' union are assured of a livelihood in art. Their mode of operation—be it teacher, painter, or theatrical designer—has its roots in the curricula of the elementary program. The nature of art activity at this level, and the way in which it prepared the students for their professional careers, will be the subject of this "outsider's" view.

The roots of socialist realism lie in a series of official statements resulting from conferences in the early 1930s, at which guidelines were set down mainly with writers in mind (the First Soviet Writer's Congress in 1934); these policies were to eventually include art education in the schools. Three concepts were formulated to direct the attention of all artists: *Partynost*, which supplied a philosophical basis and urged adherence to the ideals of the Communist party's identification of artists with the proletarian cause; *Ideinost*, which dealt with socialist content or subject matter of art works; and *Narodnost* (in a sense, a subdivision of Ideinost), which suggested that the folklore and lifestyles of the general Soviet people, as opposed to the interests of the educated elite, be considered as sources for art. Highly individualistic or experimental works, such as abstract or conceptual art, are therefore considered deviations from socialist realism because they serve the artist more than his public. The Western artist who sees himself working on the outer edges of his field has no delusions about communicating to the unsophisticated eye; the Soviet artist, on the other hand, is expected to communicate to the factory worker who happens to find himself in the contemporary wing of the Tretyakov Gallery (Moscow's leading museum of Russian art, founded in 1881) on a Sunday afternoon. As Sjeklocha and Mead have noted, "In the Soviet view, then, art is not solely an 'image' of man's intellectual perceptions, but must serve as an image of the state as well." Art must become "an ideological device or instrument in the re-education of people in organization, mobilization, and activization of their revolutionary, militant consciousness."[1]

In terms of painting, socialist realism requires the mastery of those traditional techniques that can deal successfully with such subject content as historical events, personalities, eulogistic interpretations of the Russian landscape (and of those who work it), industrial subjects, public portraits on a massive scale, and the like. Also included as popular subject matter are still lifes, portraits, and family scenes. I have observed Soviet painters closely over a seven-year period and my impression is that the range of style in visual art is not as limited as it may at first appear. Contemporary painting, for example, has shown increasing variety over the past decade and has grown more receptive to changes than sculpture, which, being more public in function, is more vulnerable to socialist realist constraints. There are also painters who do not work in abstract modes yet take greater liberties with both style and content. (The Menage, Moscow's leading exhibition hall, prepared huge exhibits on the subject of still life, theater and costume design, and book illustration—most of which lacked ideological substance.)

Not all paintings reflect the heavy hand of the propagandist; more and more are working in freer, more personalized modes. There has been, in fact, a far greater range of style among Soviet artists than most Westerners realize. Arkhipov's work has a painterly bravura style, and K.S. Petrov-Vodkin is typical of those who borrowed from several European

1. Paul Sjeklocha and Igor Mead, *Unofficial Art in the Soviet Union* (Univ. of California Press, 1967), p. 33.

styles. The influence of Cezanne can be seen in the carefully structured work of Deyneka's forms and in the portraits of Solokhov and Korin, which are solidly composed works that are stylized and painterly.

ROMANTICISM AND REALISM

Notice should also be taken of the Russian sense of scale, which is so evident in its architecture and city planning and is equally evident in the numerous wall-sized canvases that one encounters in any exhibition of painting, be it in a contemporary show or in the Tretyakov Gallery, where the obsession with size and dramatic content can be appreciated in its historical context. It would be a mistake, however, to view this as a special characteristic of socialist realism, since such favorites as Repin, Surikov, and Ivanov set the tone for size and narrative content in the latter half of the nineteenth century; nor were they alone in this respect. Painters in the European capitals were similarly intrigued by the psychological effect of size (as in the Pantheon series in Paris). In searching for some distinguishing characteristics that would set the Russian historical painter apart from his European counterpart, one is struck by the distinctive Russian sense of high drama, the ability to seize moments of intense feeling, as in Repin's highly theatrical treatment of Ivan the Terrible's murder of his son. If such high drama seems lacking in the art work of the Soviet public schools, sentiment is certainly apparent. Slavic romanticism appears to bind drama and sentiment into a sensibility that is lacking in the Western societies. American art students (and, one may assume, teachers), rarely concern themselves with themes of friendship, family life, and a variety of genre subject matter that figures into Soviet school art. Unlike Americans, Russians are not afraid of their emotions—in music, art, drama, or poetry, indeed, intensity of feeling and concern for human values is a characteristic that permeates both Czarist and Soviet culture.

Despite the commendable increase in range of approaches among professionals, only the dissident artist ventures into forbidden realms of form or content. Styles that are considered overly personal and idiosyncratic are frowned upon, as are statements critical of the bureaucracy. To be a dissident is not illegal, but it is not advisable, particularly if one wants to share in the not inconsiderable benefits that are afforded the artist. Artists as a class are favored by the government, and to dissent from social realism, either through the *way* one paints or by *what* one paints, is to place oneself outside the pale of the establishment. Realism, therefore, in one form or another, is the route to communication with the masses, since immediate recognition of subject matter requires no special empathy with the flow of movements that characterize the rapidity of visual breakthroughs of twentieth-century art. That tolerance of, indeed, that eagerness to embrace breakthroughs of vision, which characterizes the aware Western viewer, is lacking in the Soviet public and is reflected in the art of the schools.

The Soviet art teacher begins to prepare the consumer for socialist realism in the early grades. Subject matter in the schools, as in the world of the professionals, avoids pure design, experimentation for its own sake, planned accidents, collage, exercises in abstraction, or concentration upon the formal elements of design. The first stages of instruction rely very heavily upon the experience of the child and upon carefully selected "themes." An informal inventory of paintings of children from the ages of six to ten revealed such topics as "Building a Snowman with my Friends," "Ballet Class," "My Best Friend," "Walking in the Woods," "My Backyard," "Reading," and "At the Circus," and showed visits to factories and farms—all subjects which were at one time quite acceptable in the United States but which now exist primarily in the early rather than upper grades in American schools. The Soviets add drawing and painting from observation in the middle and upper grades, and use poetry, folk art, story illustration, and costume design as sources of art. Since the content of art draws upon observation and memory, there are suggested procedures for developing pictorial skills which are part of a sequenced curriculum. Added to this is sequenced instruction in use of a relatively limited range of media—water color, tempera, printmaking, collography, linoleum cuts, and clay modeling.

In striving for control of media, the Soviet art teacher has a tendency to produce work that would appear overworked and lacking in spontaneity by U.S. standards. Attention to detail, skill in shading, and use of perspective and pictorial space are competencies that are consistent with what lies ahead in the realm of socialist realism.

Lenin stated, "Art belongs to the people. Its deepest roots must reach into the very thick of the broad working masses. It must be comprehensible to the masses to be loved by them. It must unite the feelings, thoughts, and will of the masses and inspire them."[2] His wife, Nadezhda Krupskaya, had a working relationship with children and art and was influential in formulating policy for preschool and primary school children. She set down the following as a kind of credo for their art instruction:

I. The artistic activity of children is creative activity. In a drawing, a child can transmit his view of his surroundings, a living image created on the basis of observation.

II. The basis of guidance of art activities is observation of surrounding

2. Boris Johanson, "Teaching of Art," in *Soviet Education* (USSR, 1979).

reality, which in turn is based on the development of the cultivated senses.

III. For the successful development of artistic capacities, various methods must be used to shape the children's plans and stimulate their thought, initiative, and self-sufficiency.

IV. Children's weak technical skills in drawing constitute an obstacle to the development of artistic creativity. To eliminate this, it is essential that children systematically be instructed in drawing techniques.

V. Drawing instruction should be of a general nature. Children must be taught to separate the common features in objects, features that are typical for all of them, and, subsequently, in the typical features, to see what is characteristic and differentiates one group of objects from another. They must be led to the perception and awareness of the expressiveness of individual objects and phenomena and of their individual properties. (M.A. Vetlugina, *Artistic Creativity of the Child*, 1972)

Although contemporary specialists in early childhood education are far more sophisticated and consistent with Western thinking and research (see M.A. Vetlugina, *Artistic Creativity of the Child*), many of Krupskaya's recommendations appear to be followed in the upper grades.

In the classes of the student art centers and Pioneer Palaces, academic training is intensified while more imaginative projects are assigned. Puppetry, sculptured tiles in deep relief, paintings based upon still life, and city scenes were all observed by the writer.

The elementary experience, however, is not the only art education program offered to public school children. There are two major opportunities provided for children who are gifted not only in art but in sciences, languages, sports, etc. These are the specialized classes at Pioneer Palaces for youth and at the student art centers, where artists live and work on the premises. Here children receive additional time in art instruction during their six-day school week. To be accepted, children must pass an initial art examination to earn a place and compete yearly. Their two-day entrance examination consists of three parts: drawing a portrait from a plaster cast, painting a still life, and creating a compositional study. At the secondary level there are art schools for the artistically gifted that have live-in accommodations and accept students from a wide geographical area.

A lesson observed by the writer in a class for twelve-year-olds at a student art center in Moscow appeared to be typical of a balance that Soviet art teachers try to maintain between guidelines set by the teacher and freedom of expression for the child. In this case the students were instructed to first apply transparent washes in watercolors. When this dried, they were asked to draw in pencil an imaginary machine that could exist either in outer space or deep within the earth. Upon completion of this object, the forms were filled in with tempera color, thus creating an effect of deep space between object and background. In a secondary school for the gifted, a typical problem is to "create a composition in tones of gray of a group of people caught in the rain."

The secondary "magnet" schools prepare the best of their students for such professional training grounds as the Surikov Academy in Moscow or the Muchina and Repin Academy in Leningrad. The training at Surikov extends for six rigorous years, during which time the students study academic subjects, anatomy, theory of color, and design; the final year is devoted to a major work that is presented to a committee for critical evaluation. In all classes the author visited, the human figure was the major focus of concentration, with many retired "pensioners" serving as models. Since the number of art academies in the Soviet Union are few by comparison with the United States, acceptance to an art school is highly competitive. The work produced by the Soviet art student reflects exceptional competency, in the technical sense, by the standards of most U.S. art students. It should also be borne in mind that art training in Russia, as in most European countries, does not exist in the university as it does in the United States.

The pattern of a mandated art program in the elementary school, with special art schools available after school hours and arts-oriented secondary schools lying between public school and the academy, is followed in most Eastern European countries as it is in the People's Republic of China.

The Soviet art teacher's vocabulary may be very similar to that of his American counterpart ("creativity," "aesthetic education"), but his reading of these terms, as well as his philosophical options, differs in interpretation. What others can learn from the Russians resides in the seriousness with which art is taken as a part of the total educational process, in the Soviets' regard for the gifted,[3] and in the esteem in which the society holds its artists.

3. Al Hurwitz, "The Artistically Gifted Child in the Soviet Union," *The Gifted Child Quarterly* (Winter 1976).

MIDDLE EAST AND SOUTH ASIA

Afghanistan Art Curriculum Issues in a Developing Nation

Arline J. Lederman

ISSUES FOR ESTABLISHING CURRICULA

The concerns involved in forming an art curriculum where none has existed is a challenge for any art educator. This is especially true in a country, such as Afghanistan, where rich traditions and fierce pride coexist with limited economic wealth. Those who address problems in art curriculum design and seek a synthesis of traditional cultures with the arts of the twentieth century must work in a context of educational, economic, and social planning. Such is the case in Afghanistan.

Kabul University is the only college in Afghanistan. Most secondary school teachers are graduates of Kabul and are the cultural and political leaders of the country.

An art curriculum designed and planned by the Kabul University has considerable impact on the values and opportunities in the arts in Afghanistan. Since less than fifteen percent of Afghanistan is literate and as late as 1975 less than five percent of high school graduates entered college, an art curriculum organized by the university is extremely important.

Between 1920 and 1973 there was only one art course taught at Kabul University, an art history survey course taken mainly by architecture students. There is, however, a system of six teacher training schools throughout Afghanistan which teach art and where future teachers study for two years. Art programs in teacher training institutions and in public schools consist of drawing, some painting, and the applied arts. Drawing classes involved students in copying drawings and working occasionally from nature. The applied art classes have included the traditional crafts but have emphasized European-based design. Individual creativity was little understood or rewarded, but the applied arts showed the greatest vitality and skill in carpet weaving, embroidery, woodwork, and ceramics.

The arts have existed in the national school curricula of Afghanistan thanks to the teacher training programs in art throughout the country, which were developed by Columbia University under the sponsorship of the United States Agency for International Development. The valiant efforts of Mildred Fairchild of Columbia to establish the arts as an essential part of a school's curriculum were outstanding.

Curriculum decisions for the one and only university in Afghanistan were critical. The chance to establish priorities, principles, and viability always offers a unique opportunity for positive and creative action. It is also an opportunity to awaken the nation's sensitivity to the rich traditions of both the tribal artist and all the arts of Afghanistan's past, for the arts of Afghanistan have always existed on several levels. Most noteworthy have been the traditional tribal crafts created by women who wove carpets, did embroidery, and learned traditional crafts from their mothers. Other artists such as craftsmen, jewellers, calligraphers, metalsmiths, and potters were usually men whose work reflected Islamic traditions. Such men were trained in the apprentice system by their fathers, while still others contributed to the arts by being trained by Western art styles. Artists producing art for the tourists also existed. This work mimicked traditional crafts and ranged from photo-realist paintings to stonework copied from Italian and Indian sources.

Basic Economic Considerations

The question of manpower needs in the arts in Afghanistan is fundamental. Though it could be argued that not all decisions need be made upon employment possibilities, Afghanistan's limited resources, one university, and national concern for manpower is necessary and correct. In developing countries often an underemployed educational elite forms the backbone of revolutionary discontent. Education in Afghanistan is entirely government subsidized; therefore, the country's society expects the useful application of the education that it provides for its fortunate few. Those who work for their education by diligence and application of their natural gifts expect to find a reasonable source of employment.

To ascertain the economic needs of a developing country, the directions of the society and the economy need to be considered and questions need to be asked. Will rapid industrialization replace traditional artisanry? Would this be desirable? Will there still be a large nomadic-agricultural population? Will rapid expansion of the economy result in the need for industrial design, packaging, and publication skills? Will there be rapid expansion of the educational sector calling for trained teachers? The answers often come through consulting with agencies like the manpower planning sectors in the government, the United Nations agencies, and the World Bank, which gathers estimates on projected growth. Independent judgements, based upon an individual's knowledge of the arts, must also be made since the possibilities of the arts are often missing from the calculations made by consulting agencies.

The reliance of an art program upon local materials and concerns from importing technology and materials are additional problems for curricula in developing countries. These reduce themselves to such issues as whether a commercial artist should be trained to work with advanced photo processes and materials that may produce fine results but must rely on imported machinery, chemicals, and supplies, or whether simpler processes of reproduction available locally would be better. In the case of Afghanistan, Pakistani oil paints and excellent Chinese brushes make an oil painting course a viable option.

Consideration must be given in an art curriculum to the use of local resources such as marble, clay, iron, copper, and coal, or paper—or even vellum in a country rich in sheep but with limited supplies of wood. An investigation of the relations of trade and cultural exchanges of developing countries will provide curriculum designers with yet another series of factors for consideration. If trade and cultural exchange are mainly with countries of traditional values, such as Pakistan and Saudi Arabia, then attitudes towards art would be differently defined than attitudes that would develop with either a socialist or Western capitalist society. Trade with a country like India, with its rich folk art traditions and profitable economic development, will influence Afghanistan.

Basic Social Considerations

Often the key to an art curriculum is the role that higher education itself serves in a country. Learn who the people who obtain education are and what they expect and others expect of them. Discover what factors will change these attitudes or needs in time. Consider if it is desirable to alter the patterns at present and what the side effects of such alterations will be.

A primary factor in the Afghan culture is the role of religion in society. The religious spectrum is considerable, with over ninety-eight percent of the country Islamic. Interpretations of art have long been an aspect of

Islamic doctrine. Occasionally these prohibited all representations of life, including flora. At other times, portraiture, landscape paintings, and all natural forms were freely included in the visual arts.

Another social factor to be considered is role expectations and personal cultural orientation. It is possible within one society—and often within one family—to have people identified with progressive, radical, international, traditional religious, or socialist religious elements.

In addition, those persons who identify with a tribal traditionalism and those who identify with a national approach account for another variable; some of these persons may identify with the West and others with a long history that includes the ancient past. Many of these identities carry with them judgements that affect interpretations of the roles of art and of the educated person in society and the goals for the society as a whole. The choice of role models for development depends in part upon people's identities and allegiances. These allegiances may focus on places from China to Turkey, from Saudi Arabia to Egypt, from Switzerland to Cuba, or from Iran to India. Parallels exist in many societies, and this multiplicity should not be unfamiliar; such parallels result, however, in difficult identification of the major societal goals. In a developing society this is especially important since thrust and impetus are to be added to the foreign aid and other support provided towards a chosen direction. Thus, the natural richness of the developing country is affected by direct intervention by foreign aid.

These problems extend to the definitions of art. Though not necessarily restricted to broad cultural identities, the arts that are worth teaching and preserving are the arts that people prefer. Afghanistan has the arts of Islamic past, contemporary or classical European forms, politically laden art, and the tribal arts of the rural.

Along with problems of definition in a developing country are problems of opportunities for the educated person and their own role choices. Individuals subjected to the same education often choose different paths. One might enjoy painting; another might feel the labor of creating faience tiles socially prohibitive for him. A woman might consider teaching art in a girls' school but would never consider working as an artist in a commercial firm because of the respect she shows her family's conservative view. On the other hand, another woman might consider pursuing a year at MIT for a masters degree and do so with her family's blessing.

Personal possibilities are complicated by other variables. Vestiges of the caste system are inherited from the northward migration of peoples on the subcontinent. Certain types of work are traditionally done only by certain peoples. Most Afghan Moslems would deny that this prohibition exists since all are supposedly equal in Islam, but there is evidence in Afghanistan that professions such as woodcarving in Nuristan and musicianship in the cities are considered by some people as inappropriate for others outside of the kinship group. This prohibition is sometimes used as an indication of separate class status by cultural anthropologists in developing countries.

INFLUENCES UPON ARTISTIC HERITAGES

Historic, educational, economic, and social factors need to be considered when planning art curricula for a developing Afghanistan, where a dichotomy of traditions in the arts exists.

Historic Factors

Consideration of the artistic heritage of a country in which the arts are practiced is influenced by the arts of the ancient past and of nearby cultures which interact and affect a country's traditions. Along with these influences are questions about the roles of modern art. Is international modern art truly an international language? The arts practiced by rural people can be considered a valuable authentic traditional body of art. However, it is frequently not the art of the educated. The educated in a developing country form a complex group that includes traditional scholars, young people educated abroad, older people educated abroad in more traditional times, those disdaining the arts, and those supporting the premise that cultural values should include the arts of the past but not of the present. A curriculum designer must learn to discern major threads from the culture while separating successful tourist art from the high art of this culture.

The art of the West is often exciting and stimulating to the young people in a developing country. Consider it along with some national references of motif and color and its potential to become the new national art form. Are there other options for a country? These concerns are followed by no particular answers but must be weighed, considered, and analyzed carefully.

Educational Factors

The role of higher education as a force of development and an influence must be considered. Is the role of higher education in a developing country to train an elite or the many? Is its main aim to be educating the teachers and engineers that the country needs for growth, or does it allow for cultural considerations at the same time? Carrying on with the refinements of a civilization in times of great pressure for technicians and office cadres can be a problem.

There are additional complexities. What methods and content are taught in the university and what is taught elsewhere? Is recognition given to tribal arts at the university or are they left to be taught, as they always have been, by parent to apprentice child? At what point are people trained to recognize, cherish, and preserve the traditional arts for the society as a whole?

Developing a curriculum which, as it grows, can continue to be relevant to a changing society is a challenge. Building on previous knowledge and experience, yet transforming it all into a meaningful and cohesive whole, is still another issue.

The pressures created by the individual interest and skills of the people available and of those in power are also additional factors to consider. Though a curriculum designer may wish to have appropriate translations of traditional arts on a university level, such manpower may not exist.

Balancing the pressures that shape the curriculum with a clear evaluation of national priorities are without doubt major concerns that must be undertaken with great sensitivity in curriculum planning in developing countries. These considerations are relevant to all developing countries, no matter what political and economic spectrum. In summary, there is a need for sensitivity to the existing arts and awareness of the cultural patterns of the historic past, and a realization of the educational needs of the society. Careful evaluation of priorities and maintenance of flexibility to accommodate variations are therefore essential. In some sense, these are problems that administrators in all cultures have. These are also the problems of management or systems analysis applied to curricula. The difference is in the lack of alternate options once decisions are made.

Economic Factors

The economy of Afghanistan is mainly pastoral and agricultural. Fruit, wheat, and sheep are the basis of livelihood, with about one-fifth of the population being nomadic. The nomadic arts, whether practiced in towns or on rural campus, represent excellence in the current arts, with textiles as a major art form. There are contemporary artists, tourist art workshops, and some industrial arts; the use of commercial art is increasing in Afghanistan. Industrialization is minimal but growing and has created some options for advertising, packaging, and product design. There are also foreign-trained modern artists and traditional artists.

There is a prime need for teachers for the rapidly increasing Afghan school population. Education is a clear priority. Demands from the commercial sector promised jobs for students with increased product acceptability and opportunities that will positively affect the society. The traditional arts may prove eventually to be a valuable economic strength, tapping precious hard currency with their export value.

Problems of supplies, materials, and techniques are to be considered. Foreign currency is at a premium, and too much reliance on it is unwise as a long-term policy.

Social Factors

Educated Afghans are a diverse group, with people trained in Turkey, Egypt, Germany, France, Switzerland, the Soviet Union, the United States, Japan, Czechoslovakia, Australia, and Italy. This diversity is a result of the history of foreign scholarships, trade relations, and personal connections. Represented are a variety of attitudes which, in part, are reflected in the approaches to art that the foreign-educated elite represent. The vital traditional Islamic court arts such as calligraphy, bookbinding, and carpet making cross cultural boundaries.

Interspersed in the population is interest in the rich history of the country, which was host to the Zoroastrains, Scythians, Kushans, Hellenic Greeks, Buddhists, Sassanians, Mongols, and others. Each of these groups left its mark through great art or great destruction on Afghanistan. Each brought influences still evidenced today in the artworks of the country. Post-Islamic Afghanistan interacted strongly with the Arabic world, conquered India, and had a broad network of influence still evidenced today that forms the basis of the elite's current aesthetic taste.

The most vital arts of the country are the textile traditions. Textile art originated on the Central Asian Steppes and was brought to Afghanistan with the Turkoman, Uzbeks, Kazaks, and others. Tribalism sustained these arts through centuries, and they still survive today in Afghanistan.

There are over fourteen major tribal groupings in Afghanistan, the Turkoman, Pathan, Tajii, Aimaq, Hazara, Quizilbash, and a few others being the major ones. The Pathans, or Pashtuns, of the south have been the politically dominant in recent times, and their name, "Afghan," was used to name the country. They have a warrior tradition, are fiercely independent, and are located in both southern Afghanistan and northern Pakistan. Their visual aesthetics have been strongly influenced by the

Children's fabric design and painting on exhibit in Afghanistan. Photo by Arline Lederman.

less-refined aspects of Indian taste, an abundance of tinsel, bright colors, and bold forms. The Hazaras, currently a mostly poor people, are of Mongolian descent and inhabit the mountainous center of the country. Because of poverty, their aesthetics are limited to essential forms with elaboration appearing only in children's clothes and occasionally in party finery. Nonetheless, their work displays excellent workmanship, seen in simple stable forms executed in a direct manner. Because of their minority Islamic beliefs, which are akin to the Iranian Shiitesi, and because of their very poor land, unsuited for much agriculture, the Hazaras suffer from second-class social status. The Turkomen, on the other hand, enjoy great prosperity as a result of good land, skill in carpet making, and successful sheep raising.

Balancing tribal pressures has been the diplomacy needed for governing the country. Tribal pride is an important aspect of the culture and should not be bypassed by the educational process in the interests of national identity. Gradual urbanism has slightly modified the tribal identities.

Providing for and perpetuating respect of the tribal art form in a national educational system is not a simple issue. Much would have to remain in the hands of the parent and child, as it is now. Awareness and respect, however, can be communicated and endorsed by the educational process.

EDUCATIONAL CONCERNS

Artistic training requires direct experience, discovery, and exploration, but this is both essential yet very alien to a tradition that still is based on rote Koranic learning. A curriculum cannot presume previous artistic experience. It cannot even presume respect for the arts or knowledge of their scope.

Direct work with one's hands among certain groups, especially the Pathans, is considered appropriate only for the lower classes. It affects many areas of education—for example, engineering—as well as the arts. If children have not seen their parents making things, and believe it is beneath their dignity to work with their hands, it is very difficult to encourage such work beginning at the college level.

To resolve the dilemma of complex needs and values, a four-year, four-track curriculum for art was introduced in Afghanistan. The aim of such a curriculum is to retain traditional cultural forms while preparing art educators, commercial artists, and creative artists for contemporary understandings, options, and experiences. A common first year includes world art history and basic design; the second year for most students includes Asian art history; and the third year involves Islamic art history for all students. Calligraphy, a major Islamic art form, was emphasized throughout the curriculum. Special concern for Afghan art history and craft forms was also included.

Actual events led to the development by 1977 of a fine arts department at Kabul University, headed by two American-trained Afghan artists of considerable technical ability. Their training and their curriculum emphasized contemporary Western formalist values. Traditional Afghan forms were originally left to the populus at large and to the teacher training schools, not being considered appropriate for the university.

After the Soviet invasion in 1978, the foreign-trained Afghan heads of the art department left. Schooling of all sorts has continued to be disrupted; that which continues is strictly in the Soviet mode, while thousands of young people are being sent to the Soviet Union for training. Social realism has become the newest alien influence in Afghanistan.

Concern for economic, social, historic, educational, and cultural factors remain primary considerations for art curricula in developing countries. Specifically, the culture of Afghanistan, as in any other developing country, is the appropriate guide for art curricula in its universities.

Egypt Modern Methods and an Ancient Tradition

Mahmoud El-Bassiouny

ART EDUCATION AND HISTORY

The Environment

When thinking of the art education taking place today in Egyptian public schools, one can easily recognize the effects of the ancient Egyptian civilizations, which have endured more than 7,000 years, upon the development of each child. The history of Egypt and the characteristics of the Egyptians have been reflected in the art, architecture, popular art, crafts, and minor arts and industries that have been produced in the various epochs of Egypt. The design of the curricula is for children who are a product of the environment and its long history, a history in which each epoch left behind buildings, temples, tombs, pyramids, churches, and mosques. These and other treasures have been collected and are exhibited in the museums of Cairo and of cities in upper Egypt.

Evolutionary Stages

Art education in Egypt has passed through evolutionary steps, starting from copying samplers, to learning perspective, to free art expression initiated by Franz Cizek and his follower in Egypt, Habib Georgy. The Egyptians drew from modern concepts in art education based on the research theories of such authorities as Herbert Read, John Dewey, Thomas Munro, Viktor Lowenfeld, Helga Eng, and G.H. Luquet. The effect of these writers on the philosophy of art education, together with the influence of other authorities on modern art, has been transformed

locally to meet the evolutionary needs of the Egyptian environment and
Egyptian history.

MODERN EGYPTIAN ART EDUCATION

Aims

The aims of art education in Egypt may be summarized as involving the
development of (1) self-expression in various art media; (2) creative attitudes in handling art materials; (3) a sense of appreciation and art
criticism; (4) cooperation through processes of collective art work; (5) an
acquaintance, through processes of creation, with art traditions of the
past and present, especially those which were born and flourished in
Egyptian soil; (6) world-mindedness through the international values of
art; (7) an active attitude in utilizing leisure time, which adds to the
happiness of whoever undergoes the processes of art; (8) an awareness of
social, political, and cultural trends of Arab nationalism and unity
through practices of art; (9) an aesthetic attitude toward transforming
the waste materials into functional art objects; (10) an economic attitude
through the transformation of raw materials of less value into priceless
art objects; (11) an all-round and integrated human being through practices of art; (12) an individual's cultural and aesthetic knowledge as a
result of the practices of art; (13) gifted children in art by special teachers
and programs and the appropriate care of the exceptional children and
the handicapped; (14) consciousness of the relationship of art to other
school subjects; and (15) a sense of appreciation of modern art and folk
art, which affects the needs and choices in everyday life.

Each of these aims realizes its true meaning through the professional
art educator who is trained academically to teach. If art education in
Egyptian public schools is dealt with by a teacher who is not professionally prepared, his interpretations and practices of these aims will reflect
different meanings. His practices may even reflect deviations from what
is originally planned. Untrained teachers enter the system when there
are not sufficient teachers to fill the jobs available. The ministry of education appoints graduates of colleges of fine and applied arts to overcome
such gaps, but continues to train and adjust them, while they are in
service, for the comparatively new profession of art education.

The main source of the professional art educator in Egypt at present is
the college of art education at Helwan University, where the student
studies courses for five academic school years after leaving the secondary

schools. The course contains one more year than it did a few years ago, when this college was called "The Higher Institute of Art Education."

Curricula Major Areas

Transforming aims into practices at various levels and stages of development is the core and essence of the curricula in the Egyptian public schools. These goals consist of five major areas: (1) free art expression in various media, (2) design construction in various media, (3) study of nature, (4) collective art work, and (5) appreciation and art history. These areas are intermingled and are looked upon as unified and related to each other and to other subjects in the elementary schools (which is six school years). As the children progress to the preparatory (three school years) and the secondary schools (three school years), these areas are often treated separately with two or more teachers for the two-dimensional and three-dimensional arts. This division in schools is seen in the timetable according to grades by giving each teacher the responsibility of one grade with its many classes. In the first four years of elementary school, art education is left to the concern of the general classroom teacher. Art, in these classes, depends on the extent of art experiences these teachers have had in their general training at the training schools. In the fifth and sixth grades, art education is taught mostly by a specialized art teacher.

Each of the areas mentioned in the curricula has its details and specific meanings.

FREE ART EXPRESSION

From the early stage of development, in nursery, kindergarten, and elementary schools, children are encouraged to express themselves in various media. These can be pastel colors, wax crayons, gouache, dyes, color inks, dust colors, acrylic colors, chalk, sand, clay, and local and waste materials. The subject matter is derived from the environment and may be imaginative or visualized from concurrent incidents such as festivals, national days, historical events, religious stories, popular anecdotes, and myths. Subject matter is also derived from school activities or from life outside the school, and from family life, from the streets, markets, seashores, a lunapark, or from a visit to the zoo. Sometimes the children's thoughts about these subjects are developed with the help of the art teacher. The teacher widens the possibilities by always discussing such subject matter with the children and getting them to share in the formulation of pictures.

After making art, the children practice art criticism, thinking mainly of

Drawing by
Egyptian child,
age 6

composition, color relationships, form of expression, and the relation of
the foreground to the background. These results reflect the general attitude prevailing in the preservation of each child's personality, his
unique style, and his distinguished color sense.

Egyptian children take their time in finishing a picture. They try their
hardest to get it perfect. No alien standards are allowed, and the teacher
does not force any foreign idea or impose any personal pattern upon the
child. Teaching is derived from the work of children themselves and is
inspired by them, though the teacher may use his knowledge of tradition
to help in deepening the artistic vision of each child. The quality of child
art is seen in the use of bright colors to reflect the uniqueness of the
Egyptian environment with its sunshine and clear blue sky.

Students in preparatory and secondary schools are guided by the art
teacher. The teacher helps the students to overcome the effects of an
often limited public aesthetic culture. These limitations may include the

parents, the teachers of other subjects, and the common man in the streets. The teacher may depend on art traditions in order to preserve the spirit of art and help the students to achieve better standards.

DESIGN CONSTRUCTION

For creativity in design, all possible media can be utilized, such as wood, metal, paper, waste material, threads of wool or cotton, clay, plaster, wire, and plastics. Rural environmental material has also a very unique place in design construction. Design (which includes crafts) is a search for functional relationships in a suitable medium and is a training in aesthetic constructions. Through these constructions, children are trained to use various tools, understand geometrical drawing, and discover the techniques suitable for handling each medium. Elementary woodwork, metalwork, weaving, tapestry, ceramics, sculpture, poster design, and decoration are included. The art teacher chooses media and activities according to what is available in each of the schools.

Supervisors and teachers observe the children to discover each child's standard of achievements, in each medium, in each stage of development. The standards of achievement involved in children's painting, clay modeling, and linear drawing are becoming well known, but little has been written about children's standards of achievement in design construction using various media. The difficulty for not settling this matter is perhaps the limitation of facilities: media, tools, equipment, room space, means of registration, and so on.

Usually, each school has a special room for painting and another for design construction and crafts. In large secondary schools, there may be more than two rooms: one for art and a second for carpentry, a third for ceramics and sculpture, a fourth for weaving and fabric printing, a fifth for metal work, and a sixth devoted to the art museum. This last room has a collection of children's art works, art reproductions from various periods, and samples of popular art.

Design in various media is mostly affected by the taste of the Bauhaus, which has some link to our geometric and abstract tradition.[1] Geometricism is a major trend in design education, but the search for organic form is another trend. The organic form trend presents the third area in the curriculum: the study of nature. This area affects, in one way or the other, design construction. Nature is an important source for the inspiration of design in Egypt.

STUDY OF NATURE

It is believed that nature is the source of inspiration for creative ideas and that a good work of art is a result of interaction between the subjective and the objective. The objective is usually derived from nature. Students in Egypt are trained to draw from nature and to discover its unified forms and its order, rhythm, and harmony. Each student must learn to observe the objective reality with sensitivity. The achievement of good drawing signals that draughtsmanship has occurred not only in art but also in other school subjects.

Any study of nature is a transformation of reality into formal structure, where relationships are thought of in terms of the whole. Subjects of expression derived from nature include plants, vegetables, fruits, birds, animals, fish, butterflies, shells, rocks, and countless others. In the study of nature, emphasis is placed upon the discovery of aesthetic order and may be extended to bones and skeletons that are analyzed scientifically in classes of natural history but are treated aesthetically.

In the study of nature, each student's style is preserved. The various visions of the different schools in modern art are recognized. Visual aids such as photos, slides, and films help to understand order in nature. Using a lens or looking into a microscope widens experiences with nature by facilitating observation. Therefore, the study of nature leads to a work of art that embodies aesthetic principles. It includes a search for relationships in various styles.

In previous times, the study of nature meant producing only a copy of a rose or a branch of a tree. The student used to put his object in the middle of the page and make mechanical and imitative drawings. This practice has now been abandoned. Nature study presently may lead to a visual, symbolic, or abstract picture, depending on the guidance of the professional art teacher, whose role is to widen and deepen the aesthetic experience of each child through interaction with nature. If the teacher limits his students to academic methods, only mechanical responses can be obtained, which hinders aesthetic development.

COLLECTIVE ART WORK

Group art work is also considered of vital importance in the Egyptian public schools because of its social and educational effects. Children are trained to work together as a team to solve problems that require many hands, such as making a stage curtain, a mural painting, a wall panel, or a craft project. Themes are derived from school activities, industrial life, or national festivals, and are sources for the subjects of such collective art expression. Responsibilities for collective art are distributed democratically among members of each group, so every member has a responsibility which fits his potentialities, which he adjusts for the benefit of the group.

In collective art work each student learns valuable attitudes such as: to adjust individual merits for the benefit of the group; to learn to be tolerant as one deals with other group members; to know that the group's success depends on the success of the individual—as does failure; to be ready to learn from others and let others learn from you; to accept criticism with an open mind; to be cooperative and to acquire skills in working with others, thus achieving a common goal. Collective art work has a role in training students through the plastic arts to be socially cooperative individuals who are responsible and handle situations with other members of the group. This is fundamental to educational training that emerges from sharing a creative activity with others. Each member has a role similar to that of a player on a team; the final result of each situation depends on the loyalty of each team member. It also depends on the democratic relationship of the total team toward each of its members.

APPRECIATION AND ART HISTORY

Each secondary school student in Egypt has to learn about the art of his ancestors in his country. In Egypt scattered remnants of various civilizations date from 7000 B.C., and several museums have collections of rare art works of these epochs.

In secondary schools a pamphlet is written, with illustrations, on the history and appreciation of art from earlier times up to the present. While teachers give instruction on these periods, they also ask their students to deal with practical problems related to those initiated in each epoch. Through practice, discrimination between styles and schools of art is realized. Such visual aids as projectors, movies, art reproductions, and colored illustrations are used. Visits are conducted to museums of art and to ancient monuments and exhibitions. Students collect clippings from newspapers and magazines and construct albums with selected reproductions, making comments on each.

Throughout the public school years, art appreciation is addressed in the preschool, infant, nursery, and kindergarten grades by showing works of art from modern and primitive art. The child gradually becomes more conscious of formal approaches through analysis, comparison, and perceived relationships to the student's work and to the other traditions of the arts and nature.

INFLUENCES UPON ART EDUCATION

Art education in Egyptian public schools occurs in lower and upper Egypt but is controlled and directed in each zone by supervisors. These supervisors provide an official influence upon art education in Egypt.

Influences from outside of the schools began in the 1930s and 1940s, when a union of art masters was established with a plan of organizing meetings and exhibitions and issuing quarterly magazines and pamphlets; all this activity achieved the desired effect of enlightening the standards of achievements in public schools. This was organized by the late Shafik Zahir and Mohamed Abd El-Hady and other leaders.

Night courses were also organized in the higher institute of art education for the art teachers in service who had no professional qualifications. Youssef El-Affifi established such courses, which also accepted the standards of achievements in public schools. The ministry of education has also established training courses for those eligible for higher jobs in art education, which has affected the art teachers' own practice of art work and education about the latest developments in the field. These innovations have raised the general standard of achievement of art education in Egypt.

EXPERIMENTS IN ART EDUCATION

Experiments in art education, as reported in *Experiments in Art Education,*[2] show solutions of work, in various media, handled by art teachers in the Egyptian schools. These experiments were also reported at INSEA meetings, and a selection of results have been exhibited at the Museum of Modern Art in New York.

Georgy Children's Sculpture

Habib Georgy initiated a group of illiterate children to express the themes of the rural area in clay modeling which was then fired in the form of ceramic sculpture. This succeeded at placing an emphasis on children's sculpture in art education in the public schools. This work is now exhibited in a museum in the village of Hourranieh, near the great pyramids of Egypt where Weissa Wassif's experiment in wall carpets still is taking place.[3] Georgy's experiment with children's ceramic sculpture was reported in several magazines (one of them was UNESCO's magazine) in the late 1940s, when he had been able to have an exhibition of the work in Paris. Children's sculpture was also developed in a model experimental school in Quobba Gardens in 1945–46, where educational emphasis was based on Georgy's achievements.[4]

Hourranieh Children's Weaving

Habib Georgy's daughter Sophie, who was married to the late architect Weissa Wassif, was able to share her husband's work in developing child art on wall carpets, extending Georgy's experiment in weaving by hands. Sophie was responsible for continuing the weaving after her husband's death. This experiment had much to offer the field of art education and attracted many tourists and art educators from many parts of the world. Results were exhibited in the Louvre and in London. A book translated into foreign languages, *Weaving by Hands*, published with color illustrations, tells the story of the experiment and offers some analysis of the work of each artist. Georgy's experiment is evidence of the possibility of preserving child art regardless of age changes, which indirectly gives clues to the art of adolescence. It has also transformed child art into a functional and economic purpose, as the worth of these wall carpets have realized high prices in the international art market. This experiment is a result of the direct contact with the peasant environment, where its artists live, are educated, marry, and have children. These artists are surrounded by goats, sheep, camels, donkeys, cows, and buffaloes, and different kinds of birds such as pigeons, ducks, and geese. The environment has various trees and there are peasant homes made of sun-dried bricks; there is also a canal. This is a very thrilling and stimulating environment for artistic expression. Its scenery is reflected in the wass carpets, which show a link to some of the ancient Egyptian reliefs and paintings and also to coptic art.

ART EDUCATION PUBLICATIONS

In the last thirty years an evolution in the publications on art education in Arabic has taken place. In 1936 only one book on art education, written by the late Habib Georgy, existed; as of 1950, however, the Arabic library had seen more than sixty books. Mahmoud El-Shal and Abd Ed-Ghani El-Shal were prominent writers. These publications, showing links between art and education, philosophy, psychology, and methods of teaching, have helped in spreading the knowledge of modern practices of art education. Such publications in art education in Arabic are becoming the main force for transfusing culture in this area of Egypt and the Arab world.

THE PRESENT STATUS: PROBLEMS AND PROSPECTS

Although much has been done to foster art education in Egypt, many problems remain which have to be faced in order to reach a better standard. Since 1948 Egypt has entered four wars; the effect on the country's economics has, in turn, affected the facilities for learning in general public schools, in which education is free. Budgets for materials, supplies, equipment, visual aids, reproductions, publications, exhibitions, and travel are much more limited now than before. Professional teachers who are trained specially for the job try individual solutions to each problem. But in schools where professional art teachers are rare, a low standard is maintained. Some teachers prefer to do other jobs or to work in the Arab countries. This diffuseness affects the general standard of achievement. When the government thinks seriously of the teachers' problems, school facilities, rooms, equipment, materials, visual aids, examinations, and so on, there might be expectations for a rise in the standard of achievement.

CONCLUSION

The effects of the Nile River—the actual green strip but also its banks and the accompanying sunshine, blue sky, peasant life, fields, animals, and birds—are all reflected in the type of art work produced by children at the various public school levels in Egypt. Boats making their way along the Nile, from upper to lower Egypt and back, with their very particular goods and cargo, are also noticeable in the art of the Egyptian children.

The publication of colorful and well-illustrated books containing samples of the Egyptian child's art activities are anticipated. Such books would serve to widen the general understanding and appreciation of children's arts, developing awareness of children's art in one corner of the world.

NOTES

1. Cf. E.H. Gombrich, *The Sense of Order (A Study in the Psychology of Decorative Art)* (Oxford: Phaidon Press Limited, 1979), p. 50. Gombrich discusses the bending of wood in three chairs; one is by the Thonet brothers in the nineteenth century, whereas the other

two are Egyptian chairs. He concluded by saying: "The road from here to the Bauhaus is still a long one, but it is ultimately one road."

2. Mahmoud El-Bassiouny, ed., *Experiments in Art Education* (Cairo: The Higher Institute of Art Education, 1964).

3. Cf. Mahmoud El-Bassiouny, "Style of Adolescent Art in the Exhibition of Wall Carpets," *Artistic Culture and Education* (in Arabic) (Cairo: Dar El Maarif, 1965), pp. 204–9.

4. Cf. Mahmoud El-Bassiouny, "World Unity and Child Education—With Special Reference to the Function of the Schema" (Ph.D. diss., Ohio State Univ., 1949); idem, "Stories in Clay by Children Under Ten," Paris *UNESCO Courier* (July–August 1951); idem, "Traditional Culture and Artistic Form," *Education and Art*, ed. Edwin Ziegfeld (Paris: UNESCO, 1953).

India　A Changing Pattern in Art Education

Promila Sen

In India the arts have always been educative and have traditionally occupied an essential place in the native's life. These traditions of India's artistic heritage, in all their rich diversity, have been passed from generation to generation, thus assuring a cultural framework within which "art education" would take place. In India today, expanding technology and industrialization and a changing pattern of demographic, economic, and political elements are affecting social structure, individual lifestyles, values and goals, and the quality of education.

In order to assess changes in Indian art education, the position of the arts in ancient India must be understood. For more than 2,000 years (in early Brahmanic and Buddhist times), and even in prehistoric India of 3000 B.C., art was closely connected with religion and ritual. In fact, art was not separate from life; it was an essential part of the daily living process. Through the arts of painting, sculpture, poetry, drama, music, song, and dance, traditional values found expression and were woven into the day-to-day activities of the family, imparting vitality, creativity, and a sense of completeness to life. In their daily expression, the arts reinforced age-old traditions, strengthened cultural identities, and made for more harmonious social relationships. Ritual, as a part of religion, was (and continues to be) an important part of daily life in India. Through the arts, ritual remained visible, making the connection between abstract philosophic thought and the daily creative gesture.

The artist's position in ancient Indian society was equally important. His function was that of an intermediary between man and God; he was referred to in sacred texts as *sadhaka* (worshipper), *mantrin* (he who has the knowledge of ritual verses), or *yogin* (he who by contemplation can achieve "harmony or unity of consciousness").[1] The skill of the craftsman (shilpan) was also analogous to yogic practice: the "arrowmaker's con-centration" was proverbial at the time. The artist occupied himself solely with his theme. The beauty or aesthetic emotion (rasa) was a result of this state of contemplation.[2]

The status of the artist and of the craftsman was assured for life. An artist was trained from childhood as his father's disciple and followed his father's profession as a matter of course. He was a member of a guild under royal patronage and was protected from financial worry for life.

The basis of the traditional art education system, and especially that of music, was known as the guru-shishya-parampara—continuity of tradition from the master (guru) to the student (shishya). Through a ceremonial initiation student and teacher were symbolically bound for life. The student-musician kept in mind (a) his guru, for whom he always had affection and respect; (b) vinaya, or humility, a "complete surrender-ing of the self"; and (c) sadhana, or his practice and discipline. A student could stay for years with the guru, learning from and serving him, im-mersed in music, absorbing to the fullest the guru's tradition and style, which he would later pass on.[3]

The value of this traditional guru-shishya education in music and in the other arts led to a mastery of the technique; a sense of both humility and service; self-confidence—the student sat behind his guru at concerts and joined in the performance when invited; and freedom from economic worry—the student lived with and served his guru as a member of his family.[4] Unfortunately, in India today this valuable teacher-student rela-tionship is changing to a more casual one, and often far less time is spent on training in the arts. In fact, the tradition is in danger of disappearing unless an effort is made to preserve it.

Government backing of "cottage industry" has given a new impetus to traditional crafts, which must be guarded lest they lose their quality amidst the growing need for mass production. Among these crafts, which are regional and distinctive, are textiles done in batik; woven, printed, tyedyed, or embroidered textiles; the "blue pottery" of Delhi and Rajas-than; the Kalamakari and pichwai ceremonial, painted banners; objects in a combination of metals, such as brass, copper, and silver; clay and weed toys of Bengal and Orissa; cloth dolls of Gwalior; and masks and puppets, typical of every region in India.

The arts in Indian villages form an integral part of the villager's life. Annual temple festivals, devotional and folk songs (namely, the kirtan, bhajan, and baul of Bengal), the "dance-drama" (the Kathakali of South India), folk dances, and puppet shows (the putulnach of Bengal and the Yakshagana of South India) bring philosophy, myths, and epics—through legendary heroes, gods, and demons—into the daily life of the

Ink and wash drawing by Indian child, grade 7

people. Thus, even a simple villager, without any formal education, is able to participate in this informal learning through the arts, thereby getting a sense of belonging to a larger cultural setting.

From the late nineteenth century, art in the city, like education, went through a significant period of Westernization under British colonial rule, while rural folk arts remained untouched. There was a cultural break from an ancient heritage of classical literature, music, and art. However, city art schools developed a structure for art education. In art schools in the city—the Government Colleges of Arts and Crafts in Calcutta and Madras, the Delhi Polytechnic School, the fine arts department of the University of Baroda, and the Sir J.J. School of Art in Bombay—whether government sponsored or private, art was taught in the academic style of British and European art schools.

During the 1940s, in the wake of Mahatma Gandhi's independence movement, a fusion took shape. On one hand, an older group of artists—Amrita Sher Gil and Jamini Roy, among others—had begun to paint in an "Indian" style, characterized by intense color, symbol, simplicity, line, stylization, and strong pattern. Along with Poet Laureate and educator, Rabindranath Tagore, of Bengal, who created the *Shantiniketan* center for educating children through the arts, these artists helped make the connection with India's rich artistic heritage.

Younger artists like Husain, Laxman Pai, Hebbar, and Chavda, who left India to study and paint in the climate of the modern movement in Paris, returned enthusiastically to independent India in the 1950s. They combined new techniques with Indian subject matter, thus carrying this "Indianness" forward.

In the absence of art as a special subject in schools, except in private schools, the artist and art student once again come together in an art education situation. Children's expression in the arts is encouraged through music and dance recitals, plays, and exhibits of paintings. Children's art contests are held every year in the city (for example, Shankar's International Children's Art Competition in New Delhi for painting, poetry, and story writing and "on-the-spot" art contests).

An international perspective on art education is essential in India, for it helps to foster an "Indian" system that can refer to internationally tested techniques and be based upon philosophy, with a methodology, objectives, and modern resources. These resources include audio-visual materials; a suitable, sequential curriculum; an artist-in-the-schools program; and museum experiences. Finally, to be relevant, a successful art education system in India must grow from a uniquely Indian experience, related to specific needs and to a specific environment.

Educators in India, with traditional and modern resources available to them, have a most challenging task ahead. Tangible results are possible only if the administration, scholars, teachers, and artists cooperate in their efforts to bring about change in the pattern of Indian art education.

NOTES

1. Ananda Coomaraswamy, *The Dance of Shiva* (Bombay: Asia Publishing House, 1948), pp. 44–56.
2. Ibid.
3. Ravi Shankar, *My Music My Life* (N.Y.: Simon and Schuster, 1968), pp. 11–15.
4. Ibid., p. 15.

Israel An Integrated Approach

Harriet Goitein

To understand the special relationship between a public secular form of education and a public religious one, it is necessary to look back to the first development of a national system of schools in Israel.

Organized education developed in Israel in 1913 when politically supported institutions joined together to make a national school network using Hebrew as the language of instruction. Education in Israel first patterned itself after the "modern" European schools of the day.

In 1920 a second stream, *Mizrachi*, wanted a modern school that included religious precepts and was the product of the main religious party. In 1926 a third stream developed, patterned after progressive schools in the West that developed after World War I and formed by the Labor faction, whose backers were from the Histadrut and many of whose members lived on communal agricultural settlements known as *kibbutzim* and *moshavim*. Independent activity and trust between teacher and pupil were among its innovations. The kibbutz program of today, one of the outstanding features of Israel, is still motivated by these ideas. In 1948, with the establishment of the State of Israel, a fourth stream was added, the ultra orthodox or *Agudath Yisrael*.

In 1953 the State of Israel put an end to pluralism in education and created one uniform system with a religious section alongside a nonreligious section.

Presently, schools in Israel are divided into the following levels: elementary *(Amami)*, grades 1–8; junior high *(Hativat Habeinayim)*, grades 7 and 8; and high school *(Techone)*, grades 9–12. The population has a choice of two kinds of school: public secular and public religious. On the high school level, there are schools which specialize in (1) academic subjects, (2) technical and manual training, and (3) agriculture.

After some years of stagnation there are new ideas in science and math, and questions are being asked about the literature being taught.

The art curriculum is a part of this new change, and art enrichment for the culturally deprived has taken on special importance.[1]

Curriculum committees write programs in Israel and consist of directors of departments and supervisors. The art director, however, is an advisor to the minister of education. The minister of education has the legal authority to publish the curriculum and present it to the Kenneset (Israeli parliament) for approval. The curriculum, therefore, must conform to the educational principles passed by the Kenneset.

Often, parents and principals influence how much art is taught and, consequently and indirectly, what is taught. A minimum standard of materials and techniques are set by the ministry of education; a budget is allotted to every school, with equality in mind. In addition, a yearly fee is charged to the parents of each pupil to cover material and peripheral expenses. Since some schools have a population from a high-income bracket and a comparatively larger amount of yearly fees, a broadening of the art program can occur if the principal and parents so desire. This may take the form of (1) additional and higher grade art materials, (2) school programs, or (3) visits and classes at museums and exhibitions. The Israeli Board of Education makes up this inequity in other schools by allotting additional money to underprivileged schools and by providing them with additional enrichment programs and/or granting extra teacher-hours for art. However, the program is largely dependent on the level of the principal and art teacher and whatever emphasis they choose.

Until recently the classroom teacher has presented the art program in the first two grades. A relatively new innovation of the last seven years has been the implementation of trained art teachers working with the first and second grades for a period of forty-five minutes once a week. This program continues through the third grade and in many cases through the sixth grade. The art-enrichment program is augmented by an additional handcrafts course, beginning at about the fifth grade, in which a more definite division is made between crafts, industrial arts, and fine arts. Girls are taught weaving, appliqué, and various forms of stitchery; boys work with wood and metal. In both cases the emphasis is on creating a functional item.

In the secular high school there is a growing importance and acceptability of art, as reflected in art's inclusion as a specialization on the high school matriculation exam. In many cases the high school no longer provides an applied (fine) arts program, and students wishing to have this experience must go to an outside source. The Israel Museum has developed a program for these students and works with them as they prepare their final project. The vocational high schools in Israel prepare students for futures as blue-collar workers and tradespeople. Graduates are trained in all phases of the fashion industry, including weaving, fabric design, pattern cutting, and fashion design. Training for other occupations is also offered, for example, in the fields of aviation, furniture manufacture, shoe manufacture, or the printing industry. Art classes in vocational high schools are structured to provide only vocational training.

In other schools, such as in the agricultural schools, art is taught in a manner similar to that of the public high school. A fine arts program is offered in the lab schools that are connected to the universities, but there are less than a handful of these in all of Israel. Even less applied art might be found in the religious schools. Religious sanctions against figurative images in both the Jewish and Moslem religions have resulted in a view of art in the religious schools as a form of handwork essential for training a productive housewife. Macramé, stitchery, weaving, knitting, and crochet are typical subjects taught in a religious girls' high school.

THEMES: AN INTEGRATED APPROACH TO ART

The theme of the art lesson closely follows the regular course of study. In the early years of self-awareness, studies are made of phases of family and community relationships: one might see a life-sized drawing of a neighborhood, made of cardboard and painted wood-scrap, stretching from one side of the room to the other. Later, such themes are addressed as life-styles—city versus the coop farms (kibbutz and moshav); then, from the fourth grade through the eighth grade, each year is given to studying different aspects of ancient peoples. Here the art classes are often involved in recreating oversized sculpture, wall decorations, architectural modeling, mosaics, and so on, as a method of illustrating material studied in history. Another use of art in conjunction with the curriculum can be seen in the national stories and poems used in the classrooms. One can see this even on the first grade level, where the children begin to learn about Israeli poets. Puppetry is taught during all the levels of elementary art education. Throughout the year, events which have to do with the national history of Israel become natural themes for art work. In preparation for Independence Day, one can see every school filled with flags, parades of children, or tanks lining the halls and stairwells, painted or printed pictures of battle scenes, and large posters showing themes relating to peace.

ARAB SCHOOLS

In the Arab communities, schools teach a general history of Israel as well as the history of Islam and its leaders. The art curriculum in these schools uses this material to try to recapture Islam's rich artistic heritage. No matter what religion, holidays are an important part of the art curriculum. Since Moslem, Christian, and Jewish children usually attend separate schools, decorations can be made for religious holidays without infringing on any particular group's beliefs. Classrooms are decorated; gifts are made for relatives: the religious event is depicted in murals and individual drawings. Within each of the main religious groups and educational systems, there are many separate ways of thinking. In the secular schools holidays are taught with special emphasis placed on their historical importance. A recent trend is to infuse the curriculum with more religious emphasis, since more and more Jewish Israelis are turning away from traditions. In the secular religious and private religious schools, holidays are taught with a special emphasis on their religious importance. In both the Jewish and Moslem religious schools, quotes from the Bible or the Koran are a popular theme for posters and painting.

Such sections of the population as the Jewish, Orthodox Jewish, Arab Moslem, and Christian are supplemented by other minorities living in Israel, and all groups desire to sustain their particular heritage. Many churches meet this need by setting up church schools such as those for the Armenians, Greek Orthodox, and Russian Orthodox. In addition, there are a few villages of Druse, a Moslem sect, which teach their religious beliefs in separate schools.

Even within the Jewish sector there are differences, but these are more cultural than religious. A dichotomy exists between the second and third generations of Israel-born children of Western extraction and the second generation of Israel-born children of mid-Eastern extraction. The Jews of Oriental background (mid-Eastern) have much the same tastes as the people of the indigenous Arab culture from whose lands their families came. Arab influences are seen in the rich colors, the fine ornamental lines, the illustrative approach to painting, and the inherited designs in handcrafted items that are a part of their artistic heritage. In contrast, children of Western parentage are freer with the brush and are willing to experiment and demonstrate greater individual character in their work. One reason many oriental children come to school without any clearly defined artistic sensitivity or awareness is because they no longer see the articles from the former country of their parents, and nothing of equal taste and quality has replaced them.

Despite this loss, there is a definite oriental influence in Israeli art. One can see in the elementary school, before teachers have influenced the children, fine and repetitive border decorations and illustrations on most reports and stories.

The Arab children have not lost their heritage to such a degree, if at all. They work in striking color and ornamentation. Their unusual patience allows them to enrich their work with full detail. Illustration and lettering are always present; in fact, calligraphy is a major artistic endeavor.

THE ROLE OF GROUP ART IN ISRAEL

In any Israeli school forms of group activity are envariably encountered. There is a gradual implementation of group seating and the use of a part-time teacher's assistant in the first and second grades—depending, however, upon whether the annual educational budget allows for such assistants. The class, always over thirty-five children, is divided into five or six groups and, although the rooms are sometimes crowded (since they were not built for this arrangement), group art projects are thus ideal. Such projects as murals, wall-sized prints, and cooperative model building are possible in the large area created by six combined desks. This new emphasis on group work fits in with the communal spirit Israeli educators are trying to build.

The idea of group work along with the new methods in math and science are a part of the recent reinterest intellectuals have shown in changing the former outmoded curriculum.

COMMUNITY RESOURCES: THE ISRAEL MUSEUM

Aside from the ministry of education and its particular school program, there are other institutions involved in developing the arts among the youth; the YMCA, community centers, and city-sponsored youth houses are examples of a few. The Tel Aviv Museum, through the youth-art program, has been the leader in art education for the past ten or more years. The Youth Wing of the Israel Museum in Jerusalem has steadily built a unique and far-reaching program.

Under the direction of Ayala Gordon and employing forty teachers, the Youth Wing offers tours and studio work in over eighty weekly afternoon classes. More than 1,450 children participate. It also offers the public a large archival collection of reproductions and slides, and creates one or two major exhibits for children a year. Financial support comes from the municipality, the ministry of education and culture, and private funding plus student fees. The childrens' cost is one-tenth of what American students pay for equivalent courses and is barely enough to pay teachers' salaries. There is a scholarship fund for children of limited means, and the municipality contributes funds for several programs. One of these co-sponsored programs busses needy children for weekly art classes. Such children account for twenty percent of the afternoon's participants.

Another program of the Youth Wing is the workshop and teacher training program, which prepares public school teachers, who are not specialists, to use the materials and museum resources when teaching historical and archeological subjects. Most of these teachers return to the museum with their classes to participate in several of a series of courses given to visiting classes. Schools from all parts of Israel attend these classes, the museum being within one-half of a day's travel from any point.

The curriculum of the Youth Wing depends upon the age group. In the first and second grades a broad program is offered within one course as mixed media: painting, sculpture, printing, and so on. There are also classes in just drama or dance for this age group. Specialization increases from the third grade on; ceramics, constructions, and a course in puppetry are added. Teenagers can choose from courses in photography and film, etching, weaving, batik, and architecture or archeology.

The museum's goal—to bring the cultural and artistic heritage to the people—has been the philosophy behind its Youth Wing. The director explains, "We decided from the start that we would not be a school for talented artists but [we would] aim at education for all."

The museum's collection affords the possibility of observing original objects and works of art; these are used for a lesson's theme or as a point of departure. The Youth Wing's exhibits are also a major source of inspiration. Teachers guide their pupils through the exhibit, and objects are discussed and often drawn. An example of a past exhibit, "Children of the World Paint Jerusalem" was offered in 1977. During this exhibit the museum pupils were exposed to various usages of materials and to unusual techniques that children of their own ages had created from all parts of the world. In the exhibit "Mesopotamia," offered in 1976, classwork was concentrated upon imitating style and subject matter—this was similar to the way "Guernica" was taught in 1974. A huge reproduction of Picasso's painting covered a wall section at that exhibit, and students were constantly seen sketching from it, either with their classes or

ילה כוצר יץ-כמחהל-גבעת חיים פאוחו

Woodcut by Is-
raeli child, age 16

alone. A source of great fascination, it inspired discussions of the artist's meaning even at the first grade level.

"The Wonderful World of Paper," an exhibit offered earlier, provided, on the other hand, a great opportunity to work strictly from the imagination. A small exhibit hall was built over many weeks' time into a paper wonderland. There were trees, imaginary animals, and flowers; the floor, walls, and objects hanging from the ceiling were all made of white paper, but the paper was of a multitude of textures and weight. The "Film Making" exhibit offered classes the opportunity to produce their own three-minute animated film, with characters and scenery on superimposed transparencies, and to create slide shows by drawing directly on films with magic markers and treating them with chemicals and transparent materials. Probably the most popular exhibit to be offered in the

Youth Wing was the "Land of Dolls" exhibit. Here, authentic dolls in appropriate costumes were displayed in settings that included vintage furniture made to scale. There were little houses for the children to play in and dolls for them to play with. Several of the projects which evolved out of this exhibit were the making of hand-sewn rag dolls, miniature doll houses, and toy cars, while ceramic classes set to shaping ceramic puppets and dream houses.

"Our Pupils at Work" is an on-going exhibit, which shows the students' work from the museum. Works chosen are those which express most freely an individuality and innovation with materials or ideas. The great interest shown in these works by adult and student visitors may have inspired the recent opening of two new wings in the Youth Wing, providing more specialty rooms and exhibition space for permanent and temporary displays. The Ruth Rodman Frieman Youth Wing is attached to the Israel Museum at its entrance. The Paley Center is an addition to the Rockefeller Museum in East Jerusalem, serving Arab and Jewish children from both parts of the city.[2]

NOTES

1. Zvi Lamm, "Ideological Tensions in Education," *The Jerusalem Quarterly* (Winter 1978).
2. Ayala Gordon is the curator of the Youth Wing and began its first class eighteen years ago in the old Bezalel Museum. "Ten Years of Work in the Youth Wing at the Israel Museum," *The Israel Museum News*, no. 11 (1976); from "The Youth Wing: Looking Back and Planning Ahead," *The Israel Museum News*, no. 13 (1978); and from my own personal experiences over the eight years I have taught in the Youth Wing.

EAST ASIA AND THE PACIFIC

Australia A Decentralized System

Ben Crosskell, Jack Condous, and Dennis Schapel

Australia is a country of contradictions. Geographically, it is an old country with a small indigenous population adept at survival in sometimes inhospitable conditions; at the same time, it is a young country in terms of settlement, having inherited English traditions that are now being diffused by an influx from other countries and influenced by the North American way of life. Vast distances exist between the major cities of Australia—they are typically about 600 miles apart; the land is rich in mineral resources, and Australia is generally known as a producer of wool and wheat. Yet, 82% of Australians live in cities and contribute to secondary industries of many kinds.

With a generally benign climate that encourages out-of-door activities, Australia has a limited background in traditional family crafts (with these crafts would ordinarily come a sensitivity and discrimination towards materials and to shape, form, and color and other means of art). Neither has Australia a background of centuries of art, which could provide stimulation and an awareness of man's aesthetic heritage.

Each of the six Australian states controls education in its own area, although the programs are similar and children are able to move from one state to another without much difficulty. Each a highly centralized system, the art education programs indicate varying levels of development rather than any basic differences in points of view.

Most states have produced, or are in the process of producing, revised courses in art. None of these is revolutionary, but all are moving steadily towards what could be described as an international concept of art education.

At the elementary school level, art activities are usually carried out in the classroom under the guidance of the class teacher, although one state has introduced art centers attached to larger elementary schools; a specialist art and craft teacher is responsible for the work in each center. Training to become classroom teachers is followed by an extension year in art and craft; many of the participants have become highly qualified in art and craft and have introduced a professional outlook that is encouraging. Classroom teachers generally have insufficient time during training to become adequately informed about art education. The emphasis during training is on the teacher's development of a personal sensitivity to art and art materials. It is a tribute to those who train teachers that so much enthusiasm is generated in such a short time.

Art activities in the secondary schools are invariably taken by specialist art teachers who have received three to four years of training in the practice, history, and appreciation of art as well as the familiar pedagogic areas. A substantial number of art teachers are exhibiting artists in their chosen area of specialization. Art teachers are trained partly in institutes of technology, where practical art activities are usually taken with groups of students who will become professional artists; on the other hand, pedagogic studies are provided in the teachers' college to which these students are officially attached. It should be understood that a teachers' college in Australia is normally created by the relevant education authority to train teachers for its own system, the education faculties of universities being independent of the state systems and responsible for providing further study in general education.

Of course, there are noticeable differences in the quality of art education in different schools, or even in one school. The problems are similar to those in other countries: the teacher must be sensitive to art and the materials of art and to children and their needs, should be accomplished in art and practice it consistently, and must somehow solve versions of the common personal problem that confronts all art teachers. This problem revolves around the issue of whether the art teacher should practice art just for refreshment and to retain and develop further a sensitivity to the art process, in order that art teaching may be enriched, or should practice art in depth, egocentric in basis, with some probable reflection of involvement with education. The idea of teacher refreshment sounds fine but could easily result in shallow art experiences that hinder personal development; on the other hand, an overconcern with personal artistic development can only be at the expense of educational involvement. Thus, the art teacher in Australia is confronted with the dilemma common to all who work in art education.

ART EDUCATION IN SOUTH AUSTRALIA*

A number of years ago all the directors general of education from each of the six Australian states met and decided to regionalize their systems. The large central system of education thus became smaller, personalized units within the total framework. More effective communication and devolution of authority was a result of this decision. South Australia has now completed all of its regionalization programs and has allied its advisory services to particular regions or central directorates, which are responsible for staffing, for programs of inservice, for research, for production of curriculum guide materials, and for the implementation of such materials in schools throughout the state. South Australia presently has ten regions, a population of approximately one million people in the state, and a teaching population of 15,000. It is small compared to many larger cities and authorities in the United States, or the United Kingdom, but there are distinct advantages in being small.

Art Teacher Training

Teacher training for a specialist teacher of art in South Australia is conducted at Torrens CAE in Adelaide. Students at this tertiary institution enjoy the teaching of a very highly skilled and professional staff who have, in many cases, been teachers within or outside of the present system. This autonomous institution has designed its own courses to meet the needs of the students in training and to educate the future teachers. Advisory boards prepare material, critique staff planning of courses, and accredit college courses introduced by the Board of Advanced Education. Many graduates have received the diploma in teaching after three years, but now, along with the introduction of the bachelor of education, a four-year training program is required. The excellence of the teaching staff in South Australia has made possible the preparation of a capable, well-skilled, and diverse visual arts teacher, able to teach in high schools throughout the state. The training of elementary teachers in art education, however, varies from one situation to another. Predictions currently reveal a decline in college of advanced education enrollment for teacher training courses; therefore, the amalgamation of some institutions is occurring.

Students of elementary teacher education in South Australia receive minimal training in the visual arts. One of the greatest changes that's happened in South Australia is the appointment of specialist teachers of

*Jack Condous authored the section "Art Education in South Australia."—Ed.

art in elementary schools. Applications were called from elementary-trained teachers for specialist teaching positions in art education. Teachers were selected in some areas, while others having had a secondary art teacher training were appointed to primary schools. Special in-service courses were held to upgrade teachers' skills and their philosophies and practices in the classroom. Colleges of advanced education are now beginning to realize the diversity of the requirements and the depth of study needed to be able to adequately teach art to children between the ages of 5 and 12. In many ways these institutions have (and still do) produced a bias and an overstress in academic requirements. Change is a fact of life but is sometimes very slow and varies between institutions. The depth of study required in the preparation of general teachers has recently been highlighted by an important national report published from a joint study of the Arts in Education by the Schools Commission and the Australia Council.

Teachers seeking appointment in the schools must go before an interview panel consisting of principal education officers from the South Australian Education Department. The teachers present themselves and their references, teaching reports, and other relevant materials at the interview. Art teachers, like other teachers, are graded according to their ability and are appointed to the available positions in the schools. A surplus of art teachers at the secondary level recently occurred, but many teachers have since received appointments on contract or relief work in various regions. A newly appointed teacher could be placed in a large department of a large school, varying in size from five to fourteen teachers, under a department head who has overall administrative responsibility for each center. However, young teachers are often appointed to smaller high schools or area schools with smaller enrollments and students varying from five to sixteen years old.

Elementary Art Education

The art program taught in South Australian elementary schools is a specified area of study; it is only a part of the junior secondary curriculum and an option for specialization in the upper senior high school years. For young children art is an expression of self that reflects and contributes to physical, emotional, intellectual, and perceptual development. Importantly, it establishes for young children an interrelationship between art and life because it permeates most human experience. Art experiences can illuminate and add a vitality to many facets of learning. One of the most important aspects of art in education concerns the preservation and development of curiosity, fantasy, and imagination. For this reason time that is made available for children to paint, draw, print, model, and construct has a significant place in education programs for early childhood.

Enrichment of the visual environment by the teacher can provide extra motivation for the child to see, talk, and feel, leading to greater involvement in visual expression. In the elementary school curriculum, art education programs are taught to provide the major opportunity to develop skills of visual communication. Art can also be a means of establishing integrated courses that could include aspects from most other areas of the curriculum. Quality of programs varies throughout the country. In some states, art at the elementary level is well established, programs are well coordinated, and good liaison and cooperation between teachers occurs to ensure that a coherent and developing range of art experiences is available to students as they progress through their schooling.

Secondary Art Programs

In the secondary art programs all eighth and ninth grade students are exposed to a broad course of art education, and as the students progress, they may begin to specialize as interest, expertise, and facilities allow. Some schools in South Australia may structure separate and sometimes alternative courses in art and design; others may have combined courses. Where the need exists, two art courses may be offered to accommodate a greater scope of art activities. Integration with other disciplines could be considered with due respect to the aims of each. Many art teachers integrate art into broader programs of education, but this must be a two-way involvement that will add to and enhance the goals of art education as well as those of other areas of education.

Teachers of art are free to design the appropriate courses to meet their students' needs. As the impact of the policy of school-based curriculum development is felt in schools, art teachers are increasingly being placed in a position to make important decisions regarding the form and content of their students' educations. Decisions about an art curriculum are made for students in the context of the school's curriculum policy, community expectations, and the limitations imposed by the availability of staff, accommodation, and equipment.

Advisory Support

South Australia has an excellent network of advisory support (as do most states in Australia). Experienced and capable teachers visit schools in the districts, armed with their appropriate check lists to leave information

Wash painting by Australian child, age 11

with their colleagues. Team teaching programs are conducted; workshops on specific techniques are given; group information exchanges and discussions are made. Consultants in art provide a statewide service, operating from the Central Curriculum Directorate, while other services—such as education officers with the South Australian Art Gallery, the Industrial Design Council, and the Educational Technology Center—also offer support for teachers.

In-service courses for teachers are currently organized on a regional basis or from the Curriculum Directorate. Many such courses have given teachers the opportunity to visit other schools, exchange information, discuss the programs and philosophies in art education, and argue for clarity and communication.

Curriculum Guides

In the past, curriculum guides produced by many departments of education throughout Australia were centrally produced and were considered as books on things to do. However, with the involvement of teachers in curriculum planning and design, with in-service programs, and with the changing needs of students, curriculum materials are now being offered as guides to teachers and not as prescriptions. Within each guide, options or alternatives are given and developments are made for the students based on their needs.

Several guides for the teaching of art are planned in the South Australian Department of Education and are available for young as well as experienced teachers.

The philosophy of the Australian art teacher in general is best stated in the following curriculum guide selection, which reflects the views of the art teachers who both planned and use it in their day-to-day activities. In content it is typical of most systems in Australia.

Art in Education: Philosophy and Objectives

Art education is concerned with the development of a student's capacity to originate, and thus with an individual's perception, sensitivity, receptiveness, responsiveness, all of which are inter-dependent and inter-related, and all of which are characteristic of the uniqueness of the individual. Each person is a special kind of artist and each person will respond to stimuli and situations in a special way. Students' work in art comes through a fusion of intellectual, emotional, and physical energies. Through such expression of their feelings and ideas, children grow inwardly in personal awareness and sensitivity, and outwardly in confidence and in their capacity to communicate with others.

Original art is based on personal experience and observation, private fantasy and imagination, and its practice is probably the most natural and successful way for adolescents to cope with experiences which have little or no creative release. The impulse to explore and examine the environment in all of its aspects, together with the ability to give concrete expression to ideas, images, values, and aspirations, should be encouraged and nurtured.

Techniques, which are a part of art education as much as any other discipline, are seen not as skills to be mastered for their own sake, but as contributing to the act of creation. An acquired skill must bear upon the experience to clarify and communicate it. Techniques aid in showing the individual the variety, flexibility, and potency of a visual expressive language.

View-points change, but the challenge to art teachers over the next decade is to prepare students for a rapidly changing environment and to help them cope with the pressures and the values of an increasingly complex age. This has become evident by a growing recognition of the importance of art in the school curriculum as shown in the more recent history of education in South Australia and in the document "Purposes of Schools" published in 1975.

Art is a subject where the past can be related to the present, where the new does not invalidate the old, where the understanding of man's cultural history helps to provide a personal and cultural identity for the individual.

Art should not be seen as a body of knowledge, isolated and removed from daily life. Such a viewpoint tends to reduce art to a series of objects and events that are "studied" in order for the participant to become "educated." This is in direct opposition to the idea that the arts are a symbolic expression of what individuals feel, think, and know.

Budgeting

Budgets are a constant problem for all the schools in Australia. Schools in South Australia have now been given basic grants based on the overall school population. School-based funding has allowed decisions affecting the needs of schools to be made by school staff. Teachers have found they can purchase materials and equipment according to their needs but, of course, finances have been shrinking and the purchases of a dollar have been getting smaller. As in every country, art teachers have become masters at using their materials, using scrap material from industry, recycling materials whenever possible, and spending wisely in the best interests of their students. Teachers do charge art fees, and schools receive $1.00 per child for art as a base-line allotment.

Facilities

The well-designed buildings in South Australia have been generously supported by interior designs made from sketch plans that were based on the working needs of students. Many schools with an enrollment of 1,000 at the high school level would have five or six art teachers, with five rooms fully equipped and used for both two- and three-dimensional work. Sculpture courtyards have been designed in addition to open flexible areas, supplied with storage facilities for tools, materials, and major equipment. New schools use open-plan approaches, with a suite of adjacent art areas.

PROBLEMS IN ABORIGINAL ART EDUCATION*

Dots, lines, and cross-hatched patterns painted on the surface of iron or stringy bark with earth ochres and white pipe clay has become a traditional form of art, widespread amongst northern tribal Aboriginals in Australia. The paintings are symbolic of the land, birds, animals, and fish in relation to their mythological meanings. As such, bark paintings are a way of recording and preserving cultural information.

Other traditional art forms used are carved wooden figures and spear heads, woven mats and baskets, bags formed from handmade string, feathered ornaments, rock painting, and ceremonial body painting. In the desert areas sand drawings and incised rock or stone drawings are used in ritual ceremony. Recently these Central Australian Aborigines have turned to stretched canvas and pigments with startling results. The dot and line designs and colors now being used are steeped in symbolic Aboriginal meaning.

Aboriginal art education in the tribal sense is not a formally taught situation as we know it; rather, it is a part of the ritual of sacred ceremony and mythology in which all participants are involved. It is not until circumcision and a series of other ceremonies have been experienced that an Aboriginal boy has been allowed to participate in the making or painting of sacred objects and symbolic designs. It is not until he is considered an adult that he learns the designs through helping and participating in ceremonies. Aboriginal girls do not have the role of making or painting sacred objects; instead, they will weave and dye mats and bags for everyday use.

Today, bark paintings and carvings and such art products are produced by adult Aboriginals for sale in controlled outlets and can be a vital source of income. The subject matter of the barks and sculptures is not of a sacred nature, but is a description of the artist's environment as he knows it. Children, however, are not encouraged to participate in the making of nonreligious art.

Besides laws, there are so many tribes, clans, and "skin" groups governing behavior that to arrange programs of training in traditional art forms for children is almost impossible and, in most cases, is contrary to tribal custom and therefore undesirable. Not all Aboriginal communities have retained their sacred customs. Many are in danger of losing their art forms; some have already lost them; and some are in process of trying to form an identity by salvaging a little from the past.

*Dennis Schapel authored the section "Problems in Aboriginal Art Education."—ED.

The question therefore becomes, "What, then, should or could be done in art education for Aboriginal children?" The existing solutions depend upon the types of Aboriginal community aspirations, which differ across Australia, and the types of educational situations in which they are involved. Three identifiable approaches toward art education appear to exist: (1) preservation of cultural traditional art forms; (2) development of art forms from *secular information* and designs stemming from Aboriginal cultures; and (3) use of Western materials and techniques to express the present-day life and environment. The nature of the Aboriginal educational situation determines which approach is employed.

Schools Within Aboriginal Townships

Townships are composed of various tribal groups usually having the resources of a school hospital, a store, and a town administration office. Townships are governed by an Aboriginal council. The schools, while encouraging traditional art forms, attempt to teach art based on a Western view of creative expression. This is justified in part by the need to become familiar with the properties of Western materials that are part of their daily lives and environments, as are concepts of time, measurement, and space.

Schools on Outstations

Outstations consist of tribal groups living on their land away from townships and striving to govern their own development. The schools, which are generally very small, employ Aboriginal teachers who have usually been trained at the Aboriginal teacher training centers, which encourage the use of secular images using simplified Western techniques of painting, printmaking, and sculpture. However, preservation of ethnic traditions is important to these communities.

Transitional Schools

Transitional schools are designed for Aboriginal children who are identified as academically capable of achieving in a high school or a trade training course. Here they learn Western techniques to provide an easy transition to high schools or trades. Aboriginal artists have come to such schools as artists in residence, to help students sustain an ethnic identity in a Western milieu.

Schools Within Urban Centers

Aboriginals attending schools within urban centers are usually from mixed ethnic communities within suburban areas of cities. These students are usually seeking identities within the city. Teachers here also use Western techniques while encouraging the use of native art forms whenever possible.

Aboriginal Teacher Training Centers

The Aboriginal teacher training centers, or colleges, prepare their trainees for teaching positions in the Aboriginal schools using their own languages. While Western art techniques are taught, the use of secular images peculiar to the trainee's ethnic background is encouraged.

An Aboriginal-Based Curriculum

From birth, the Aboriginal child is usually in constant contact with Aboriginal painters and their concerns, and therefore has an innate sense of his native art. A program developed by Cynthia Venn at Elcho Island in the northern territory uses secular Aboriginal knowledge and methods to teach from traditions while striving for a developed form of art. Some examples are as follows: (1) The stencil method of blowing paint over a hand to make a print is a traditional method and image used in rock painting. By first watching as an Aboriginal painter shows the method and then trying it themselves, the class is able to progress to a mechanical spray gun and to use objects other than their hands to form the stenciled shapes. The process eventually leads to screen printing. (2) Aboriginal children know how to imitate the tracks of animals in sand. By first imitating the tracks and then reproducing them with paint on paper, the students make a variety of printed images, not only from the hand but from other shaped surfaces. (3) In the same way, traditional methods of weaving and dyeing lead to original fabric designs.

Such activities are examples of experiences that can lead to developed art forms which have direct links with Aboriginal culture. Venn produced a short film, *Art with Aboriginal Children*, which featured these methods.

Aboriginal children possess a deep knowledge of the land and the things which live within the land. They are taught from an early age to be highly perceptive, and their knowledge of the habits of the wildlife is unsurpassed. Aboriginals have names for all types of species of plants and animals, birds, and insects. Those students in the coastal regions often know the migratory habits of the sea life. Many of their dance forms reveal their intimate knowledge of the wild and their understanding of symbolic cultural meanings. Therefore, the subject matter of the paintings of the Aboriginal children is directly related to a knowledge of the environment, even though the colors chosen and the methods employed may often be Western in nature.

Small industries have been developed in some townships, and these are influencing art education in the schools. "Tiwi Designs" on Bathurst Island in the northern territory produces printed Aboriginal designs on cloth which is then made into clothing and wall hangings. Similarly, a pottery industry is developing.

In outstation schools, Aboriginal traditional forms of art are being preserved by the Aboriginal peoples in the intricately balanced web of the total ethnic culture. Art educators, recognizing the importance of such tradition, encourage the preservation of visual ethnic elements. Of course, Western methods are also needed in communities where the aspirations are consistent with integration with Western society.

The development of elements from within the Aboriginal cultures appears to fulfill an emerging ethnic need by providing an avenue of identity within today's world.

China Tradition and Change in the People's Republic

Shirley Wood

China's school system was patterned decades ago somewhat like the American—six years of elementary school and six (three junior and three senior) of secondary, or middle, school. Elementary school children are given drawing lessons in each year. These start with drawing apples, oranges, and bananas, and progress to flags, houses, trees, and people. Later the students do pencil drawings of cups and teapots with shading, and they learn about perspective and other elements of drawing. Depending on the capability of the art teacher and the thinking of school leadership, a junior middle school will require one or two years of art studies.

Besides classroom instruction, school children are taken to art exhibitions. The schools enter their pupils' better art work in local and provincial exhibitions of school art. Although the course itself does not get strong emphasis in the curriculum, it can give children a foundation and bring attention to talented children.

The Russian (essentially, European continental) influence, felt after 1949, promoted the development of conservatories for art and music, taking gifted children on the basis of examinations. Aside from this, the Children's Palaces of Culture in the bigger cities and the Madame Sun Yat-sen's China Welfare Institute in Shanghai provide first-class after-school instruction in the arts for interested children.

This formal special education is entirely insufficient in a country the size of China, where a small county seat has a population of 20,000. However, away from the big cities and their billboards advertising pink pills, Eurasian ladies, and machine parts, the provinces, where a few big names do not overshadow everything, have an enormous amount of respectable art to offer. There are three reasons for this: Chinese calligraphy, the traditional master system, and the art market.

From the third grade in elementary school, children start writing with a brush and ink. They learn large characters an inch and a half in size, then small characters half an inch square, written with brushes of different sizes. Besides the school exemplars in standard book script, others can be bought in various scripts, many of them prints from stone rubbings of texts by famous scholars. Calligraphy, considered an art in China, gives meticulous training in control of a brush. The Chinese character itself is an object of art, and pen and ink calligraphy is also much cultivated. Children are bombarded with examples of fine calligraphy, in children's picture books and magazines, on shop fronts, in brand names, and on school prize certificates, filled in by one of the better writing teachers. Children may enter junior middle school already noted among their schoolmates for their large or small characters.

Aside from written characters, artistic "lettering" is widely used. Like letters in the Latin alphabet, the square Chinese characters are capable of all sorts of distortions. Squares may be rounded; horizontal and vertical strokes may differ in width, as in Gothic script; or characters may be distorted in width or height. Such art characters are used in colored chalks for blackboard headings, and a higher primary or middle school class puts out a blackboard as often as once a week. Such a blackboard utilizes several pupils for the writing as well as the editor and those who contribute poems or short compositions. At least one pupil who makes good small characters takes part in copying the material, while headings are the task of another who is adept at good large characters. The masthead is done in art characters by yet another. Between them, the students manage flowers and ornamental dividing lines, unless a picture is called for.

Cutouts are another form of art characters. When something more formal than black on white is called for—on special days, to welcome VIPs (the home team gets black and white), or for big meetings—red cloth streamers are brought out and yellow paper-cut characters pinned or pasted onto them. These may be in any form of art block characters or "grass" (longhand) scripts, so long as all parts are slightly connected for cutting and pinning. Big characters may be two feet high. By middle school, drafting these is the students' job.

The traditional system of learning anything in China was to apprentice oneself to a master. Although there is now a universal public school system and various specialty schools, this tradition is still very alive. The interested young person can always find a competent master from whom he can get criticism and learn a few pointers. The most satisfying work for art teachers may be done with such pupils after school, or the master may be the gym teacher, school counselor or gateman, or perhaps a neighbor who may have exhibited or done commissioned paintings or even taken prizes or had a folio printed. At the least, the master's work is much in demand among friends.

A great art tradition in Chinese society is that many well-known artists are professionally employed in some other capacity, leaving them free to be generous with their art. They are also generous with their teaching, particularly of the young. In China the greatness of a man is judged partly by his students. If an artist finds special talent in one of his disciples, he gives special encouragement and instruction, and sometimes art materials, and if necessary promotes him with an art institute or a better teacher. Although the best way to become a good artist early is to be born in an artist's family, the wide dispersion of artists in society enables even rural children to benefit from individual instruction.

There is a wide demand for art work in society. Books in China are cheap and are heavily illustrated. A novel may have half a dozen full-page illustrations. Furthermore, the flood of children's books are heavily illustrated. A story for twelve-year-olds may have a small drawing on every or every other page. All books are paper backs and are cheap and sell in large numbers. A twelve-page book for smaller children, with color illustrations on every page except the back cover, may cost twenty-eight *fen* (an aluminum coin of China; this amount is equal to about seventeen cents). Illustrations may be in cartoon styles or in realistic or Chinese traditional painting. The serial pictorial, about four inches by five in size, is made up of detailed lined drawings, one per page, with a short text below each. These books for readers of all ages include European classics, Chinese opera or history (a top-selling, three-volume historical novel has been kept up within a series of these small pictorials), fairy stories from all nations, and children's stories. Anderson's "The Little Mermaid," with eighty-seven drawings, sells for eleven fen. Art institutes have a special course in serial pictorial drawing.

Well-known illustrators make a good living from this work. The large number of publications in provincial publishing houses brings work to nonprofessional artists and even to unknown young people.

Drama is very popular in China, and every county seat has a professional opera troupe. Part of the staff is one or more artists for set painting. There were fewer billboards in the past, and these were repainted at least once a year with propaganda posters often featuring flowers, children, scenery, or figures costumed to represent nationalities. This practice, which kept a number of artists on city payrolls, is coming back in some cities. The design and labor involved in China's widespread arts and crafts also absorbs artistic talent.

Young people to whom art is essentially a hobby can find ways of showing their work. For example, a young man could get a clerking job in

Ink and wash draw-
ing by Chinese child,
age 15

a new sweetshop, serving candies, cakes, canned goods, and wines downstairs, hot sweet soups or beer and ice cream upstairs. One by one his
paintings could appear on the bare walls—landscapes in oils above the
show windows downstairs, Chinese traditional between the windows upstairs, the Great Wall at the landing. Railway stations, big hotels, and
restaurants commission well-known local artists, but the department,
hardware, drug, and grocery stores, for example, depend on their staffs
to cover the bare spots on the walls or make up fresh and striking window
displays with dramatic backdrops or modeled and painted clay figurines.

The way to master art is by practice, and what better practice than
painting for friends? The work of budding artists is often introduced to
society on the walls of private homes, and original painting or calligraphy
from a local person is the personalized gift. Artistic talent is much admired among one's peers at all ages.

All this work varies in quality, of course, but some of it is quite good, the artists having shown in local exhibitions and having made a name for themselves among those who pay attention to art.

In most areas of China there are coteries of those who pay attention to art. Another Chinese tradition is that artists know the ball scores and ballplayers discuss the merits of paintings. Television, which shows exceptional artists at work from child painters to young students or workers to well-known elders, gives all an opportunity to see a variety of works.

The rural areas are not behind in art. Rough murals on adobe walls in some areas attest less to the level of rural art than to its existence, while in other regions there is a strong art tradition. Calligraphy in urban schools lags behind that in rural, where it is the major sign of scholarship. Good calligraphy is much in demand for holidays and special days, characters for luck and prosperity on red paper diamonds, or couplets to be placed on either side of the door, with a four-character line to finish them off across the top. Middle-school students talented at calligraphy are besieged with demands from neighbors and acquaintances; they are also sought to do the lettering for social functions.

At national exhibitions of children's art, one can see some remarkable work. An artist of six may have shown works in foreign exhibitions, or a twelve-year-old may have had his own show in a major city. These achievements have behind them a massive social appreciation of art; exposure of children to good art works creates the social background that can help the formal art teaching they get in school to be of real effect.

Two Views On Chinese Art Education by American Teachers

Brenda Lansdown and Thomas Slettehaugh

Boys and girls of junior high school age and even younger in China draw figures of people in complicated actions so well that an American high school art major would be proud to do the same. Nursery and primary school children skewed the "draw-a-person" scale by about two years, and a trained American visitor overestimated the age of each young artist observed. There are immense and accurate details in many pictures of young Chinese. Some ten-year-olds have fifty or sixty people in their drawings, each person presented in a different action, although each child draws all faces alike. No violence, war scenes, explosions, or any acts of aggression were seen in their art. There is much representation of cooperative interrelationship. Hands and bodies are posed in gestures of helpfulness. From the age of eleven or twelve, children draw hands which function strongly and accurately.

The child's personal interpretation of a collective society appears clearly in most drawings because most of the citizens' lives are dedicated to building socialism. Consummate skill in handling tools and in fine muscle control is perhaps explained by the facts that all children are educated in the difficult craft of Chinese calligraphy and that from kindergarten on, they all take part in some productive labor necessary for the life of their commune. For example, five-year-olds may spend ten minutes a day, three times a week, folding paper boxes or placing flashlight bulbs in small egg carton sections.

Here again one realizes that art reflects the lives and attitudes of the people. Certainly our children's art in the United States does this, too. We foster expression of individual feelings which may come out as abstract color patterns or lines but which show no reference to social reality. On the other hand, American boys often draw star wars and guns in action, while girls picture fashion models. The objective theme of American and European children's art is one's own personal experiences, memories, and feelings. China is a collective society where the major concern is the group to which the individual belongs and is protected by, but each young Chinese student represents this in his or her own idiosyncratic manner. What is emphasized is *your* view of working together as a part of your life and *your* experiences of "serving the people." Therefore, pictures of children cooperating with heavy loads, of a People's Liberation Army "uncle" carrying buckets on a shoulder pole for some peasants, or of masses of crocks storing grain are often the subject matter of Chinese children's art.

Traditional Chinese art also influences children's art in several ways. A glance at a group of child art evokes the comment, "Just like the Hu Hsien peasant painting!" It is the same gestalt-type recognition that enables us to categorize a French Impressionist work. Chinese art even older than the Hu Hsien works often represented perspective as higher on the page. Chinese children also use this convention. However, even quite young children draw distant objects with a Western-type perspective. Repeating objects as an area design is another tradition; for example, there may be rows of cabbages or a mass of people in neat array. These also show a fine attention to detail and could be an outcome of much practice in writing Chinese characters—really a most exacting requirement—as an adult novice discovers by trying to copy a character and then showing it to a Chinese person.

Children have contact with many books and many professional artists. Children with various abilities go to the children's palaces after school hours for special training in all manners of cultural expressions. The obligation of those chosen is to pass on to their schoolmates the knowledge they have received. Professionals in all art fields visit commune schools after the academic hours and teach those children who wish to learn.

The emphasis on people rather than on things, along with a cultural tradition thousands of years old, the universal emphasis on "we" instead of on "me," form the matrix of Chinese children's art. Each child then creates his or her interpretation of the total social perception.

Calligraphy in China, as in all Eastern and mid-Eastern countries, plays an important part in the total art program. The use of the brush to create these symbols aids the young children in developing the skill for writing and communication and for fine arts projects. Hand and eye skills are needed for traditional Chinese painting classes that come later both in the school curriculum and in all types of painting used in the factories. Older boys and girls and their teachers work alongside the younger children, at tables for eight or less students. Every art teacher is a specialist in the area they teach—the Western concept of a "generalist" is unknown.

Western-style art classes have been developed for the talented youths, ages seven to seventeen, based on the Soviet Union's special school system where the children can create art products two to three hours a day, six days a week, for ten months of the year. In a typical situation, half of the students in the drawing room face one direction and draw the still life while the other half of the class face the opposite side of the room to draw their still life. The same system can be observed in any number of Soviet student art centers.

Traditional Chinese painting is done in classes where the child can stand and work on a flat top of a table using the brush and black color ink blocks. As the child's work advances, other colors are added to the palette. One basic technique used by the children is to lay a piece of transparent rice paper over a painting that was made by the teacher or an older student and trace over the lines. Sometimes the older children are given a picture post card to look at and then enlarge into a painting of their own that resembles the picture on the card; in other instances it may be a large reproduction of a "master" painting.

Children also do cut-paper designs with a pointed knife on a single piece of paper using this same tracing technique. Concerning subject, content, and media, some of the tasks previously noted were as follows: painting acrobatic activities; tug-of-war with a narrative story; sports and games in the scratched crayon technique; Western-style fabric collage; flat figure representations with a Chinese landscape; cut-paper technique using a single piece of colored paper; representation of the head and two lines for the body; Chinese opera; Western-style landscape crayon drawings; repetition of the horse using change of color and reverse imagery; depictions of outer space and the Great Wall; paintings like x-rays, using the sea subjects of a boat and fish in the net under the water; a telephone call to the moon and rice patties in perspective or time space sequence; and picking fruit from the trees.

The elementary craft projects are models of airplanes and/or ships that have been made into kits; the children can follow the instructions, assembling the model and then painting it when they have finished. These projects develop skills that can later produce art work in the form of feather cutting and mother-of-pearl pictures, made in large shadow boxes and to be displayed on trains and in public buildings.

Junior high crafts include small cloisonné bowls, fabric stuffed animals, traditional figurative stone sculpture, traditional ceramic animals, traditional animals created from cloth, carved jade table lamp bases, traditional wood carved figures from the Chinese opera, traditional Buddha stone carvings, traditional Chinese paintings with a change to some modern Western techniques, Western-technique wood carvings using perspective, traditional block prints, and rubbings from the tile roofs of the Ch'in and Han dynasties. In the secondary area, a conscious effort has been made to incorporate folk crafts into the school curriculum.

The Cloisonné Factory Art shows why children are trained to follow directions in the arts when they are young. A pattern made by an older factory worker is passed to a younger worker, who cuts and bends the flat copper wire to the plans of the drawing. This pattern is then given to the next person, who uses a gum to hold the wires in place on the copper bowl. Silver solder is sprinkled on and the piece is soldered by a torch expert. The powdered glass colors are added by the next group of workers, and the pieces are then fired. After the cleanup process is completed, the pieces are brassplated and ready to be sold. Workers in the jade factories use the same process whereby one person designs the piece of jade using a brush and paint, and another person refines the larger piece according to this design into more defined planes and areas. The piece is then passed on to others who complete the details; then it goes to the polishers, who finish the traditional work of art. School art is clearly designed with vocational ends in mind.

An artist making a Western-style landscape watercolor painting at the Lungmen Caves of the Buddha carvings was the only example observed of an individual using his own ideas based on the hand and eye coordination technique. Chalk drawing on blackboards is the most contemporary technique used for a work of art and can be seen throughout China in the factories, at schools, and in public buildings. Nursery school children use wood blocks to build with and try to match the preconceived patterns on the paper that is placed beside them on the table. Workers in the porcelain factories do some special carving in the clay pottery as individual projects; however, most of the pottery is made in the form of the rice bowl.

Japan   A National Tradition in a Shrinking World

Frank Wachowiak

In a country where the major department stores provide generous floor space for continuing displays of international art, where menus are prepared to delight the eye as well as the palate, where there are as many colorful festivals *(matsuri)* as there are days in the year, and where master artists and craftsmen are honored by their government with the title *Living National Treasure* (Ningen Kokuhō), it is quite understandable that a rich and varied art curriculum in the schools, especially at the elementary and middle school level, will have the strong support of the citizenry. This has been the story in Japan for the past quarter of a century.

Child art in Japan permeates the daily atmosphere and environs of the elementary school. Every classroom, corridor, principal's office, and school entrance is a showplace for the students' creative efforts. The grounds surrounding the school serve as display areas for plaster and brick sculpture, both two- and three-dimensional. Exhibitions of child art, sponsored by a growing number of business firms, are scheduled throughout the year in a number of cities.

The most commonly practiced studio art techniques in Japanese schools are drawing, painting, collage, printmaking, ceramics, and three-dimensional construction in paper, wood, metal, and plastic. Sketching trips are scheduled frequently for classes at all grade levels. It is a common sight in Japan to see school children from grades one through nine drawing or painting in parks, zoos, aquariums, fish markets, harbors, ship building yards, museums, and in the vicinity of Shinto shrines and Buddhist temples. Almost every school maintains a flower garden and some even boast an aviary where the youngsters may find immediate inspiration for their sketchbook compositions. Although school uniforms are not as much in evidence in Japanese schools today as they were in the past (actually, some uniforms in prestige elementary schools have become more elaborate over the years), the use of painting smocks in art classes, especially in elementary schools, is quite common.

Drawing is a basic component of the art program. Preliminary drawings in pencil, pen, or brush precede actual painting in most instances.

On an initial visit to Japan in 1964 I observed children at sketching sites so absorbed in their drawing that they were immune to distractions. During more recent travels, discipline was found to be much more permissive, the behavior more boisterous. Socializing during classtime has increased correspondingly.

There are at least 1,000 professional painters in Japan, a large percentage of them still influenced by the French Impressionists and Post-Impressionists. Unlike painters in Europe and America, they are often affiliated and in most cases exhibit as membership groups in annual shows. Many younger, avant garde artists, however, display their creations in one-man shows in the scores of modern art galleries of Japan as well as abroad.

The interest in pictorial art that has been part of the Japanese heritage for hundreds of years, exemplified in the traditional *kakemono* or *kakejiku* (the seasonal paintings and calligraphic poems that are exhibited in the living room *tokonoma*, or alcove), is still very strong today, so that painting continues to be a basic and vital part of the school art curriculum. Opaque and transparent watercolors in tubes are employed in both elementary and secondary schools. With the generous time allotment given to art classes, the youngsters soon develop a mastery in creating tints, shades, and neutralized hues. From the first grade on, children learn to mix their own colors, utilizing a palette. A collapsible, plastic water bucket is a typical example of the ingenious and practical art tools available to Japanese children at nominal costs.

Japanese legends and historic feats of honored heroes keep recurring as themes for painting projects in elementary school art. There is a fascination with classic stories they can identify with, such as *Gulliver's Travels*. The children are proud of their industries and growing economy, and include many illustrations of ship building, deep sea fishing, automobile factories, undersea exploration, and skyscraper construction in their drawing and painting repertoire. A wealth of characteristic detail is recorded in such paintings, which is a result of strong eidetic imagery and recall. Much of this painstaking effort in recording minutiae is no doubt attributable to their patience and their persistence, but it is probably more related to their singularly contained culture and to their quest for excellence. Every aspect of their lives is a fair subject for documentation: the holiday excursion to a shrine or a temple, the viewing of the cherry-*sakura*-blossoms, the sumo wrestling matches, the school's annual competing events, the visits to the department store, the thousand-and-one festivals and parades, the predawn fish market, the crowded subways, and the constant traffic jams.

The beauty and variety of Japanese paper *(washi)* has been recognized universally; therefore, it is no surprise to find a multitude of paper projects, both two- and three-dimensional, emphasized in the school's art repertoire. Paper, clay, and bamboo appear to dominate the Japanese world of crafts. Packaging and gift wrapping have achieved the level of a unique art form; indeed, it is customary in Japan to admire the beauty of the wrapping before opening the gift. We are all familiar by now with *origami*, the Japanese art of folding paper to make three-dimensional forms. There is little exploitation of origami in the elementary school, but instances of its use can be seen in related projects in middle and high schools.

Who among us has not heard of Hokusai, Hiroshige, and Sharaku? The beautiful woodblock prints, sometimes called "ukiyo-e," of Mt. Fuji, *The Great Wave*, and Kabuki scenes are familiar to all art students. Printmaking, in all its varied forms, is a major part of the art curriculum at all grade levels in both the elementary and middle schools. One finds a wealth of found object and vegetable printing, stenciling, collography, monoprinting, woodblock printing, and paper etching. Children begin cutting woodblocks as early as the third grade. The late Shiko Munakata, one of Japan's most renowned printmakers, claimed he was so accustomed to using the woodcutting tools of his elementary school days that he continued to employ them in his professional work, expending them by the dozens in the cutting of his giant woodblocks.

A popular print technique generally associated with Japanese child art and certainly emphasized in their elementary art curriculum more than in any other country in the world, is the collograph, or paper relief print. This printmaking process is introduced with simple cut shapes in the first grade, but the subject matter grows in complexity as the child moves from elementary to middle school. However, perhaps the most unique and most sophisticated print technique, usually for fifth or sixth grade and middle school classes, is what the Japanese refer to as "paper etch."

Paper etch is basically an engraving process where cardboard is substituted for the metal plate. A glossy-surfaced cardboard, manufactured especially for this project, is available from Japanese art supply companies together with the special engraving tools—stylus and cutting knife—used in the paper etch process.

In the paper etch technique, the cardboard is incised for the linear and patterned design; then, areas which will be dark in value in the final print are cut and peeled off. The cardboard plate is then inked, wiped off, and printed on moist paper that has been soaked in water and blotted. A

Paper etching by
Japanese child,
grade 6

metal roller press is employed. One of the reasons for the high quality of
the Japanese school print is the fact that oil-base rather than water-
soluble ink is employed. In projects such as the collograph, monoprint,
woodblock, and paper etch, the oil ink remains moist a longer time on the
plate, generally ensuring a darker, richer print.

A plethora of diverse art materials and tools is made available to Japanese children. These comprise paint in tubes; a variety of modeling sub-
stances and tools; armatures; stone sculpture and wood construction
tools; painting palettes; collapsible water containers; art technique
paperback handbooks for each child; painting smocks; paper, both colored
and plain, in dozens of choices; as well as the customary oil pastels,
adhesives, brushes, inks, brayers, presses, and kilns.

Ceramics plays a major part in the art curriculum in Japan. From the
first grade on, Japanese children explore a multitude of ceramic possibilities: animals, both real and imaginary; acrobats; sumo wrestlers;

clowns; athletes; sea castles; and wall reliefs. In the upper grades they experiment with portraiture, outdoor sculpture, masks, and pottery. A large variety of ceramic tools is available in all classes, including turning wheels and armatures. Thus, the Japanese tradition in clay carries on, from their ancient Jomon and Haniwa funerary pieces to present-day teapots and tableware. Their history of ceramic production—Imari, Satsuma, Kutani, Oribe, Kiyomizu, and Bizen—is a long and illustrious one, influencing the life of every school child and teacher in Japan today.

The story of Japanese art education would not be complete without reference to what is considered unique in their teaching and implementation of elementary and middle school art—the Japanese employment of graded arts and crafts handbooks. These colorful paperback art guides, Zuga Kosaku, were introduced into the school programs over a quarter of a century ago; what makes the Japanese experience with them so noteworthy, however, is that, unlike the case in U.S. schools, where their utilization is sporadic and minimal, these handbooks have been in and on the desks of the elementary and middle school art students continually since 1950.

The government gives every school child in grades one through nine a copy of the arts and crafts handbook, which may vary in length from 32 to 38 pages. These beautifully designed paperbacks include graphic descriptions of a variety of art projects, both two- and three-dimensional, appropriate for the particular grade level involved, as well as reproductions of creative work by master artists representing both Eastern and Western cultures. A few pages are devoted to descriptions and uses of the tools of art. In the middle school the emphasis of the handbook shifts to the practical arts—to lettering; poster making; container, furniture, and fabric design; architecture; and city planning—with greater coverage especially in the third year of middle school to art history and art appreciation.

There are at least four different editions of these paperback handbooks, which are revised every three years by selected groups of art educators and professors of art. Teachers in the schools then choose the particular edition they wish to use. In Japan's elementary schools, where the classroom teachers have a limited college preparation in art, these guidebooks are a vital source of motivational inspiration for the children.

Evaluation of the children's art in Japanese elementary schools is required and a letter grade is generally employed. For promotion, the same importance is attached to art as to the other subjects. Art in the Japanese elementary schools is taught as a rule by the classroom teachers, although schools attached to a university may employ special art teachers. This holds true for private and middle schools as well. The classroom teachers receive course instruction in child art in the teachers' or educator colleges *(kyoku daigaku)* they attend. There are over fifty of these in Japan. No specific textbook is used in these courses, and the reference reading may include well-known English and American art education authors such as Read, Richardson, Lowenfeld, Ziegfield, and D'Amico. Fine arts universities are located in Tokyo, Kyoto, Kanazawa, and Kita-Kyushu. The Women's Art University in Tokyo has a director of art education and offers courses leading toward a teaching certificate. Many Japanese art educators and professors of art have visited schools or themselves studied in England and the United States.

The teacher *(sensei)* is an important element in the Japanese order of things. When someone does something extremely well in Japan, the first question usually asked is: who is your teacher? One such teacher is Professor Kozuma, who emphasizes the following guidelines in teaching contour drawing: observe intently, draw slowly, press hard with the pencil, do not erase. In the attached elementary school affiliated with his university, the fortuitous results of his teaching are seen in the sensitive contour drawings by young children. The benefits of this master teacher's philosophy were once manifest in schools throughout the whole city of Osaka and its suburbs. The influence of this teacher, now retired, is still evident today.

Japanese art teachers meet annually in a nationwide conference. Their national organization, Zenkoku Zokei Kyoiku Renmei (the "National Creative Education Society") is similar to the NAEA in the United States. In addition, there are smaller regional art teacher organizations on separate islands, such as on Okinawa, Kyushu, Shikoku, Honshu, and Hokkaido, as well as an active branch of INSEA.

There are two national periodicals dealing with Japanese art education practices and research that teachers may subscribe to. Both *Kyoiku Bijutsu* (Educational Arts) and *Biiku Bunka* (Society for Art Education) are subsidized by art supply companies.

Art education instruction in the Japanese senior high schools is, unfortunately, minimal. There are a few high schools in larger cities, especially those affiliated with prestigious universities and those in affluent communities, that may offer basic courses in painting and design. Some secondary schools include courses in calligraphy and flower arrangement. The emphasis on passing rigid college entrance exams which stress the "solid subjects" has traumatized secondary education and practically eliminated art in the high schools. Those students hoping to make art a career must wait until they can enroll in one of the fine arts universities. Still, the high quality of Japanese art instruction, and the generous time allotment given to it in both the elementary and middle schools, provides Japanese youngsters with a sounder and richer foundation for an art career than can be found in most countries.

Japan's expanding economic growth in the past three decades, the impact of the Western world on its culture, and the growing emphasis on material things has subtly, yet indelibly, affected the quality of the art practices and performances in the elementary and middle schools. Today, there is not always evident the deep concern with qualitative aspects of child art that was the hallmark of past decades. Some of the current art emanating from the Japanese schools today, as documented in their recent periodicals on art education, is not of the calibre of the children's work in this collection gathered in past years; it reflects more often the practices of an international culture, where, sadly, the popular criterion seems to be "how quickly can it be done; how quickly discarded."[1]

What has been minimized and, consequently, is being jeopardized, not only in Japan but everywhere in the world, is the children's precious gift for noticing things sensitively, their patience and persistence to record every detail in its singular beauty, their commitment to do the very best they can to capture the essence of an experience, and their joy in discovering—through the magic of line, color, value, shape, and pattern—the continually expanding world around them.

NOTE

1. *Young Art from Japan*, two filmstrips, International Film Bureau, Inc., 332 S. Wabash Avenue, Chicago, Illinois, 60604.

AFRICA

Ghana Cultural Renaissance

Emmanuel C. Nyarkoh

Africa is a huge continent with diverse cultures and variant systems of education. The mere size of the African continent indicates the dangers of generalization, especially in matters of education in modern Africa.

Art is considered one of the most important components of the culture of the traditional African society. In fact, traditional arts form an integral part of the citizen's social, religious, and political life. To the African, "art is for life"; it is not merely "for art's sake."

Perhaps the greatest contribution Africa has made so far to the cultural heritage of mankind is its richly varied arts, especially its sculpture. Sculpture, and to a lesser degree painting, often served in tribal Africa as a kind of cultural mirror, since it was largely produced in response to religious and social needs, and consequently reflected and gave visual expression to certain fundamental aspects of life (Mount 1973, xv). In most African societies, architecture was a form of art that exhibited many artistic skills and cultural symbols.

Traditional education throughout Africa has, therefore, always involved the teaching of the arts. Education in music, drama, literature (folklore), and in crafts such as wood carving, weaving, pottery, metal works, and leather works formed a major part of the enculturation of the African child.

Various African societies have their own traditional festivals and ceremonies in which they show their artistic skills, their values, and their beliefs through art. Fafunwa (1967, 75) maintains that "art and music touch the spirit and soul of the child, and African art and music form the foci of African culture." He asserts that African art and music are more than aesthetic and artistic expression; they express, in most cases, the African philosophical and religious views and systems. In short, they express the African psyche and personality.

Modern education in Africa since its introduction during the eighteenth and nineteenth centuries has failed to emphasize art in the school programs. The content of the curriculum in the "European schools," even the general ethos of the educational systems planted in Africa, failed to recognize the vital role of the arts in the African culture, excluding them from the subjects taught. African students were discouraged from participation in their traditional arts, thus creating cultural alienation among the educated Africans. Therefore, colonialism in many forms, including religion, imposed a new culture upon the African. In those early years the African "elites" looked upon African arts with scorn because of the indoctrination of the early missionaries; the values of the African world were disturbed by the early mission schools.

It was not until after the First World War that serious doubts arose about the educational policy and the content of the African curriculum. Two official British Colonial Office papers, one published in 1925 and one in 1935, publicly raised the question of the divorce of modern schooling from African culture and its disintegrating effect upon the African communities (Cowan 1965, 357). By the twentieth century, however, Europeans had begun to appreciate the African arts. The naive ideas about African art had changed with time and the gaining of knowledge. Willett (1971, 27) reports that during the twentieth century "the liberating and refreshing effect of African arts on Western art has been immeasurable." He further states that the revolution of twentieth-century art was set underway by this influence.

SYNTHESIS OF AFRICAN EDUCATION

African culture is always changing. Likewise, the cultural arts have been undergoing exciting and dynamic changes since many African countries gained independence. As the societies grow, the occasions when traditional art forms are required become less frequent; however, there are demands of a new kind, to which African artists are responding. Western art schools expose Africans to Western techniques, values, and traditions, thus allowing them to investigate and draw upon other interesting traditions. Eclectic experiments in the arts are being conducted by Africans in their quest to develop a "new African art." In fact, many of the writings in African literature reflect the problems of a changing society, both in taking a retrospective glance into the value systems of the past and in seeking new values for the future.

The variety and richness, the high quality, and the innovations one finds in contemporary African arts are indicative of cultures that are changing and evolving in their own unique directions (Wahlman 1975, 21). Throughout Africa, one finds that, though school art is ailing, the traditional and modern arts are vigorously alive in many areas outside of the school. The coexistence of traditional and contemporary art in Africa seems healthy, and its continuation should be promoted in the African schools. In Ghana, for example, there are now several festivals and recreational activities at which an observer will clearly see the combination of modern and traditional arts in vogue.

It is easy to discover that "the culture of present-day Ghana is not only an aggregate of diverse traditional forms but also a composite of old and new, indigenous and foreign. . . . Thus, Ghana's cultural and social life, instead of being absorbed by foreign elements, has selected only those elements which have enriched it and endowed it with the strength to develop and grow" (*Ghana: Studies and Documents on Cultural Policies*, 16).

SUPPORT FOR GHANAIAN ART

Ghanaians, as well as all Africans, are becoming more aware of the need for a cultural renaissance in which education in the arts will play a predominant role. Those persons interested in or charged with education in African arts can no longer remain passive to the changes taking place in the cultural life of the people.

A growing awareness of the value of African traditional arts and culture is gradually becoming evident among the educated people, especially among the youth, who had been culturally alienated because of the influence of a colonial education that touted the supremacy of the European culture and its arts. Ghana today is culturally awakened; her rich cultural heritage is evident in many spheres of life; and her cultural arts are being renovated.

DEVELOPMENT OF ART EDUCATION IN GHANA

The art department of Achimota College, the first of its kind in British West Africa, was opened in the early 1920s, inspired by Governor Guggisberg and Dr. Kwegyir Agarey, the first African vice principal of the college. The training of art teachers began in 1927. The Achimota School art department has made a substantial contribution to the development of art education in Ghana. Meyerowitz, Michael Cardew, and other British art educators converted the department into a school of arts and crafts

Painting by Ghanaian child, age 11

that offered a three-year specialist arts and crafts teaching course. Most of the pioneer students who completed the course received scholarships for further training in the United Kingdom.

During the 1940s and especially in the 1950s, arts and crafts and music were recognized in the curricula of the country's schools and colleges. Records show that systematic art training provided in the schools and colleges followed the British pattern of art education and disregarded the African cultural outlook. It has been charged, however, that the neglect of "Africanness" in the education provided during the colonial era was a form of "education of cultural imperialism." Fafunwa (1967, 75) has pointed out that the effect of the school systems' neglect of African traditional arts, considered "vital aspects of a truly meaningful and extremely pertinent educational process, is to kill the very soul of African education."

Since independence was gained in 1957, Ghana has made many changes in its educational system, and these have affected its art education. Gradually, the curricula of art education has been given an African bias, and traditional arts and crafts are now being recognized as important elements in the school system. More institutions of higher learning are offering courses in the arts. The art college at the University of Science and Technology, which was created out of (Achimota) School of Art, now offers degree programs in fine and industrial art and in art education. It has graduated many art teachers and industrial designers. The Winneba Specialist Training colleges, established in the 1950s, have supplied many specialist art teachers for the secondary schools. Recently, three more art colleges have been established to train more art teachers.

The regional and district offices of the ministry of education have an inspectorate team of art specialists who supervise art education in the schools and teacher training colleges. They also offer in-service training for the regular classroom teachers—who are ill-qualified to teach art and music but are still required to instruct their students—to improve their skills.

The introduction of African studies in Ghana's universities since 1959 and the cultural bias that is being provided as a basis for the Ghanaian school curricula are gradually providing fruitful grounds for more interests in the traditional elements of Ghanaian culture. The need for a cultural renaissance in Africa has not only been seen by politicians such as the late Dr. S.B. Danqual of Nigeria, Dr. Kwame Nkrumah of Ghana (in his famous rhetorics on the concept of African personality), President Sengher of Senegal (who, along with others, has written about "Negritude"), or Dr. Nyerere (who developed the political philosophy of African Socialism); famous Ghanaian artists such as the late Kofi Antuham and Vincent Kofi, who received their artistic training in the Achimota School of Art and in England, have also always portrayed the dynamism of a new African art which serves as a cultural prop for the African renaissance.

Recent continental festivals of art have aided the emergence of a cultural renaissance in Africa by bringing together all the African peoples, including those in the Americas and in the Caribbean West Indies. The Dakar Festival of Negro Arts (1966), the Pan African Cultural Festival in Algiers (1969), and the recent Festival of the World Black and African Festival of Arts and Culture (Festac) in Lagos, Nigeria, were celebrations of African culture. Such celebrations indicate that a cultural revolution has been born in Africa. Education in the arts is unquestionably the only potential force which, when utilized and well directed, could give the revolution the necessary support it needs to survive and abound.

COMMUNICATION OF THE ARTS IN GHANA

The main organ through which the ministry of education and culture in Ghana has been fostering, developing, and disseminating cultural information of various types to the general public is the Arts Council of Ghana.

This council is responsible for developing, promoting, and disseminating knowledge of the arts throughout Ghana and for developing an appreciation of all forms of Ghanaian art and culture. Its particular concerns are for preserving, fostering, and developing the traditional arts of Ghana. There are three cultural centers in the country, situated in Kumasi, Accra, and Tamale. Established in 1951, the National Cultural Center at Kumasi has provided avenues for promoting the cultural arts in the country. It has patronized annual interregional and national festivals of the arts. Plans to establish cultural centers at all the regional capitals will enable the organization of annual festivals of the arts rotationally, from region to region.

In Ghana, as well as in other African states, the cultural arts are receiving much public attention. National competitions organized by the Institute of African Studies of the University of Ghana awards prizes to outstanding artists. School art exhibitions are also organized at national and regional levels. The Ghana Film Corporation has an up-to-date infrastructure for film production and a program for in-service training of technicians and artists. The Museum and Monuments Board is instrumental in preserving the cultural monuments and other works of art. The traditional chiefs and people of the various ethnic groups in the country do cooperate with the government in the promotion of the cultural arts.

The African governments are also becoming more aware of the need for cultural awakening in the arts. Most have been providing the necessary encouragement, funding, and facilities for cultural development. Cultural centers, or art centers, have been established in many African countries. The creation of art departments in the new universities and the training of more art teachers have been supported by African governments. Organization of annual nationwide art exhibitions and the awarding of prizes by the education ministries in many countries is noteworthy. Also, many museums and art galleries have been established.

Those persons in charge of the development of art education in Africa would agree that the major problems facing most African countries include the following: (1) a shortage of qualified art teachers; (2) insufficient teaching materials; (3) a dysfunctional, outmoded curriculum; (4) not enough involvement by traditional artists and craftsmen in "school art"; (5) a lack of proper supervision and direction of art programs in the school system; and (6) inadequate research in African studies and textbooks and literature on art education for schools and colleges. Reform and improvement of the curriculum and teaching methods of art education in Africa is long overdue. Modernization or improvement of the program would require a proper balance or synthesization of what can be considered as the best of cultural elements, both old and new, which will guarantee an "African bias" in the various systems of education.

AN AGENDA FOR THE FUTURE

The new art education in Africa calls for a new philosophical base. Its programs need to be enlarged to cover all the various cultural studies that may interest and serve the needs of individual students. The dichotomy between the fine and applied arts or arts and crafts, music and dance, should be broken down. Art in education needs to be emphasized and art teachers have to prove their worth as cultural catalysts. The talents of traditional artists and craftsmen must be utilized in the school art programs. Preparation of textbooks on the history of African art, among other cultural studies, should be given priority. The provision for new instructional materials, including films, tapes, and even the television, must be considered. The importance of the use of local materials for the production of art works needs to be pointed out.

Art education is not only useful for the "gifted" but is an essential field of study for all people and should not be left out if we mean to develop the entire human potential in creativity. All the African nations should devote attention to the training of specialist art teachers for the schools. Certainly the dynamic transformations taking place in Africa to promote cultural development in the continent would be incomplete if education in the arts is left behind. The success of future art programs will be determined largely by the economic, social, and artistic traditions of each African country. The scope, context, and orientation of such programs, as well as natural and human resources, will influence the educational goals of all of Africa. It is hoped that all agencies, governments, and educators involved in art education in Africa will do more to raise the present status of cultural arts in African educational systems.

REFERENCES

Cowan, L. Gray, et al., eds. *Education and Nation-Building in Africa.* New York: Praeger Publishers, 1965.

Fafunwa, A. Babs. *New Perspectives in African Education.* Ibadan: Macmillan, Nigeria Ltd., 1967.

Ghana: Studies and Documents on Cultural Policies. Paris: Unesco Press, 1975.

Kaplan, Irving, et al., eds. *Area Handbook for Ghana.* Washington, D.C.: U.S. Gov. Printing Office, 1971.

Mount, Marshall Ward. *African Art—The Years Since 1920.* Bloomington: Indiana Univ. Press, 1973.

New Encyclopaedia Britannica, The. 15th ed. Vol. 1. 1976.

Wahlman, Maude. "Why Study Contemporary African Arts?" In *Contemporary African Arts.* Chicago: Field Museum of Natural History, 1974.

Willett, Frank. *African Art.* New York: Praeger Publishers, 1971.

Nigeria Priorities and Problems
Ruth Coron Omabegho

INTRODUCTION

Viewed realistically, Nigeria, an energetic country of about eighty million people, can be seen as being in the midst of a transition phase, a period of friction between old and new values. The following excerpt is from a brochure published recently by the Nigerian ministry of information:

> The tumultuous events in Nigeria since 1960 have shown that society undergoing acute structural changes at such a pace that all who are involved in the drama, to survive must make corresponding changes in their lives. In this the arts have shown an almost infinite capacity for adopting to everchanging conditions, deriving energy and vision from the depths of social realities.[1]

SETTING THE SCENE

The glorious heritage of Nigerian art antiquities, including the stylized terra cottas of the early Nok Culture (900 B.C.–200 A.D.), the naturalistic terra cottas and bronzes of Ife (900 A.D.–15th century A.D.), the intricate bronzes of Igbu Ukwu (9th century A.D.), and the magnificent bronzes of Benin (1200 A.D.–1897 A.D.), leads one to expect that contemporary art

Dr. Garba Ashiwaju, the chief cultural officer of Nigeria, is responsible for government publications and for most federally sponsored cultural programs in Nigeria. To obtain data for this chapter, interviews were done with Ashiwaju in his office at the modern National Theatre.

and art education would be on a comparably high level or an even higher level.

The reality of the situation is that the Colonial Period effectively destroyed the art and craft traditions while it decimated the art treasures. When people are taught not to value traditional patterns of living, they certainly cannot esteem the art that these produced. The psychological and physical hangovers from this period have not been adequately researched and analyzed. Thomas Munro notes:

> Receptiveness to foreign cultures can be carried too far. It does so when elements of value in the old native tradition are rejected and lost through extreme adulation of exotic influences. This often happens when a people is conquered or otherwise subjected to overwhelming influence from a more advanced and powerful neighbour. On the other hand, conquered people have exerted great cultural influence on their political and military conquerors.[2]

In the colonial schools African art was not taught from a historical perspective but was relegated to an extracurricular activity such as "handicrafts." It is still regarded by many Nigerians as "cottage industry" or as something done by a child in a village. The missionary view that was perpetrated by Africans who taught in the schools was that African art was heathen and pagan, a form of idolatry that should be stamped out. They saw no value in it.

My husband, who was an art major in a Nigerian secondary school, recalls that, while no formal courses were offered in African art history, several were offered in European art history. It was not until he came to Cornell University in the United States that he studied African art history in any formal way and began to appreciate his own art heritage.

In general, Westerners have tended to express the most interest in what seems to them exotic or bizarre in African arts and culture. Perhaps this is because they found such things as fetishes, rituals, and masked dancers most intriguing or because these objects and practices satisfied their preconceptions in regard to the "dark continent."

As a result, the fine arts were not given support. Craftsmanship was also not encouraged and handmade things were demeaned. Europeans were more interested in promoting and selling their own products. The quality of the beautifully designed and rendered traditional decorative and functional arts and crafts—including weaving, dyeing, pottery, leatherwork, carving, and furniture making—deteriorated under these conditions. While the Africans began to value and desire machine-made products over objects of their own manufacture, an opposite trend took place in the Western world, where handmade objects were in vogue and thus in great demand.

Nigeria has been free of colonial rule for twenty years and should have been able to correct the damage in that time. However, many other factors enter into the picture. The country's civil war (1967–70) destroyed life and property, and left a residue of tribal tension. The current period is one of massive population growth and economic and political change and movement.

Crowded Lagos, the capital of oil-rich Nigeria, has many of the characteristics of a frontier boom town in the United States during the gold rush era: money flows abundantly; fortunes can be made overnight; inflation is almost impossible to control; the electric power, water, and telephone services are erratic; and transportation is difficult. All this is happening at a time when much of the world has reached a high level of technological efficiency.

NIGERIAN ART EDUCATION—PAST AND PRESENT

Ritual ceremonies have traditionally acted as teaching devices in Africa. They utilized a fusion of dance, drama, music, sculpture, and self-adornment, and integrated them with the spiritual, political, social, educational, and economic life of the group. Distinguished Nigerian scholar Emanuel Obeichina describes the role that art formerly played in the lives of the people: ". . . in the traditional society, artistic education, like other forms of education, was derived from the broad flow of cultural life. Its members participated in this common culture and absorbed its artistic tradition by seeing and doing and experiencing. Art was to the individual part of his social experience and was shared with everyone."[3]

The urban child today is far removed from the inherent design, aesthetics, and order of traditional architecture, self-adornment, household implements, ceremonies, and sense of space, as well as from the pure beauty and colors of the natural forms of plants, animals, land, and water. As a result of the increasing and denser population in modern times, caused by the dynamics of migration patterns, the age-old methods of educating the young that were effective in the past are no longer viable.

In traditional Nigerian village life, the chief or *oba* was principal client, patron, and impresario combined in one motivating and supportive structure or force. He commissioned, sponsored, used, and paid for most of the art that was produced, much in the same way that the church did in the Western world. The new agent of aesthetic awareness and education is the government, through its public spaces, buildings, mass media, programs, expositions, parks, museums, libraries, and, primarily, its

Jane is stading oulside her house

Drawing by
Nigerian child,
age 6

schools—their physical plant as well as their educational programme. Although much has been said about the importance of teaching the arts in the schools, much work remains to be done toward setting standards and implementing quality art programs.

The Nigerian government recently demonstrated its commitment to the country's arts and culture, indigenous as well as contemporary, by sponsoring and hosting Festac '77, the Second World Black and African Festival of Arts and Culture in Lagos. For an intense and exciting— albeit brief—period, Lagos was inundated with performers and artists from all over the world. A visual, aural, and intellectual feast resulted, with offerings of dance, music, drama, colloquium discussions, canoe regattas, horsemanship shows, and many fascinating exhibits including visual arts and crafts from the various participating zones, traditional costumes, architecture, instruments, and crafts of Nigeria, and "2,000 Years of Nigerian Art." All in all, it was a memorable and moving event, but one that needs to be examined critically.

Singing and dancing were the only arts that were encouraged by the former colonial administrators. Festac reflected this attitude, since emphasis and support were primarily directed toward music, dance, and theater about the visual arts. A similar attitude also prevails in the universities, where more space and financial support are provided to the performing arts.

Soon after the festival ended, a postgraduate art student currently teaching in one of the better Lagos secondary schools assigned his students a drawing project involving a cultural motif. Almost without exception, they drew the ivory mask from Benin that had been used as the symbol of Festac. Before and during Festac, good and bad reproductions of this mask were seen all over Lagos, in store windows, on light poles, and on every publication connected with Festac. It would therefore seem that, for these students and for many Nigerians, Black and African culture began and ended with this mask, since it is all they saw of the festival.

In truth, with skillful teaching and discussion, young people can be helped to draw on their own image and information banks for other evidences of indigenous culture. These banks, however, need substantial deposits of images and information. There is a dearth of material available for teaching about Black and African accomplishments in the arts and sciences, especially at the primary and secondary school levels.

APPROPRIATE CONTENT AND TEACHING MATERIALS

Those persons who understand the dynamics of the situation continually emphasize and reiterate the need for books, audio-visual aids, art supplies, and other teaching materials at every level in the arts. Whereas until recently Western art and culture were esteemed, there has been a movement striving toward rejecting that which "was imposed by foreign colonialists" and exalting only the indigenous culture. Certainly, during Festac such comments were heard.

In fact, the pendulum has now swung to the other extreme in the visual and other arts. Only that which is considered indigenous, in either form or content, is encouraged. At the University of Nsukka, the department of fine and applied arts adheres to a philosophy that "believes in evolving art with uniquely Nigerian identity or character through the fusion of the old (cultural heritage) and the new (contemporary culture). . . ."[4] On the other hand, there is another group that "believes mainly in the artistic" and accepts that "the reflection of cultural heritage or the objective contemporary culture could be irrelevant as long as art, good art or art with high standard is produced."[5]

This conflict, which is prevalent in Nigeria, is somewhat reminiscent of the attempt in the United States to divide American Black artists into "Mainstream" and "BLACKstream," a movement that was largely unproductive, unfair, and irrelevant to individual artists. A subtle and serious problem is caused by the prevailing attitude held by influential people in the arts and government. This attitude tends to espouse the external and encourage a depiction of the genre in Nigerian life rather than an understanding of the essence or true aura of African art.

Several of the persons I have interviewed on this subject, though they were of course interested in furthering Nigerian culture, expressed a much more balanced and world-conscious outlook when questioned. A. Ajepe said:

> Our culture cannot exist in isolation. If education is to help us grow and develop broader outlooks, then we have to see our culture as something which cannot be contained. Culture should be exposed to other external influences while retaining basic elements of traditional forms. We have to take what is good in other cultures and graft it on to our own.

Y. Grillo observed: "In any environment the art educator has a duty to expose to students that which is around him—the traditional art of Nigeria, first and foremost. One ought to know about his own background—even if he will not be an artist." And E.J. Alagoa declared: "The base from which we must grow should be our own indigenous history and arts, but we are living in a modern time. We cannot isolate ourselves from the techniques and ideas of the rest of the world. We have to use them, incorporate them, and make them our own." This view would seem to agree with the following statement by Munro: "In its own school system, each people has a primary duty to select, preserve, and impart the best in its own cultural tradition, including its arts. In that way it can make its own best contribution to world civilization. Its secondary duty is to select and impart to its own people what seems best in foreign cultures."[6]

These sources regard modern African culture as a dynamic entity that should emerge from a synthesis of the evolvement of traditional forms and those coming from the outside, originally alien, influence.

PRIORITIES

A major problem is the issue of priorities. Many people view art education as a luxury in a country where the majority of the population is illiterate. There is little understanding of the part that the visual arts play in the day-to-day lives of people. It is also not apparent that education in art will provide a livelihood for those who are pursuing it.

The government is trying to eliminate illiteracy through UPE (Universal Primary Education), but only those persons who are aware of what art education is really about understand the connection between training in visual perception and literacy. Grillo said: "It is definitely a mistake to view art education as a luxury. Education through art is a very true and real philosophy. In fact, art is the basis of education. One could only hope that people will be exposed to good educational training so this view may be changed." Alagoa remarked: "I can't help comparing the kind of thing done for sports in this country with arts. The government built the National Stadium. Sports have been accepted in the educational system, into its curriculum and programs. Similar attention must be given to the arts. . . ." Whereas J. Ojugunyigbe observed:

> Often, the tendency for the headmaster is to put funds for general improvement of the school into areas other than art, so the art teacher doesn't have the necessary money to run his program. Allocation of rooms is also a problem. Other subjects are assigned rooms first, so the art teacher will have to carry his material all about the school, wasting time. . . .
> I think that it [art education] is a necessity for everybody. Judging from the aims expressed by art educators, especially making pupils creative in approach and developing their interest in things around them, I feel that art education should be encouraged.

ART IN THE SCHOOL CURRICULUM

Underlying many of these problems is the need for specific "government policy stating in broad terms the percentage allocation of grants to subjects taught in the schools every year."[7] Some persons agree with G.O. Talabi (who lectured at an induction course for art teachers) when he says that "Ideally, the highest influence should derive from . . . ministries of education, where lies the machinery for effecting the desired change."[8] Others look to the universities or artists' organizations for leadership; for example, Alagoa believes that "the policy making level is where some problems are created because of the uncertainty over who should be responsible for decisions. It is not yet possible to make coherent policies." Ashiwaju observed: "Cultural development by the government started very recently. After the Civil War, the budget was 40,000 pounds (approx. $80,000) for arts and culture; now we talk of millions. Consciousness in development of culture requires political action in the sense that the government has to define its course." Grillo remarked: "The Federal Ministry talks about instituting art programs. We hope that the practical manifestations won't be long in coming." And Ojugunyigbe maintained: "There are many schools where there is no art program at all. Where there are art programs they are not well effected. I feel that the Ministry of Education should be more concerned. Government should be more involved."

In this somewhat glorified description of existing conditions in Nigerian arts (produced for the Lagos International Trade Fair to accompany an exhibition of student work by the history of art section, department of fine and applied arts, University of Nigeria, Nsukka), problems are minimized and positive directions are maximized:

> Though art is yet to be properly and fully integrated into all our institutions and though art teaching could be made more meaningful, the position of art in the Nigerian educational system can be seen as promising. . . . our art institutions are reasonably rich, though a lot is still greatly desired— particularly in forms of material/equipment, space, etc. . . .
>
> Without doubt, art has come to stay in our educational system. The question about what one can do with art can now be answered by a larger number of people; the negative attitude of parents to art is fast diminishing (in fact, many parents now encourage their kids to make this highly expressive mode of culture their life concern); the society is recognizing the great difference between intuitive or airport art and meaningful or intellectual art; many intellectuals and government officials are beginning to see the educational values of art and its role in technology or industry, in commerce or media, in the household and society in general. Briefly, art is being recognized as an inescapable aim of national development and an integral part of culture and cultural evolution.[9]

PROBLEMS: THE PRESENT SITUATION

The reality is that art receives very little attention in the school curriculum from the nursery level through the university education. Art programs are practically nonexistent in primary schools except for in a few private and privileged institutions. The quality of art teachers in secondary schools generally ranges from poor to excellent, and the art programs reflect this range. In addition, these programs are plagued by inadequate facilities and a shortage of supplies.

The art educator or would-be art educator is likely to encounter many problems and deterrents; these may be caused by physical conditions, lack of administrative cooperation, insufficient materials and funds, public and governmental apathy, or, in fact, their own inadequate training. Ajepe has said: "The problems are tremendous. It will be a long time before we have the facilities, equipment, and materials. The government places its priorities in development of technology." Grillo revealed: "In the primary schools one can write the art program off as nothing. With UPE, up to 60 pupils are in one class with one teacher teaching all subjects. There is no provision for art rooms, crafts tools, materials, etc. Such activities as copying a duck from a blackboard are common." And Ojugunyigbe commented: "When you sit together in the staff room, other teachers look down on you as somebody who is just collecting money for nothing. There is a general lack of understanding, even among educated people, about what art education is really trying to do."

Throughout the country there is an acute shortage of art teachers because of inadequacy of training programs and the lure of other fields, such as business, which offers the tangible reward of more money. It is probably true that "many of those presumed to be art teachers are technically not proficient to handle the subject" and, in fact, "a good many . . . have merely an edge over the children they teach. . . ."[10] Ajepe maintained: "All the teachers who man the primary schools and teach all subjects need adequate provision in art so they can teach art, music, and drama. . . . Art education courses should be required for certification. It is probably more convenient to hope for the classroom teacher to have training in art at least for the foreseeable future." Furthermore, Ojugunyigbe reported that "there are quite a lot of unqualified people teaching art in the schools and, because the administrators are either unconcerned about art or unaware of what good art teaching is, nobody does anything about it. If the teachers manage to keep the students quiet, then the administration is satisfied."

Recently an art education program at the University of Lagos was introduced under the aegis of the faculty of education; this was designed to: expose future and current classroom teachers in early childhood through secondary schools to art, train art teachers (primarily for secondary schools, since only a few exclusive, private primary schools have art programs), and prepare those teachers who will teach students in teacher training institutions. However, the program is being taught under conditions that are not conducive to the development of art education due to the following: undergraduate courses are not yet required for a degree in education (students can only elect to take them without credit after registering for the rest of their program); a shortage of space restricts the art education courses to a room in which a maximum of eight students can work at one time; besides there being no running water in the art room, there is often no running water in any of the taps—therefore, water has to be stored in pails; electric power is more often off than on, creating situations that are not only uncomfortable but require a last minute change of plans; and art materials are expensive and difficult to obtain.

On the other hand, the undergraduate students who elect to take the course are very enthusiastic and hard working, and the graduate students, who have degrees in fine arts from Nigerian universities, are of a high calibre, produce excellent work, and are truly concerned about art education in Nigeria. Before their study here they have had no art education courses.

In the absence of qualified, trained art teachers, classroom teachers can use local people. Craftsmen can be brought to the schools and students can visit them in their working places. Traditional potters; weavers; gourd, wood, and ivory carvers; tie dyers; metal workers; leather workers; and basket makers—all still operate, using ancient methods passed from generation to generation, in the various village locales where these crafts forms originated. Insofar as what is produced is still used by the people in their households, these crafts remain viable, though somewhat static. Unfortunately, the poorly designed and crudely executed "airport art" produced for the tourist market abounds. This has little of the nearly perfect form and workmanship for which ancient Nigerian art is noted.

When almost all art materials and tools have to be imported, a lack of supplies is inevitable; however, there are local alternatives to complete reliance on manufactured products. One can find, near at hand and free for the taking, natural materials that are traditionally used for crafts. Clay, reed, and raffia, to cite a few, are available in abundance. Art materials can also be made from food stuffs such as starch, which is suitable for papier-mâché paste and finger paint. Banana leaves make excellent wrapping for keeping clay moist, and so on. There are also the usual industrial discards that are available in all urban areas of the world.

When I first came to the University of Lagos in 1975 to start a program in teacher training in the arts, I had several talks with Professor N.O.A. Durojaiye, dean of the faculty of education. Durojaiye told me that he appreciates the important role of art in education and lends his support to teacher training in the arts. However, he emphasizes the need for training classroom teachers in art, as opposed to training art teachers. He asked me to go to the university staff school to observe the art program— or, more accurately, the lack of it—and to devise a means of helping the teachers to integrate art into their classrooms. (There are plans for a new school building sometime in the future, but for now there are only small, overcrowded, and ill-equipped classrooms.) There, the teacher, the principal, and I planned together for several teachers' workshops, centered around activities that could be undertaken with a minimum of materials and space. Those decided upon were making puppets, working with papier-mâché, weaving with natural materials and a simple loom, printing with "junk," tie dying, making magazine mosaics, and so on. The teachers were dexterous and involved to the point that they had to be reminded several times when the allotted time had passed and the workshop was over. Thus, it appears that in most cases art is not neglected by design but because of lack of awareness and skills. There is an unexpressed hunger for art teaching techniques and processes that surfaces when the opportunity to have it satisfied arises.

My experience with students at the university has been similar. As has been mentioned, the arts course presently bears no college credit, yet many students have willingly taken it as an elective. They rarely miss a class and are a gratifying, responsive group, very anxious for what they deem to be "practical know-how." I have made no attempt to introduce anything of an avant-garde nature, for I fear it will not be understood or needed in this time and place.

THE SECONDARY LEVEL: THE SYLLABUS

To be awarded a secondary school certificate (a GCE) in Nigeria, each student chooses six subjects in which he will be examined by the West African Examinations Council (WAEC). Art is one of the fifty-three subjects considered acceptable for the certificate. A student is expected to select three papers to complete in art, including at least one from both section A and section B and at least one in color.

Section A	Paper 1	Drawing or painting from still life
	Paper 2	Drawing or painting from nature
	Paper 3	Drawing or painting from a living person
Section B	Paper 4	Imaginative composition in color
	Paper 5	Design
	Paper 6	Craft work
	Paper 7	Art appreciation

The art syllabus, which is also distributed by WAEC, must be closely followed in order to prepare for and pass the exams. The crafts areas included are the traditional ones—puppetry, gourd decoration, textile design, pottery, weaving, basketry, and leatherwork—and others such as bookbinding, theater design, wall decoration, and printmaking. Few, if any, students elect to take the paper in art appreciation; neither is this paper encouraged by teachers, possibly because they are not prepared to teach it. Students who choose to take paper 4 are instructed that any style or technique, including that which is traditional in their own country, may be used.

Thus, it can be seen that the secondary school curriculum is fairly well structured and standardized (at least as regards program if not quality) for all of West Africa by WAEC. Actually, West Africa is divided into two zones for WAEC's purposes; one includes Ghana, Sierra Leone, and Gambia, and the other is Nigeria alone.

Somewhat less uniformity exists in the primary schools. Ajepe stated, however, that "we cooperate with WAEC and use their syllabus. . . . The WAEC syllabus is essential because of the standards that it establishes. . . ." WAEC establishes curricula and administrates qualifying examinations; it may raise standards to a uniform level in some cases, but this standardization also prevents the individual schools or teachers from deviating or creating personal programs. Teachers are forced to gear their curriculum to the prescribed one so that their students will pass the WAEC examinations.

The Nigerian educational system as a whole is based on the English model. Of course, this presents certain advantages and distinct problems; however, as Ajepe remarked, "Even though we've inherited our system from the British, we don't have to repeat their mistakes."

While supervising students doing practice teaching in a variety of subjects, I realized that rarely or almost never was an interpretive question that required individual, critical, or creative thinking asked of the pupils. Generally speaking, education is not geared toward imaginative development in Nigeria. Creative thinking does not seem to concern educators, either for themselves or their pupils. It is difficult to know whether this has been inherited from the authoritarian British colonial schools or from other sources; however, Professor Nwosu of the University of Lagos maintains:

> If education stops at mere cultural transmission without developing in the individual the ability to add to his culture, then it isn't education. Education should not only transmit the culture but should create new cultural forms itself. We cannot be satisfied with learning what others have done but must create the ability to innovate. At the moment in Nigeria, education doesn't play the second function. We indoctrinate rather than educate. *Educo* in Latin means "I lead." The extension of this is the ability to bring out potentialities of the individual. Civilization is all about the creative spirit of man. When he loses this, he ceases to be a Homo sapien. There is a spiritual aspect to creativity in addition to the material one. Man becomes one with nature when he is creative. . . . Education must focus on this creative ability.

ACHIEVEMENTS, ASPIRATIONS, AND FUTURE DIRECTIONS

Despite the many problems confronting art educators in Nigeria, many hopeful and positive accomplishments can also be cited. It would seem that the authorities now see the importance and relevance of the arts in modern life. The National Theatre, Festac, additions to the National Museum, and the new Museum of African Art are evidences that the authorities are making some efforts toward integrating the arts into the lives of the people.

Almost all Nigerian universities now have art departments and centers for African and cultural studies. The federal government established a cultural division in the ministry of information and a National Council for the Arts, and each of the nineteen states has an arts council. In addition to these, several organizations outside of the government structure are working to promote art and art education—for example, the Museum Society, the Society of Nigerian Artists, and the Nigerian Society for Education Through the Arts. These organizations would accomplish a great deal if they were to unify their efforts.

During this transitional time of extremes and contrasts, there is striking individual beauty even amidst the ugliness of the city environment. Personal adornment is traditionally an emphasized area where energy, time, creativity, and money are invested. Intricate, elaborate hairstyles—which are, in effect, mobile sculptures—are seen everywhere. Men and women alike wear magnificent fabrics that are woven, embroidered, printed, tie dyed, or stitch and resist dyed, and are fashioned into voluminous agbadas, wrappers, and head ties. Indeed, a highly developed aesthetic awareness is demonstrated in regard to one's personal adornment. All this lends a dazzling passing beauty to the untended and neglected environment.

The opposite is true for architecture, interior decoration, and other such areas. There is a rising upper-middle class with money to spare, but what they buy is usually either locally produced furniture that represents a crude attempt to imitate badly designed European prototypes or overlarge settees and chairs and phony gilt antiques—all of which are entirely unsuited for local climate conditions and needs.

Although that which is Western is supposedly being discouraged, it seems that some other bad aspects of Western culture are sought after, such as motion pictures which glorify violence, showy cars, and Western fads such as high heels and thick-soled shoes for men (which are carried to the extreme here). The list could continue ad infinitum with further examples of poor taste and conspicuous consumption often found in developing nations. There is clearly a need for art education to play a role in influencing a new aesthetic that combines the best of contemporary art, technology, and design with the timeless beauty of traditional African art forms.

People in the arts are now attempting to extend their influence to improve the general environment. This is an area with infinite possibilities for organizing programs that could modify the thinking of people and government, establish aesthetic standards, and bring on action. Grillo stated:

> The art societies are able to educate the public through popularizing exhibitions and art events, highlighting worthwhile examples of decorations in buildings and monuments, quality controls of the aesthetics in manufactured objects even to the level of crockery, textiles, etc. From my experience I have found that public lectures are not effective. People don't attend. We must use other means. . . .
>
> A cross-section of various government agencies could help establish aesthetic standards: the ministry of industries for manufactured items, the ministry of information for mass media, the ministry of works for buildings. If we had a ministry of culture, it could be a coordinating body for all of this.

Art educators are faced with the problems of how to revive and revitalize the traditional arts so as to reveal the best examples of the African arts that have been lost or forgotten and how to make the present practices meet what they were in the past; at the same time the arts must not remain static but must be modified into new forms of comparable quality (not bastardizations pumped out for bulk sale to tourists). This requires an analysis of art history and a search for the best works of living craftsmen.

Undoubtedly, a complex mosaic of forces are at work, and it is not within the scope of this paper to analyse them. Rather, this essay has been an attempt to set the scene and to survey some of the opinions of both those who are influencing policies today and those who are affected by these policies.

NOTES

1. Edith Uche Enem, ed., *The National Theatre and Makers of Modern Nigerian Art* (England: Pelican Colour Graphics Ltd., 1977), p. 22.

2. Munro, *Art Education—Its Philosophy and Psychology* (New York: Bobbs-Merrill, 1956), p. 167.

3. Emmanuel Obiechina, *Culture, Tradition and Society in the West African Novel*, Cambridge University African Studies Series (Cambridge, 1975), p. 77.

4. Department of Fine and Applied Arts, University of Nigeria, Nsukka, *The New Director—Experiment on the Training of University Art Teachers* (November 1977), pp. 1–4.

5. Ibid., p. 4.

6. Munro, *Art Education*, pp. 167–68.

7. G.O. Talabi, "Problems of the Art Teacher and Possible Solutions," *Nigerian Society for Education Through Arts* 1, no. 2 (August 1976): 7.

8. Ibid., p. 6.

9. Department of Fine and Applied Arts, University of Nigeria, Nsukka, *The New Director*, pp. 1–4.

10. Talabi, "Problems of the Art Teacher and Possible Solutions," p. 8.

South Africa   Teaching the Zulu

John W. Grossert

VIEWPOINTS FOR ART EDUCATION

Africans see two cultures in society: one is scientific, unemotional, and rational; the other is emotional and irrational. Both form one culture in reality. The scientist and the artist in Africa endeavor to extend the understanding of experience using creative imagination subjected to critical control. Both use their rational as well as intuitive faculties in varying degrees and report their explorations and discoveries in the print media of their respective disciplines. Science and art are therefore considered two facets of the coordinated activity of man. The empirical approach can be found in crafts and in a less obvious way in art. Aesthetic factors, however, are also present in the advanced branches of science. Within the field of pedagogy, education through art influences both science and art. Unlike African education, the bureaucratic educational systems of Western civilization dichotomize art and science into opposing areas of study.

Education through art in Africa extends from kindergarten through the highest grade of school. It begins for the young child, like art in palaeolithic times, before the individual has a structured language. Art and the artifacts that the child and the man make embody the totality of their knowledge, intellectual growth, emotional development, and awareness of their environment, gained through sight, touch, hearing, smell, and taste. Art education in African schools takes place when pupils make original personal statements in visual symbols, forms, and constructions. Arts and crafts are presented as school subjects in Africa.

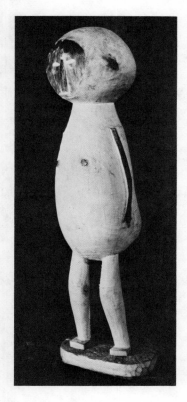

Standing figure of wood, with charred details,
by Zulu child, age 13

THE RELEVANCE OF ZULU CULTURE

In Africa, where systems of education were often introduced by a colonial
power, education was generally looked upon as a process of training for
the purpose of inducting natives into the higher culture of the ruling
power; thus, the Africans were enabled to participate more fully in the
world of commerce and industry. Little attention was given in colonial
times to indigenous types of education such as the initiation schools that
existed in Southern Africa or the less formal peer education in which
younger children were given instruction by older ones. Among the Nguni
tribes, of which the Zulu is one, small boys obtained their education
through peers while herding the family goats and cattle.

Since their lives are spent predominantly in the outdoors and close to
nature, Zulu children at a very early age become aware of the wide
variety of vegetation, insects, birds, and animals in their environment.

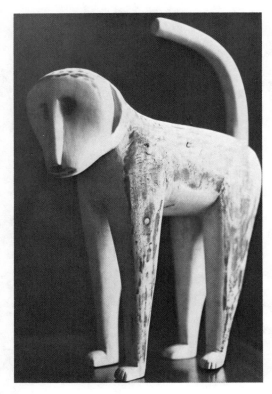

Baboon sculpted in wood by
Zulu child, age 15

Through games, the Zulu youth obtains an extensive knowledge of
botany, biology, and zoology. Studies during the period of 1950 to 1958
revealed that Zulu boys and girls, through peer education, had classified
over 450 grasses used in their crafts. This was a monumental achievement by any standard; in fact, the extent of this knowledge was unsus-
pected by most teachers until these studies and investigations revealed
this knowledge. Zulu boys learning through peer education developed
herdsmen's skills of recognizing and describing cattle so that names for
cattle of various coloration soon became a part of the Zulu language.
There are far more of these color names than the hundred or so that
every herd boy was expected to identify and recite. Zulu girls likewise
cultivated a sensitivity to the color of beads and gave names to indicate
these differences. These vital forms of peer education are genuine
methods of education in which adults are consulted but play a very small
part. Pupils assume important roles in decision making through peer

education and often, when adapted to the art course in a school, the content of an art course becomes less important than the development of individual potentialities. The art teacher (and, in fact, teachers in every subject) assumes the role of a trusted leader because of his or her greater experiences and understanding. Factual recitation conducted by authority figure teachers is not present in this form of Zulu education.

AFRICAN CRAFTS AND AN INSTRUCTIONAL APPROACH

It is feasible for Zulu pupils in African schools to design their own plans of study to be done during the school year. Since 1948 the foundations of teaching art and crafts in the schools of Natal and Zululand has involved pupil participation in the planning of art programs. Art education in Zululand embraces this approach, with the scientific method called into action through the analysis of a problem and the collection of empirical data by direct experimentation. This method is often utilized when using clay in the arts and crafts program. Education through art progresses from the initial experience of looking for the clay, to becoming aware of geographical characteristics of the land by walking over the landscape, to discovering the nature of the plasticity and malleability of clay. Through a discovery of the types and qualities of clay, as well as its characteristics when fused through sufficient firing, pupils and teachers learn geology as well as art. The aesthetic sensibility that emerges through an art experience of making things and expressing ideas is carried over into language development in Zulu education. A fuller medium and another art form in which pupils are confident and secure is therefore established.

Art teachers practicing this approach usually have a list of proposed topics or projects for the school year and, through class discussions, evolve relationships of crafts to everyday life and orientate the pupils' thinking to craftsmanship. Once motivation and recognition of the role of crafts in everyday life is established, the art teacher and the pupils find available materials; some are brought while others are off-cuts, factory rejects, and scraps. Others are found in nature and are gathered in the vicinity of the school. The special qualities inherent in the materials suggested and listed by the pupils and the art teacher, as well as the tools required to work with these materials and the techniques applied when using them, are discussed along with ideas of what can be made with these resources. Ideas are recorded on the chalkboard, which is never big enough to carry all the thoughts which a normal class of thirty pupils puts forward. Decisions on monthly programs of these proposed projects are then undertaken, following a methodology of democratic participation in an on-going debate.

The art teacher in Zululand also values the pupils' knowledge of local craft traditions. It is possible for teachers to draw upon the knowledge of children whose parents possess and practice the traditional Zulu craft skills. The discovery of traditional craft techniques is as much a part of the education-through-art process as discovering sources for art materials.

CHARACTERISTICS OF ZULU STUDENT ART WORK

Different cultural groups develop different concepts and images which are characteristic of themselves. Zulu children have an inclination to grasp fundamental and universal forms and to solve representational problems by simplification and elimination of unimportant details. Such ability to eliminate involvement with superfluous detail does not destroy the monumental dignity and strength of their forms. The Zulu children possess an appreciation of the two-dimensional surfaces when making pictures, and since they have not been influenced by creating illusions of depth, they are more intuitively aware of the patterns their figures make within the format of their paper. Zulu children do not seem to pass through the same developmental stages as European children. They begin at about the same age to scribble and then make symbols for various objects, which they scatter on a sheet of paper without spatial correlation. From here, the Zulu children move in a different direction than European and American children. Backgrounds in their art become tilted planes that provide spatial relationships between figures instead of base lines that also show the child's recognition of the two-dimensional surface of the paper. European children use the base line as an indication of a growing awareness of the three-dimensional possibilities in a picture. Zulu children, however, are influenced by two-dimensional patterns.

Art programs for Zulu children that succeed in inspiring and achieving the full support and cooperation of all involved are those designed by governmental authorities to help rather than to be imposed. A teacher who respects materials, the student, and the environment helps Zulu children find their own way by helping them to draw upon traditional influences and their personal styles of expression.

Brazil Emphasis on the New

Ana Mae Tavares Bastos Barbosa

THE TYRANNY OF THE NEW

The lack of knowledge about the past is leading Brazilian art educators to excessively value the "new." Most things that are considered novel by a group are adopted enthusiastically. Supposedly new objectives, methods, and strategies have been successively introduced in the art room without concern for their interrelationships. These objectives have been proposed without the necessary renovation of methods formulated by former cultural periods and are used unreflectively, and vice versa. This lack of internal structure in the art teaching that was intended to be innovative is leading to a conception of art as nonsense, a kind of doing without meaning. In a recent newspaper interview, a child (Rosangela, eighth grade, Colegio Gilberto Amado of Rio de Janeiro) gave the following description of her class:

> She [the art teacher] orders us, and we keep doing as she orders. In one task, she ordered us to wrinkle a sheet of cellophane paper, then afterwards to stretch and glue it on a piece of cardboard. When I finished she said that it was beautiful. But she knows what it means, I do not.[1]

Colegio Gilberto Amado is considered a *model* public school in Brazil.

Art education objectives to modern art educators in Brazil are seen as a kind of bureaucratic statement to be written in school projects without deserving to be rationally put into operation. As a result, a kind of collage of activities often takes place in the art room which are unconnected, unreflective, and anachronistic: a random oscillation between a rationale of skills development and laissez-faire orientation.

Paradoxically, widespread anxiety about the new results in everything looking alike in art classes. The "art school style"[2] is the same both in

Drawing by Brazilian
child, age 13. Courtesy
of The Seonaid M.
Robertson Child Art
Collection.

private and public schools despite richer materials in the former. The
activities are centered in the studio and subordinated to the same "original" use of scraps, the same conventional themes, the same cultural and
commercial symbols (Christmas, Mother's Day, etc.), the same new relationship between body expression or acting and pictorial expression, using the same exercises and similar materials or, further, subordinated to
the same superficial relationship between music and visual arts—reduced
to graphic representation of music and sounds. On the other hand, conservative currents of art teaching (coloring books), geometric figures
(lines, triangles, angles, etc.), geometric ornaments (rosettes, moulding
interlacing forms, vertical and horizontal repetitions) are still gaining
power.

Despite their psychological and social inappropriateness, these activities at least maintain internal coherence with the "traditional" concept
of art which inspired them. In addition to the ostensible presence of
declared conservatism in art teaching, art teachers enslaved by the new

are accepting, out of ignorance of the past and of theory, conservative methods often disguised by modern masks.

It is common practice that conservative methods invoking new objectives and using new figures of speech, everyday language, or even slang in presentation are being introduced to the student by modern textbooks. An example can be found in an art book for the sixth grade where an exercise of enlarging figures is proposed under the objective of developing perception. The teachers, driven by the overvaluing of the new, have been accepting such exercises, deceived by the attractive and modern graphic presentation of the book and by colloquial invitations to work such as: "Let's play photography machine." They do not know that this method was introduced in Brazil in the nineteenth century under the old-fashioned name of *rede estilográfica* and is based on a conception of visual perception as a mechanical function of the eye or the identification of visual perception with the retinal image, which was completely disproved by the scientific experiments on visual perception of the twentieth century. On the other hand, it supports the idea of art as based on mere reproduction of form. Finally, it is an exercise of eye-hand coordination. The method should be rejected not because it was used in the nineteenth century but because its aims have lost scientific and aesthetic validation. To reject methods because they were used previously would be another aspect of misreading the new.

Besides the lack of theoretical knowledge that makes it difficult to act out and evaluate the practice, the lack of historical knowledge is responsible for the anxiety about the new that is felt by many of the better art teachers in Brazil. As a result of such anxiety, the idea "I did it first" is a provincial way of fighting among art educators. It leads to the false belief that an indigenous approach to art education is being constructed which is independent from foreign concepts. Such a belief represents a theoretical, sociological, and chiefly historical misconception.

THE PROBLEM OF DEPENDENCY

Our historical experience proves that in a country economically and politically dependent, the educational system is a reflection of such dependency. The concept of dependency is more adequate in characterizing the Brazilian industrializing society than the fluid concept of "third world" and the artificially hopeful concept of "developing country."

Because of an international condemnation of direct colonization after World War II, many countries were subtly exploited through the domination of their systems of production and distribution by the metropolis. The dependency, merely an economic relationship at first, internalized, became a quality that characterizes all of a society's institutions.

The educational system is dependent as a result of the dependency of the general society that it serves, and it becomes a tool to maintain the situation of reliance. According to Carnoy, ". . . center groups in the metropole transmit models to dominant groups in the peripheral countries who decide the design of education, managing to limit the possibility of new forms of institutional development emerging."[3] Through education the same values and aspirations already reached by independent societies are transmitted to dependent societies, which are thus impeded from creating their own values. Artificial needs and demands are created to guarantee the marketing of foreign products and foreign ways of life. It is therefore evident that "the more the citizen is trained in the consumption of prepackaged goods and services, the less effective he seems to become in shaping his environment."[4]

In fact, the process of manipulating the educational system did create a cultural alienation in Latin America, which is manifested in copying everything from the developed metropole. Latin Americans became really incapable of shaping our cultural environment because we are not free to determine our own system of values. We are oppressed not only by foreign models but by judgment and validation from the outside. Our social consciousness has been enslaved by foreign educational models for such a long time that we are suffering from a kind of critical amnesia. We are accepting as national models things that have hidden foreign roots. Unconsciously, the teachers serve as vehicles to crystalize behavior, thought, and institutional development in order to guarantee the continuance of dependence. Deliberate masking of external influence by educational dictators is successful thanks to a lack of criticism by teachers.

DISTORTION OF NATIONAL-LOCAL CHARACTER

The art teacher easily believes that we are creators of our own models because this is what is said by people who disseminate the idea of exalted "nationalism." However, such nationalism is a regression to the euphemisms of the turn of the century—the praise of Brazilian natural beauty and the glorification of the land and its official heros. For example, by the compulsory requirement of folklore in the curriculum of undergraduate art education, this curriculum is believed to receive "nationalistic" validation.

"Nationalism can be a liberator"[5]—that is, it can be the force that will destroy the colonial past and project Brazil into the future, but only if it springs up from social consciousness based on diachronic and synchronic analyses of Brazilian "reality." A superficial and deceptive nationalism has been limiting the social consciousness to slogans such as "Brasil grande" and to applause of Bahian costumes in art shows and of xenophobic jokes.

THE ILLUSION OF REJECTION

The educational leaders, in order to feed the superficial nationalism nourished in the people by the dominant group that they serve, frequently distort the real foreign origins and multinational mechanism of the educational system to catch the teachers' sympathy. At a recent national meeting of art educators an important educational legislator, who was one of those persons responsible for the last educational reform act, manifested all his supposed rejection of American education through ironic and sarcastic phrases. However, this educational reform is a simplified copy of the American educational model, especially with respect to the content, which is being strategically hidden from the public.

That national conference was organized to explain and popularize the Reform of Education Act and the curriculum of the undergraduate course of art education determined by the federal government. Among the representatives were those of universities, colleges, and boards of education from all over the country. This objective, however, was not declared. It is not an exaggeration to say that the majority of the teachers who attended that conference became convinced of the nationalism of our system of education, which, in fact, is a collage of foreign influences.

The few existing historical analyses of the Brazilian educational system prove, for example, that the package solutions from France, the United States, or England imply the same grade of surrender of social consciousness. Historical unawareness is driving Brazilian intellectuals and art teachers to overvalue French or English influence as a way to minimize the value of American culture and as a strategy to fight against American influence. However, respecting cultural invasion, I agree with the authors when they say, "We cannot accept quality distinctions between cultures,"[6] and with Carnoy, who affirms: "Decolonization, or liberation, demands personal and societal struggles which go far beyond lowering one flag and raising another."[7] That attitude is only a manifestation of the self-deprecation of the oppressed, who are incapable of fighting with their own tools because they are, in the words of Paulo Freire, "convinced of their own unfitness," and are "sick, lazy, unproductive."

We cannot live in isolation, as some romantic nationalists intend, nor can we, on the other hand, passively accept educational models based on economic and/or political foreign interest or dictated by foreign cultural authority. If a dependent society, such as the Brazilian society, cannot have an educational model particular to Brazil, we have the task of fighting at least for cultural survival. At the present time, the way to fight seems to be to awaken the consciousness, to capture the nature and implications of the models adopted from the metropole, and to understand our cultural possibilities and institutional heritage. Having such knowledge or understanding can produce transformations in the "application" or operation of foreign models, to get control over the influence.

Therefore, the attempt to determine a chronology of art teaching in Brazil should be understood as an effort toward *conscientizacao* about the past with reference to the present, although this chronological analysis will be based upon the internalization of the phenomenon of dependency and "cultural invasion." The determination and characterization of the periods of art education in Brazil will be made in confrontation with the development of general education, of which art education is a subsystem.

ART EDUCATION TODAY

Today, to understand Brazilian art education or any other social manifestation, it is necessary to understand the cultural dynamics of this last period (1958–63). The most alive cultural tendencies today have their roots in this period or in the short renaissance of it in 1968.

An effective move toward emancipation in education arose from 1958 to 1963 and was related to the political, cultural, and economic openness of society at that time. Economic expansion and modernization of institutions was then the chief concern of the government. President Juscelino Kubitscheck (1957–60) gave continuity to the policy of development initiated by Getulio Vargas in 1950. While Vargas's economic nationalism found hard opposition in international capitalism and traditional Brazilian society, the Kubitscheck model, destined to internationalize the Brazilian economy, was supported by the most differing political groups. The Labor party, the Nationalists, the Communists, and the pro-Americanists welcomed Kubitscheck's move toward industrialization against the theses of "agricultural vocation" that pushed Brazil back for many years. Besides the support from the majority, the relief of pressure that spread over Western society with the end of the Stalinist and McCarthyist era made possible a political openness during Kubitscheck's government.

Consequently, with "the policy of substitution of imports, a vigorous industrial sector was established in Brazil."[8] The industrialization developed other sectors of the economy, generating jobs and goods and extending the consumer capacity of the population. This provoked a climate of euphoria. However, the state's inability to eliminate inequalities and structural distortions brought about a large campaign for basic reforms (1961–64). It was during this period of intense politicization and mobilization of student groups, workers' unions, and peasant leagues that Brazilian culture and education strove toward self-identification.

A temporary political and economical openness in Brazilian society made possible a cultural renovation that reached all fields. The Superior Institute of Brazilian Studies (ISEB) elaborated new social and philosophical approaches to Brazilian development and movements, giving value to popular culture which was springing up all over the nation.

In literature the Concretism movement, which exploded in 1957, received international recognition. Guimaraes Rosa's principal work, *Grande Sertao: Veredas* (The Devil in the Backlands), set the plans for renovation of the Brazilian novel. The New Cinema movement (Cinema Nuevo) presented a critical vision of Brazilian reality. The "Bossa Nova" gave a new orientation to popular music. The movement toward making the theater less elite was reinforced.

Brazilian architecture re-encountered its roots lost in Baroque through the work of Lucio Costa and Oscar Niemeyer in building Brasilia, the new capital.

Education encompassed the social and cultural change, and in art education, experiences in many private and public schools became significant. The University of Brasilia, to cite one example, was the first modern Brazilian university created by that time. In the history of Brazilian culture it is an example of the humanistic model of higher education. Art education occupied a relevant place at the University of Brasilia. It was intended to begin the school of education with a department of art education. Actually, the first entity to study education organized in the University of Brasilia was an art school for children and adolescents. Its preorganization involved the work of different specialists (art educators, architects, psychologists, artists, educators, and chemists, for example) during almost one year. The idea was to begin the researches and studies of education by art education, to study general education through art education: the genuine education through art.

Intensive debate on the role and nature of the university in Brazil preceded the organization of the different schools and departments in the University of Brasilia. A critic of the University of Brasilia said:

> These discussions were frequently broad philosophical discourses drawing on the past work of European and American educators and dealing with the issues of what should constitute the Brazilian university. There were rarely any empirical data, however, on the Brazilian educational system presented in these papers and conferences and never any explicit discussion of education as an economic good which could conceivably be analyzed in quantitative terms.[9]

It was exactly this rejection of technocracy and quantification that became the University of Brasilia's achievement, an irreversible conquest for the Brazilian education system. The foundations of the University of Brasilia were social consciousness and educational and philosophical principles.

When in 1965, protesting against despotic persecution and military occupation, 200 teachers resigned their positions, an unequivocal demonstration of "liberating action" generated in consciousness, the first chapter of the story of the University of Brasilia came to an end. Even their opponents had to agree that:

> Following the political changes of March 1964, the University of Brasilia experienced many dismissals and resignations among the faculty and administration at the insistence of the new government. Thus the spirit of innovation was at least temporarily checked; nevertheless, it is clear that the plans for university reform developed later in the decade were in part influenced by the experience at the University of Brasilia.[10]

Paulo Freire's actions and theoretical constructs, however, were the most powerful educational instrument for "critical intervention in reality" achieved at that time. Freire's anthropological approach, consolidated in his method of liberation through *conscientizacao*, constituted an objective achievement in the movement toward independence in education. It is the only educational model that can be considered truly Brazilian.

John Berger wrote that the movement of educational emancipation, "as all the rules induced into the system, suffered a certain rupture in continuity with the 1964 Revolution. The military government which assumed power diverged ideologically from all the attempts and previous projects, using sometimes force, leading the educational system to new ways and giving new course to it."[11] After 1964 the technocratic model took over and the concern with quantification as a system of control and expansion became predominant. The state, instead of behaving as educator in all the humanistic meaning of this function, took on the role of builder, manager, and inspector of schools.

THE CURRENT STATUS OF ART EDUCATION

The 1971 Educational Reform determined that art should be a compulsory subject in the elementary education curriculum (first grade, seven-year-olds, to eighth grade, fourteen-year-olds), and in the curricula of some programs of high school. Welcomed by all the art education researchers, this decision promoted, however, through unplanned multiplication, a dilution of the former experiences centered in quality that would have given national character to art education.

On the other hand, the government's institutionalization of an inadequate undergraduate course in art education to prepare teachers is reinforcing the march toward mediocrity in art education. These undergraduate courses, named "The Short Degree in Art Education," are producing incompetent teachers because administrators pretend to form in two years a teacher who will have the obligation by law (lei 5692, 1971) to teach at the same time music, visual arts, and drama from the first grade to the eighth grade and even in high school. That, however, is a clear example of copying from weak foreign models, of a reduced and incorrect version of the principle of interdisciplinary or related arts, so popular in the American schools during the last ten years.

There is another two-year course, the Full Degree in Art Education, that can be taken after the Short Degree. It is designed to grant the student specialization in visual arts or music or drama. This course is supposed to prepare teachers for high school; however, very few high school curricula include art. Therefore, there is little motivation to get the Full Degree.

Some states are requiring only the Short Degree diploma to teach art in the high school, and the federal government is managing to give more prestige to this degree, whose holders have job preference. Private schools do not take into consideration the Full Degree diploma and will not even accept teachers who hold it because of their higher pay scale.

There are still no graduate courses in which an orientation toward research is possible. A typical instrument of bureaucracy and standardization is the "curriculum minimum," which is determined by the ministry of education for the universities and colleges all over the country. It is possible to enlarge the curriculum, though such an enlargement first has to be examined and approved by the ministry of education. Actually, economic interests of private colleges that want to give a diploma, thus saving time for the student and money for the school, as well as the apathy of the public universities is restricting the study of art education to the *minimum* demanded by the federal government.

All of the bureaucratic elements that describe the education system of Boston during the nineteenth century are emerging in the process of institutionalization of art education in Brazil:[12] (1) Centralization of control and supervision by a federal government that determines the minimum curriculum and fiscalizes the programs of all colleges and universities. (2) Differentiation of function: the change is from requiring all teachers to teach all subjects, to the emergence of a whole corps of specialists. (3) Qualification for office: that is, appointment and promotion on the basis of the number of certificates or diplomas presented. Examinations of teachers are casually applied but are being conducted by amateurs in art education. The rules of examinations and criteria of judgment are being determined by artists whose capacity for determining the fitness of a candidate for teaching is undetermined or by educators insensitive to art. (4) Precision and continuity: routinization is guaranteed by the continuity of all tenured teachers of geometric drawing who were entitled to teach art after the removal of their specialty from the curriculum; also, there are efforts to tie the teachers to the contents and strategies prescribed by the educational administrators and legislators. (5) Retention and assessment: the evaluation of teachers is conducted by the school principal and adheres to a strict code of conduct. Any deviation from criteria established by the conventional system of general education in Brazil provides rationale for a negative assessment of the teacher by the principal. This may be based upon the teacher's performance, his or her personal life, controversial political behavior by the teacher, the teacher's active engagement in the teacher's union, or even upon criticism of his or her style of dress. Information from government or specialized agencies can also be used to devise academic assessment and to evaluate the art teachers, whose ideological positions must be considered correct if they are to retain their positions.

If a major function of art in the school is to help "students to become more human by having them value art as an important aspect of their lives," the school's latent function manages to accommodate the process of humanization of children to the cognitive and social authority of the school "as a prelude for accepting the authority of other institutions."[13] Art, thus, becomes party to the hidden agenda of repression by the school.

NOTES

1. "Risonha e Franca," *Opiniao*, 12 March 1976, p. 4.

2. Arthur Efland, "The School Art Style: A Functional Analysis," *Studies in Art Education* 17, no. 2 (1976): 37–44.

3. Martin Carnoy, *Education as Cultural Imperialism* (New York: David McKay Co., 1974), p. 55.

4. Ivan Illich, *Celebration of Awareness* (New York: Doubleday, 1970), p. 161.

5. Bradford Burns, *Nationalism in Brazil: A Historical Survey* (New York: Frederick A. Praeger, 1968), p. 145.

6. Donald Swift and Anthony Flew, *Sociology, Equality and Education* (New York: Barnes and Noble, 1976), p. 35.

7. Carnoy, *Education as Cultural Imperialism*, p. 20.

8. Otavio Ianni, *Crisis in Brazil* (New York: Columbia Univ. Press, 1970), p. 24.

9. Douglas Hume Graham, "The Growth, Change and Reform of Higher Education in Brazil: A Review and Commentary on Selected Problems," in *Brazil in the Sixties*, ed. Riordan Roett (Nashville: Vanderbilt Univ. Press, 1972), p. 291.

10. Ibid., p. 292.

11. John Berger, *The Success and Failure of Picasso* (London: Penguin Books, 1965), p. 178.

12. Michael Katz, *Class, Bureaucracy, and Schools: The Illusion of Educational Change in America* (New York: Praeger Pub., 1971).

13. Arthur Efland, "The School Art Style," p. 40.

United States Foreign and American Minority Influences

William Bradley

There is a continuing aspect of worldwide art education that is often overlooked in favor of one's own national interests, but the United States offers a special opportunity, because of its multinational origins, to see firsthand the influences brought from many countries into the history of its education and particularly the history of art education. Much of what was shaped into North American art education was shaped by personalities who were trained in other places. Sometimes these influences are subtle and overlooked, but other times they are disregarded despite their obvious nature. An examination of some of these minority influences and the personalities which represent them may direct attention toward what could be considered a third-world consciousness of sources in the world of art education.

The initial intent of this writing was to elicit responses from persons in several countries regarding their perceptions of the influences of their respective countries on art education in North America. Responses were either ones of perplexity or of surprise, creating an array of information which became either difficult to decipher (as well as to translate) or required additional clarifying correspondence. One central thread, however, was persistent: many art educators in other countries are aware of specific personalities who continue to show up in art education literature whenever some attention is paid to historical sources. It became evident that a good base for this chapter would include a call to attention of the persons in the various countries who, through their training, helped to produce the personalities whose influence aided the shaping of North American art education. Several correspondents remarked that it would be easier to speak of the influence of North American art education on their countries than to answer this question. In some countries (such as

Australia), perhaps such a view would be the only one to take. But these views are somewhat self-evident; behind them is a hidden one: the educational origins of North America owe some homage to a wide spectrum of diverse groups that have come together in a special way. While it may be true that the melting-pot nature of art education in the United States demonstrated a model which has become important in the development of programs of study in many countries, there is often a tendency to link this to only two European areas: Prussia and England.

Names such as Hungary's Laszlo Moholy-Nagy and Georges Kyepes, Czechoslovakia's Frank Cizek, and France's Le Cocq show up only briefly, for they are acknowledged more in history than in content. Yet, these people were influential in both content and method.

There have been and are many less-known influences on art education which go unnoticed. These are persons who first produced a social consciousness in art, such as Mexicans Diego Rivera and Jose Orozco. Contemporary interests in public murals (and particularly those associated with the Black movement) can be directly traced to these influences as much as to the Russian interest in social art. Art has always taken up social issues, even when painting was done only for the church and the royal courts; however, these issues have not always been a part of art education models. Abstract or theoretical interest in social art became practical in curricula structures when these contemporary social artists became an important part of the history of art education. The Russian and Mexican influence on North American art education has been in evidence for at least fifteen years.

The connection between this early social art and the contemporary interest in celebrations is intricate and interesting. The French, for example, have a long history of street "animation," which includes face painting, theater, music, painting, and construction, and is often associated with active social movements. The popular use of street art in America may be logically connected with not only the French animations (which have only recently entered into art education in that country) but also the people's art of Russia and Mexico, which has permitted an antielitist view of the function of art. The first antielitist developments in U.S. art curricula occurred during the formative stages of the so-called freedom movement, beginning around 1955. These influences, however, extend to the mid-1930s and through countries which have produced twentieth-century revolutionary movements. It is, at least, instructive to acknowledge the movement of revolutionary art and its probable formal influence on art educational curricula today.

Currently in North America, curators in museums, community groups, and (sometimes) public educators try to interpret people's art, including the art of celebrations (street animations), the painting of public murals (supergraphics; the subway paintings of Chicago and New York; the street children murals) and the curricula-included social issues such as ecology, environment, and inequality (including Women's art). The influences which brought about these interpretations are hardly recognized in conventional histories of art education. They seem clearly antifascist and prosocialist in their intent to disenfranchise a strict curriculum of high or elitist art in favor of an acknowledgement that art is for people. Mexico, France, and Russia have been leading influences in this movement.

Formalized art education in most countries assumes its posture within a stated need to provide culture-keeping activity. It subsumes in a "Future Shock" way any social movement that would encourage human freedom and thus cultural change. A national art curriculum can serve the double purpose of attending to both social movement and cultural maintenance. Celebrations, in this way, are properly years behind the influences that produced them. But it is instructive to anyone interested in the social movements which eventually produce a consciousness for curriculum development that these influences exist. They are not easily found in a history that is faithful to tradition.

Beyond the influence of revolutionary art on the U.S. curricula, there are less activist examples arising from minority countries that have nonetheless altered the face of art education curricula in North America. Hungarians are proud of their contributions, as are the Czechs. But this pride is not yet developed among the Scandinavians, Latins, Orientals, American Indians, eastern Indians, and Africans. These people hold a secret which is yet to be deciphered. In histories of art education in North America these small voices have not been included, but they are rising and insistent at America's door.

One relatively unanalyzed influence on art education curriculum in America (and throughout Europe) is that of Africa and, in particular, Nigeria, where the ceremonial wood carvings and bronzes imported into and housed in Paris and London near the turn of the century helped to create a rethinking of the nature of both the cultural and private functions of art. Because of these implantations, civilizations could no longer be measured according to a simple evolutionary development. The factors of custom, environment, religion, function, and history could now be seen as important considerations for the teaching of art. It would be nearly a half-century before these developments in the art world would take hold in educational structures. They arrived in the 1950s, as anthropological concerns entered the art education curriculum development activity of that time (for example, the Stanford group under June King McFee).

Surely two of the most direct examples of the movement toward the African image could be seen in the paintings of Modigliani and Picasso, who both made the bridge between the elongated spiritual faces of the Dogon and the tradition of western group and portrait painting. It is speculated that much of the expressionistic portraiture of public school painting classes of the 1950s and 1960s could be connected with this fifty-year-old influence on western art. This does not often show up in historical accounts of art education.

Just as the plantation songs and the development of jazz represented an exquisite and real influence on what was to become an authentic North American music, the influential movements of spiritual expression, culture-grounding, and the modern link between the animate and the inanimate can be traced to the uncovering of the African cultures. The influences are not adequately described in histories of Western art education, and Black Consciousness in America has been too overwhelmingly directed toward the *American* history of Blacks to offer much assistance in meeting this need for clarification.

Again, curriculum decisions to include watercolor and ceramics were often influenced by forces outside of the Western tradition. The impressionist movement seems clearly related to an oriental influence that ascribed a virtue to the obscure; the image was to be found in the obscurity of meaning. It is easy to locate this influence in both the public school art room and the college studio beginning in 1950. The question of the source of this influence, however, is seldom raised.

It does not seem to theorists that this move should be treated separately from a more general art developmental notion. Yet it would be admitted that much of art activity in the schools from 1950 to 1960 was, in fact, of impressionist origin, and that the announced influences of both Manet and Monet and later the paintings of Matisse, Tobey, Rothko, Michaux, and others were of oriental descent. This influence from cultural sources is often merely attributed to the general art movements of the twentieth century; in failing to recognize the origins of these influences, however, a disservice is paid to minority countries. Art education in North America, like every aspect of its developing culture, owes its diversity and strength to the many countries and cultures who collectively settled in the U.S. The Prussian and English influences, although strongly developed through personalities such as Horace Mann, Walter Smith, and Viktor Lowenfeld, were only a part of a history. The rest remains to be told.

There is today an interest in attending to the background and history of pupils in planning activities. American Indian schools, as an example, are attempting to develop programs that take into account the ceremonial history of art in healing, worship, and other religious activities. Sand painting is no longer a curious thing to do but a serious study of a private way of healing people. Psychiatrists and psychologists are showing that these methods are effective for curing anxiety and emotional problems. They should at least be recognized in the study of art in America. For pupils to recognize this role of art in the life of a community is a positive response.

The development of basketry, weaving, ceramics, and jewelry shows the general influence of American Indian culture on North American art education; not simply as media, but the uniqueness of the object formation itself has often been an unwritten part of its history. Additional content sources as exemplified in the media can be traced to India and to the islands of the South Seas. The development of wax and dye techniques and the peculiar results of batik on paper and cloth are examples. These little-recognized sources will require an extended analysis before an adequate history of North American art education can be written.

One additional influence should be mentioned. Naum Gabo, in his Washington lectures published as *Divers Art*, produced some evidence that the treatment of space in a geometric fashion was not strictly a European style from Cézanne and Braque but had an older history in the work of the Russian painter Mikhail Vrubel, who demonstrated that this perception was worldwide. This concept of space (dubbed "cubism") became influential not only in content but also in pedagogy. Many art training institutions and, consequently, public training were influenced toward a new geometrism, which is still evident in curricula today. That cubism was produced by these Frenchmen is a common and perhaps erroneous assumption. Perhaps art historians in education should deny a "father of cubism" in favor of its wider source; at the least, a history of art influences on North American curricula should be rewritten to include a much wider perspective. Geometrism as a force in curriculum development has shown up in many sources and particularly in contemporary design. Jewelry and painting are clearly influenced even today. In reviewing national scholastic awards, one finds that the function of geometrism continues to be strong. The question as to whether or not one would pedagogically begin with the cube, cylinder, and cone remains important to the field of art education.

It is not so clear, however, that such an influence should be linked solely to the French movement of the nineteenth century. After all, the use of mathematics in the training of artists is seen at around 500 B.C. among the Greeks. The Russian painters (particularly of the revolution) and the French movement are linked with a tradition which makes geometrism a multinational influence.

These samples of influence could be much more carefully expanded and clarified because there are others. Perhaps the future histories of art education will include these descriptions.

METHODOLOGICAL INFLUENCES

It is clear that the predominance of English and Prussian influences on methods was based upon the fact that influential people in education set out to educate, for the first time in civilization, 100% of their population; still, there are some small nods given to other sources. (It should be noted that 50% of the current population of North America is involved in university education as opposed to 8% in England and 6% in France.)

Some of the methodological sources were eventually abandoned, not because of inadequacy but because one would lose a particular art form. In France, for example, Horace Le Cocq de Boisbaudran, in training his academy pupils, utilized techniques for increasing memory as a part of a more general pedagogy. While some of his work is similar to the work of Kimon Nicolaides, it is at a much more sophisticated level and can perhaps be traced to a certain ancient Greek system invented by Simonides of Ceos around 525 B.C. Le Cocq's methods of remote drawing, shut-eye drawing, and drawing from other people's memories were lessons never forgotten by some of his most famous pupils: Rodin, Delacroix, Turner, Fantin-Latour, and Legros. These memory techniques came to North America by way of England and the translations of Bruce Catterson-Smith and, subsequently, the teaching pedagogy of Marion Richardson; however, whenever and wherever the training of imagination through the use of memory shows up in classroom pedagogy, it is still of French origin and linked to an old Gallic tradition.

Much of the organized play pedagogy of the nineteenth-century kindergarten of Elizabeth Peabody in Boston was based largely upon the work of German educator Friedrich Froebel. In fact, in his classic book Frederick Logan studiously describes Froebel's influence, as does Robert Saunders in his thesis on the subject. Much acclaim has been given to Froebel's "gifts" and "occupations," which were ways to help pupils form concepts of "color, texture, size, number, and creative arrangement." This pedagogy seems curious in art education study, where interest in conceptual development has again arisen.

Although the gifts are generally thought to have originated in the minds of Froebel and other educational theorists of the early nineteenth century, the curious relationship of the folded gifts and puzzles of ancient China and Japan may remind us that sources are sometimes elusive and complex. The pedagogy of gifts is likely older than the Froebelian period, particularly since the conceptual intent of these gifts was primarily mathematical. Perhaps there is a stronger connection between Froebel's gifts and the Chinese and Japanese puzzles and folds than is generally recognized.

The occupations of Froebel may also have arisen out of the need of families to apprentice their children in their own trade of weaving, tool making, jewelry, or the like. This practice preceded the institution of the medieval guild system, and this influence was thus traditionally multi-European. Froebel's use of such a practice was likely within this tradition. How these occupations, as interpreted by Froebel, influenced the pedagogy of art curricula in North America could perhaps most readily be seen in the cut-out work, color-in work, and mathematics- and reading-related work of the art classrooms in the twentieth century. These influences, although peripherally related to the stated art curriculum, often become an actual part of the curriculum and particularly when such teaching is given over to the untrained art teacher or the general elementary teacher. Such activities, as described in three highly used journals, *Arts and Activities*, *School Arts*, and *Instructor*, represent an unwritten but influential, even though unofficial, curriculum in the North American public schools. Such activity has been a part of the actual art education of elementary pupils in America for several decades.

One of the newest changes in curriculum structures for U.S. art education is the use of museums. This practice has become fortuitous for the museums themselves, as financial exigency has created both the opportunity and the need for expanding the public base of support. Public entry into museums, although new in America, has a 450-year-old history, beginning in Italy and continuing in Russia and England. Great collections in these countries (first in Italy with the Medicis) were opened for limited public viewings, setting the precedent for what was to become tours and finally educational programs within the general purposes of the collections.

This helps to show that curriculum structures often reflect goals and priorities which, because of social needs and exigency, become important. Museum education appears to be one of these. As of yet, no theoretician has placed into perspective the educational development of museum education. Most, if not all, research in museum education today remains empirically descriptive. However, minority cultural influences and the perceptions of the general population on this development should be recognized.

Other program shifts, including art therapy, gerontology, hospital work, and other community efforts, which are equally politically bound, may be found to be sufficiently linked to minority populations to suggest that a new history needs to be forged out of the new consciousness that has appeared in recent years.

These methodological influences, which may best be traced to the countries mentioned, are perhaps too tenuous to make any definitive claims. Yet it is important to begin once again the search for the roots of influence, simply because histories are as much a present way of seeing as a past way of being. Histories are a fiction of the time of their writing. A new history is due. The present has shifted in a particularly unacknowledged fashion since the beginning of the civil rights movements.

One of the more promising aspects of the International Society for Education Through Art is that, with increasing familiarity and dialogue between various countries, more will be learned about the subtle and sometimes overlooked influences which by their presence have produced content, a certain flavor of media, and certain evolving methodologies throughout the history of North American art education. Some of the influences that produced the history of a particular era in art education no longer seem to affect practices in the same way, and new traditions with different histories fall into this ever-changing vacuum.

One example of how shifts in historical influences can occur is in the concept of imitation. In art education, imitation goes in and out of favor. In the period dominated by Lowenfeld, copying was considered harmful even though prior eras utilized it as a matter of course. Today many art educators once again are examining the usefulness of imitation as art pedagogy. This is only one example of an instance which requires the shifting of both philosophical and historical legacies. It would therefore be of some consequence to continually examine the sources of content, media, and pedagogy and, at some further point, to study the relationships which exist between these shifting histories.

A history cannot forever be true because of its fictional quality. It provides a way in which a society can be assured of its own authenticity by portraying its roots, but change extends and variegates these roots. To account not only for civilization (as does the historian) but for civilization at work (as does the sociologist) would isolate the active changes of subtle influences in art education in the United States. Such an accounting would lay the groundwork for a new consciousness of sources as they have arisen in increasingly diverse cultural arenas. A new history of North American art education will depend upon this groundwork.

The following correspondents influenced the ideas expressed here, and I am grateful for their contributions to this essay: Akòs Páal, Budapest, Hungary; Felix Ekeada, Owerri, Nigeria; Aimee Humbert, Sévres, France; Boris Lichaczils, Moscow, USSR; Victor Reyes, Nextila, Mexico; Liu Kuo-sung, Shatin, New Territories, Hong Kong; Ruth Jonas Bardin, Jerusalem, Israel; and Denise Hickey, Paddington, New South Wales, Australia.

III
Developing International and Cross-Cultural Studies

Differences as well as communalities have made art education unique among various countries. The differences, however, are not so pronounced that they drastically widen gulfs and chasms, making a crossing impossible. Each country has influenced the teaching of art in one manner or another, but most have in common a rationale for the need to teach artistic and cultural heritages. This is basically universal. Part III of this book is devoted to the further discernment of these universals through research devoted to the effects museums have on art education, research on art examinations, and empirical research within the issues of cross-cultural art education.

Nowhere does the realization of a movement toward comprehensive art education become more evident than in the role of museums as essential institutions for teaching artistic and cultural heritages in cooperation with school art education programs. Indeed, there is scarcely a museum in any country that cannot indicate currently a form of involvement in art education, nor are there educational systems that do not find the resources of their museums, like those of their libraries, as centers for art teaching. In some countries—as in Finland, for example—the ministry of education along with museum directors have worked to create a total integration of museums into their systems of education, from kindergarten through vocational and adult education programs. Museums and schools have rediscovered each other and, while some administrators say that museums are actually the universities of the people, others predict that the museums are and will steadily become the art education centers of the future.

Robert Ott and Lois Jones, scholars of international art education in museums, tell about many of the recent practices in international museums in their chapter that follows. Cross-cultural influences for the acceptance of the public into museums, like those within public education, began to be felt some time ago. Italy, Russia, and England provided

Texture study of a historical subject by a schoolchild, age 14, in the Netherlands

many of these influences, setting precedents for the current educational formats within developing cultures. The methodologies of twelve countries for teaching artistic and cultural heritages in art education are reviewed in this chapter. Both Ott and Jones have based their research on many years of in-the-field investigation of museum educational programing and of universities and schools that support and develop the integration of the museums in art education. Museum education bears watching because it is, in global terms, a growth industry in art education, whereas support of art in the schools is uneven, ranging from expansion to decline. Even countries with severe economic problems continue to offer support for their museums, while art in schools struggles yet survives.

The forms of art education in museums illuminated by Ott and Jones invite an intense response to art education that transcends unemotional or mindless partisan acceptance of art and is therefore extremely appealing to the art educator. They warn, however, that art education in museums will continue to move towards accommodating both the connoisseur and the novice with the same degree of finesse as is found in the demands for cross-cultural research and effective program development in art education.

The effect of various countries' art examinations upon art education presents yet another aspect of cross-cultural research. The arguments for and against standardizing art education through national examinations are set forth by Bradley, as he examines the persistent reservations that exist over national examinations in art. A survey of representatives from twenty countries was used by Bradley in developing and evaluating the specific examples of differing formats existing in several countries. By doing so, he presents several areas for future research that promise to lead to investigations which will further an international understanding of the problems faced by art educators. Such research is the basis for assessing not only the cultural heritage of individual groups for curricula purposes, but also for evolving the traditional artistic heritages of particular cultures, thus assisting in the understanding of cross-cultural issues in art education.

National examinations in countries where examinations thrive are today under study in order to find ways of bringing to these examinations a better balance between the theoretical and the practical aspects of art within particular educational formats. Some of the committees that have undertaken such studies are investigating the possibilities of having more input from the local school systems in their national examination processes. In some countries conflicts continue between the influence of foreign powers over a national art examination and the persisting cultural and artistic traditions of a given society. Issues over choices of internal or external forms of evaluation, therefore, extend the debate over examinations. The centralization of examination criteria is often seen existing in close relationship with the field of technology in a particular country and with the standardizing influences that are prevalent within such technologically oriented societies. Therefore, issues concerning national examinations in art are not simplistic, as many art educators discover whenever such issues are viewed cross-culturally. Even within multicultural societies such as the United States there appear to be no clear-cut solutions, for organizations have attempted to identify the art values within diversified countries and have not adequately evolved criteria. The examination concept, therefore, continues to be debated in the United States, particularly by those who desire more regional and local responsibility for the development of their art programs. Exploration of the criteria governing national examinations in several countries does, however, help to bring many currently debated issues to the forefront through detailed descriptions of practices in Nigeria, Hong Kong, England, and the Netherlands.

The development of and the issues concerning the examinations, curricula, and art programs in schools, studios, galleries, and museums appear wherever art teachers engage in rigorous scholarship, planning, methodological inquiry, and reporting. This is also true with cross-cultural research, and Anderson underlines guidelines to facilitate these endeavors in one of the final chapters in this book.

The aims of cross-cultural research in art education can best be realized through inquiry grounded in a significant cultural theory that is relevant to art education, reflects contemporary social issues, and shows a promise of offering needed insights to the profession. Anderson, by careful documentation of methods in cross-cultural research, presents a means for achieving these outcomes with an analysis of the crucial steps in cross-cultural research. Strengths and weaknesses, particularly between psychological and anthropological factors, are brought to the attention of the reader, and it becomes apparent that cross-cultural research, while not as easy an endeavor as one might at first think, is nevertheless both needed and possible. Through the study of such exemplars in art education as Child (1962–1965) and the Hess-Behrens study (1973), efforts in developing cross-cultural research can be strengthened.

It is necessary that cross-cultural research be meticulously planned and be piloted well in advance of any data collecting. In order to facilitate endeavors toward qualitatively outstanding cross-cultural studies in art education, researchers—neophyte or seasoned—should profit from an adherence to Anderson's guidelines.

Finally, there are many organizations and institutions that offer excellent resources to assist the art educator with cross-cultural research, and many of these are noted in the closing portion of this book. These range from national to international organizations that have consistent publication policies and offer a wide range of services.

The preceding accounts of art education, as well as the concluding chapters of this book, have attempted to provide an introduction to the study of issues in international art education. It is hoped that these have helped to develop a broader perspective on various art education concerns. For many readers this will be a first book on art education on an international basis, and for others it may be the motivation for future research of an even more specialized and developed character.

These abbreviated and introductory accounts of the research and the art teaching activities involved in international art education indicate that considerable work remains to be done in cross-cultural art education.

Inquiry into patterns of art education throughout the world should continue by way of a continuous search for additional contributions which will adequately meet the rising expectations of societies for effective art education throughout the world. The challenge of further study awaits today's art educator.

International Museums and Art Education

Robert W. Ott and Lois Swan Jones

When young students visit art museums, they learn to perceive and appreciate wide varieties of art. This experience aims at nothing less than the full awakening of a student's potential for appreciation by blending emotion, imagination, and perceptual awareness.[1] Members of the educational departments of many museums want to assist visiting students in having this kind of rewarding experience.

Ott's in-depth study of the educational programs of major European museums indicates that museum education is now, more than ever before, a growing and major concern of the European and American art museums.[2] Development of the educational philosophies and theories of these art museums is now providing innovative learning methods in the arts for students of all ages, from the primary grades to the university level. Today, the European museum staff is concerned with art education, with finding the best way of presenting objects in the collection so that the works of art invite intense aesthetic learning experiences and do not just find a bland, unemotional reception or a mindless, partisan acceptance.

The principal child education programs of European museums are similar to those advocated by institutions in the United States: school-visitation programs and special group projects. Certain emphases, however, are different in the European museums. For example, in the United States most museum educators train numerous volunteers, or docents, to guide the students through the museum, whereas the European museums have paid professional guides or trained classroom teachers to supplement the museum educational staff. Moreover, in special group projects, Europeans exude a more club-like and free-play atmosphere, unlike the classroom aura of American museums. Some of the school-visitation programs and special projects for children conducted by the educational directors of various European museums are described in this chapter.

SCHOOL-VISITATION PROGRAM

Opportunities for children as a group to learn more about the perception and appreciation of art during the academic year are provided by the school-visitation programs run by many museums. Jones's study[3] of 110 art museums (70 in the United States, 3 in Canada, and 37 in Europe), which were selected on the basis of the size of their art collections and their geographic locations, found that of the 21 European museums that answered the questionnaire, 57% had such a program.[4] This report by Jones, which was based upon the answers to a questionnaire in addition to personal interviews with the educational personnel of a number of European and American museums, indicated that the school-visitation programs were popular at the institutions which provided them. Although a low count of 1,800 student visits per year was reported at the City Museum & Art Gallery, Birmingham, England, it was estimated that as many as 200,000 school children toured the Musée National du Louvre, Paris, annually.

Although the school-visitation programs of most of the European museums are based upon one trip per year, a few museums—such as the Szépművészeti Múzeum, Budapest—provide a program that encompasses eight to ten visits per class, with 90% of these tours being conducted by classroom teachers. One of the big differences between the European museums and their American counterparts found in Jones's study is in the use of docents, or volunteer guides. Whereas in the United States large groups of volunteers are trained to be guides for school-visitation programs, the European children are conducted through the galleries by a combined team of the museum's educational staff, paid guides, and their own classroom instructors. Since the classroom teachers often do the guiding, the educational personnel of many museums have provided assistance to the instructors in the form of booklets, slide presentations, and teacher training.

Staff members of the British Museum, London, have written a seven-page pamphlet, *Information for Teachers Organizing School Party Visits*, which furnishes the reader with pertinent data about the museum's facilities. Advance notification to the Museum Education Office of the proposed time, date, and topic of the visit is encouraged so that public lectures and other school tours will not be scheduled for the same area at the same time. Specific study galleries that accommodate parties of about twenty students are detailed; data are provided concerning the availability of folding stools and sketch boards, the proper decorum to be followed in the museum, and the lunch room facilities. The pamphlet also mentions the study boxes, which contain material pertinent to the museum's collection and are available to teachers at the Museum Education Office. Also recorded is the schedule for the twenty-minute introductory talks given by the members of the education department five days a week, in the morning and each afternoon. The British Museum educational director has also compiled, with the assistance of the curatorial staff, a series of guides for teachers to various sections of the museum's collection. In *A Brief Guide to the Prehistoric Galleries* information as to the location of the prehistoric works is provided as well as drawings and historic information on some of the objects displayed in these galleries. The twenty-page booklet includes a series of questions, with spaces provided for the answers, which the students complete by naming or drawing the desired objects. Moreover, a brief bibliography of nonfiction and fiction books is also recorded.

Although there are no formal school-visitation tours sponsored by the Rijksmuseum, Amsterdam, the School Art Committee, composed of twenty-six artist teachers, brings classes to the Rijksmuseum, the Van Gogh Museum, and the Stedelijk Museum in large numbers. To assist these instructors, the educational staffs of these museums have provided slide presentations on various aspects of the collection. Built around the principle that museum visitors need more freedom to discover objects on their own,[5] the program consists of a three-fold scheme: first, a slide-tape presentation on the collection to be highlighted; followed by the students' visit to the particular gallery that houses the collection, accompanied by their instructors; and, to reinforce the occasion, ending with the student obtaining a reproduction of one of the works and sometimes information or literature that relates to the works seen. Open to the public as well as to classes of students, the twenty-minute slide presentations are shown daily at the Rijksmuseum in the specially built Röellzaal Auditorium, which features presentations that can be narrated in ten different languages simultaneously. Programs include "Dutch Paintings in the Seventeenth Century," "The Dutch and the East Indies," and "Christmas in the Rijksmuseum Collection." The Rijksmuseum, like the Tate Gallery, publishes pamphlets that assist teachers who guide their classes and booklets that deal with special topics. These handsome color brochures are available to teachers who prepare in advance for their visits.

Because the principal guides for the school-visitation programs in most European museums are the classroom teachers, museum educational directors often put considerable effort and time into providing information and study sessions for teacher education. This is as true for the large museums as for small museums such as the Gotland Formsal in Visby on the island of Gotland, Sweden. Two London institutions—the British Museum and the Victoria and Albert Museum—have extensive teacher-training programs: courses for university students who are training to be teachers, and various programs, called "Study Days," which are designed to assist instructors who wish to bring their students to the museum. For instance, the British Museum holds sessions one day a week for seven to nine weeks during the fall for teachers-in-training. These college students attend a full-day session to learn about museum resources that can be utilized in the classroom.

The educational staff of the Victoria and Albert Museum in London are employees of the national Department of Education and, as such, are civil servants whose relationships with the administration of the Victoria and Albert Museum are both cordial and constructive. Because of this unique position, members of the museum staff have close connections with teachers in the schools and conduct extensive teacher-education programs in the museum. The Study Days program lasts six weeks and has sessions arranged for a full day of each week for teachers who are temporarily released from their teaching commitments. These teachers explore the arts of various periods in order to perceive relationships between architecture, painting, sculpture, the decorative arts, literature, and music. A normal Study Day session includes two lectures, both of which are illustrated by slides of art works. Moreover, the museum instructors attempt to use slides of objects owned by the Victoria and Albert to illustrate these lectures.

The use of the word *study* in the title of these programs provides a basis for the nature of this teacher-education experience. The literature and social history of the arts under study in these sessions are well integrated in each session and assist the teachers in providing any essential knowledge either in a framework of the social and cultural milieu of the lecture themes or with the historical period under study. Such sessions promote an intelligent response to art objects in the museum collections by presenting visual and verbal comparisons of the art works under study and by providing an understanding of the forces that have influenced their creation. The origins of words and art terms assist the teachers in building a working art vocabulary that makes them more competent at dealing with the expressive content of art works.

A personal encounter with art objects in the collection is, however, the main objective of the Study Days at the Victoria and Albert Museum. No attempt is made to dictate the mode of appreciation that the teachers should employ; rather, the purpose of the lectures is simply to provide information. The primary focus is to guide the teachers toward personal discovery in viewing and comparing various art works, with an understanding of the qualities of cultivation and a personal sensitivity necessary for sincere contemplation and appreciation. The philosophies of education resulting in a knowledgeable viewer and of briefing a teacher before exposing him or her to the collections within the museum permeate the pedagogical focus of teacher-education projects at this London museum.

In addition to the Study Days program, the staff of the Victoria and Albert Museum provide a number of short courses for teachers. For instance, a one-day session on Simple Photography of Museum Objects assists teachers in learning how to effectively photograph the museum objects. Other courses include consecutive Saturday morning sessions connected with a British television program on world history, the "Study of the Chinese Civilizations," the "Furnishings of English Homes," "Visual and Practical Approaches to Styles in English Art," and "The Embroiderer and Her Household." Conceived of as planning sessions to encourage teachers to bring their classes into the museum, these short courses provide instructors with opportunities to work on ideas and materials for postmuseum projects to be used in their own schoolrooms following a class visit to the museum.

What the educational staff or the classroom teachers do with the children once the students are on the premises of a museum falls into several categories. One method is to concentrate on the art objects, using information and perceptual skills as a primary way of dealing with an object's design or style or with a specific period of art. Others use the museum to more generally extend sensory awareness through a variety of approaches. For instance, London's National Portrait Gallery has had a program for teenage girls from comprehensive secondary schools that emphasizes the relationship between historical portraits and fashion. Following a brief introduction covering the Tudor period, students are given a worksheet upon which is drawn the basic outline of a woman's figure. From their analysis of the fashion aspects of the Tudor portraits in front of them, these students make basic drawings of their observations. Consequently, the museum visitors are learning not only that costume changes the personal image of these historic subjects but also that fashion transforms and expresses the human figure. An additional asset of this program is knowledge of a fashion vocabulary including such terms as *coif, farthingale,* and *doublet.*

The Moderna Museet in Stockholm does not mix students with regular gallery visitors; it is available for school-visitation tours only before the museum opens. No formal program is offered; the children are allowed to wander at will, though docents are on hand to answer questions and suggest activities in the spacious art studios. In Stockholm a system of assigning various grade levels to different museum centers in the city is used. Consequently, the style of instruction is related to the nature of the museum. The repository of "fine art" implies certain kinds of approaches, while the ethnic museum suggests others, such as folk dancing, ancient games, storytelling, and festivals. The question of whether the museum should be a social center or whether it should preserve a collection for study has not yet been settled.

The Staaliches Puschkin-Museum, Moscow, has a program based upon the storytelling aspects of works of art. The stories told are derived from the subject content of the paintings, which are of any origin, from Russian to European. Typical favorites, however, are from the Russian masters, especially the realist painters of Russia such as Ilya Repin and Vasili Surikov. Developed and presented by the museum staff, these programs are presented one or two afternoons per week to students who wish to come both with a school class and individually. Children from preschool age through the secondary school level are accommodated, although, at this particular Russian museum, the older students also copy from the old masters, receive formal lectures, and meet with artists for discussion.

Although no statistics are available as to the extent of this practice, some European museums have exhibitions of children's art within the institution itself. One such exhibition displayed in the foyer of the Museum der bildenden Kunste zu Leipzig, Leipzig, East Germany, included such themes as "Our Russian Neighbors" and "Children's Fairy Tales," illustrated by teenagers. At the Muzeum w Toruniu, Torün, Poland, the display space is devoted exclusively to the art work of children from all over Europe; according to Stefan Koscielecki, director of the museum, work of all ages is included and is changed several times a year.[6] The museum facilities are used for teacher workshops and student activities: children's programs have been devised on such subjects as "light" and "motion."

The exhibition "Rhein und Maas," held at the Schnugen-Museum in Cologne, West Germany, stimulated visiting school children with a display of early Christian art made along the Rhine (Rhein) and Meuse (Maas) rivers. Some of the students returned to their classrooms and proceeded to emulate some of the exquisite reliquaries they had just seen. A group of eight- and nine-year-old students constructed one large reliquary, while some of the kindergarten children made individual reliquaries using wooden cigar boxes. Constructed with gold- and silver-colored foil and a repoussé technique, these art works were subsequently placed on display in the foyer of the Schnugen-Museum. The children then acted as guides, taking their parents through both exhibitions:

"Rhein und Maas" and their own art. Thus, the exhibition of students' works generated a larger, more diverse audience for the Rhein und Maas show than would otherwise have been possible.

Perhaps one significant sign for the future can be noted in a recently convened meeting in Helsinki of the Finnish ministry of education and the directors of the museums of Finland. Here they attempted to create policy for the integration of museums into the total spectrum of Finnish education—from kindergarten to vocational schools to adult education. Whatever the patterns of relationship, one thing is clear: the museums and a new public constituency have discovered each other—the charge of museum elitism is a thing of the past. Indeed, there are signs that public demand may be in excess of what the museums can accommodate, on an economic as well as a philosophical level. The curatorial function of museums is still of paramount importance, and the task which lies ahead for museum staffs in the United States as well as in the rest of the world will be to accommodate both connoisseurs and amateurs with some degree of finesse.

SPECIAL PROJECTS

Many museums provide special programs for students—Saturday clubs and summer holiday projects—as well as programs for special children that require the student to come to the museum alone, without the school's participation. Again, many of the European programs are similar to those in America; however, in European and Soviet museums the atmosphere seems more like that of a club for students interested in art rather than like a class that meets on Saturdays or during the vacation period (although these situations also exist). For instance, many of the English museums have a Saturday Art Club. One such weekend organization, founded by the Art Gallery and Museum of Glasgow in 1945, is still limited to sixty-five members, from ten to eighteen years old. Divided into three age groups, the morning activities, which are held from October through March, include painting, archaeology, film appreciation, and puppetry. Current emphasis in these activities is on creative work, and the finished art pieces are always exhibited in the museum at the end of the year.

To join the Saturday Club at the City Museum and Art Gallery in Birmingham, England, the prospective club member must complete an entrance project. This can be a booklet of drawings of museum objects accompanied by notes on the pieces, or it can be a short essay on one of the civilizations represented in the museum collection. Club membership is open to students between eight and fifteen years of age; there is, however, a limit of sixty members. Once the project is completed and the application is made, the prospective club member must regularly attend all meetings for a period of three months; in addition, he or she must show evidence of sufficient knowledge in some special field encompassed by the museum collection before being awarded full membership in the group.

Education for children at the Tate Gallery, London, has been referred to as "Creative Appreciation." Working with innovative special projects entitled "Kidsplay" and "Tate Games," children have had the opportunity to develop a deeper understanding and enjoyment of art works. Body movements, rhythms, and extemporizations encourage the children to relate to the constructions and compositions of art works by building their own art objects on the premises. It is almost impossible for the children not to be active, not to want to do things, not to wonder about their environment, not to explore and perceive. The primary objective of the museum in arranging such an educational experience was to attract children to the museum who would not normally come on their own accord.

The Tate Gallery has also had exemplar holiday summer school projects, one of which was originally called "Kidsplay" and evolved into a program entitled "Tate Games." This project was a drop-in affair, whereby the children participated as often and whenever they wished. Basic to the conception of "Kidsplay" was the objective that anything done by the museum should focus the attention of children on the art works in the collection. In these discovery-based learning environments of the participatory exhibitions, children were encouraged by the fun-and-games atmosphere. All of the games, however, tended to be didactic experiences intended to encourage a response to works of art. These activities, strategies, and educational techniques owe their conceptions to the museum educational staff's familiarity with the way that artists exhibiting at the Tate work and think. Tate Museum educators have the opportunity to constantly meet active artists—a situation unique to contemporary art museums. This permits the educational programs at the museum to evolve from the elements of the creative process that have actually brought these art works to the museum exhibit area. Concepts of perspective, illusion, and construction systems involved in specific art works have been designed with participatory theater approaches and have served to create the environments of "Kidsplay."

Visual quotations from works of art provide the key to the special projects of education at the Tate. Paraphrased quotations of such artists as surrealist Rene Magritte and contemporary British sculptor Robyn Denny, who have had retrospective exhibitions at the museum, have provided the substance of the participatory games for children at the museum. For instance, one of the "Kidsplay" projects included an upside-down room which, when viewed from the exterior, was a form of solid geometry intruding into the gallery space but was painted atmospherically, like a three-dimensional piece by Magritte. Such an installation, designed to expose children to experiences of perspective and to perceptions of shapes and dimensions, provides the children with opportunities for the manipulation of color and the perception of illusion. Through play, children participating in these Tate Museum educational programs have discovered the excitement of creating combinations of color and shapes by design, discovery, and experimentation. In addition, these installations, such as the one in which a maze of colored glass creates an environment, have permitted children to form their images from spontaneous movements rather than from manipulation.

Such fantastic numbers of children have responded to the annual development of these educational programs that these projects have often exhausted the Tate Gallery services and currently there are less programs offered of this material at the museum. The museum found that there were neither enough lavatories nor enough eating areas; however, this has not totally stopped the expansion of their educational offerings. When the staff needed more space for the educational programs, the director had a large circus-like tent erected on the lawn in front of the Tate Gallery, thus creating individual galleries for the use of these educational experiences. In these well-designed, temporary modules, the museum educators accommodated the massive artistic response of the children and assisted the students through exploratory experiences and encounters before the actual art works on exhibit in the museum were viewed. These learning environments were not an aside to the effective gallery operations but were the heart of these museum experiences. Such modules continue to be used today, but only for exhibition purposes.

Like their American counterparts, some European museum educators have developed certain programs for disadvantaged visitors—children as well as adults. The Musée National du Louvre and the Victoria and Albert Museum conduct tours for blind students. However, one of the best facilities for the visually handicapped is the Blinden Museum in the Staatliche Museen Preussischer Kulturbesitz, Dahlem, Berlin, Deutschland (West Germany). An area about the size of a classroom was enclosed on all four sides by shadow-box cabinets encircled by a railing. Lined with foam rubber, each shadow box contains one of the objects that is part of the exhibition. The objects are loosely affixed to the shadow boxes by wires so that the visitors can handle the pieces, but they cannot be removed from the display cases. Moreover, the foam rubber protects the art works. Standing out from the shadow boxes, the railing acts as a guide for the blind students going from one exhibit to the next; it also provides a place from which a cane can be hung. The Braille identification plates in front of the objects and the informative recording concerned with the exhibit provide the students with the opportunity to visualize the exhibit independently and at their own pace. Begun in December 1970, the Blinden Museum has had such exhibits as "Jewelry of Non-European People," "Spoons and Dishes from Africa," and "Sculptures of Non-European People." All objects are original pieces of art, and the museum has more than one sample of each. The director of the Blinden Museum has found that the best exhibition pieces are objects whose surface structures are not too complicated and diversified; also, art that is not commonly used in Europe is popular, since these types of objects often stimulate the visitor's curiosity.

SUMMARY

The educational staffs of international art museums are striving to provide the stimulation for learning and discovery that can only come through contact with actual art objects, with the creative works of artists, and with the great minds and ideas that have produced these works.[7] Through these public-accessible institutions, all types of students are offered living, concrete proof that human beings are capable of restoring, consciously and on a level of meaning, a blend of the sense, need, impulse, and action characteristic of the human being. Today, the international art museum is an art education institution that offers art as a conscious idea and as the greatest intellectual achievement in the history of humanity. It is also an active facility for teaching the artistic and cultural heritage in society.

NOTES

1. Robert W. Ott, "Teaching Art Awareness in Museums," *Art Teacher* 7, no. 1 (1977): 18–19.
2. Ott, "Art Museum Education: Issues and Methods for Aesthetic Education in the Art Museum" (Post-doctoral thesis, Univ. of London, 1975).

3. Lois Swan Jones, "Volunteer-Guides and Classroom Teachers in School-Visitation Programs in European and North American Art Museums," *Studies in Art Education* 18, no. 3 (1977): 31–41.

4. Questionnaires concerning the school-visitation programs were answered by the personnel in the following twelve European institutions: in Deutschland, Staatliche Museen Preussischer Kulturbesitz, Berlin; Aussenreferat der Kolner Museen, Cologne; Museumspädagogisches Zentrum, Munich; in England, City Museum & Art Gallery, Birmingham; British Museum and the Tate Gallery, London; in France, Musée National du Louvre, Paris; in Poland, Muzeum Narodowe w Warszawie, Warsaw; in Scotland, Art Gallery and Museum, Glasgow; in Sweden, Göteborgs Konstmuseum, Göteborg; Nationalmuseum, Stockholm; and in Hungary, Szépművészeti Múzeum, Budapest.

5. Gerard Van der Hoek, "De Educatievedienst van het Rijksmuseum," *Bulletin Van Het Rijksmuseum* 3 (1970): 104–25.

6. Koscielecki's book, *Wspolcaesna knocepcja wychowania plastycanego*, is based upon the visual learning laboratory that is part of the museum program.

7. Ott, "Art Museum Education: Past and Present Issues," *The Penn State Papers in Art Education* 1 (1977): 105–23.

National Examinations in Art

William Bradley

The concept of examinations as they are currently applied in various countries did not directly derive from art teaching practices nor from a particular need of the art world to make assessments of their own pupils and students. Examinations in art were eventually deemed important, following along with general concerns for normalizing instruction toward agreed-upon standards. These concerns were at first directed toward general literacy in reading and writing and reflected the growing recognition that certain pedagogies seemed superior to others in instructing increasingly diverse abilities.

When there had developed a serious interest in establishing a way of identifying individuals who are capable of pursuing university studies, the form and content of general examinations were set by the various academic areas concerned with the political and social interests of established governments, such as those of England, the United States, and France. Of these three countries, only England and the United States remained resolved in their social interest in art instruction for more than seventy-five years. Many other countries, as a result of various political upheavals, have not exhibited a consistent development of examination policies, and formerly colonized countries continue to alter, change, or abolish previous examination structures in favor of a newly rising social consciousness. Some countries, such as Germany and Denmark, have never established national art examinations at the precollege level. Until recently the United States had also avoided any concerted effort to develop nationally standardized art instruction.

Such reservations against examinations that systematically remove local control over curricula are not uncommon, even in countries where such examinations have a long history. These reservations continue to be centered in the art education world itself, despite external pressure for the art curricula to fall into the more acceptable and general pattern of the examined pedagogy. Some of the reasons for these persistent reservations will be discussed later in this chapter.

Examination can be linked to the history of formal and symbolic logic in that, at best, it implies a search for causes of behavior and, at worst, it assumes that causes of behavior are known. This history may also be linked to the replacement of the delicate nature of human valuation by a concept of service to technology and society. As such, it is not remarkable that fields such as visual art, theater, dance, and, in some ways, music have resisted a heavy reliance upon examination to determine either curricula or developmental growth. But more instructive, perhaps, is the persistent agreement exhibited in all the reports of examinations I have read, that to arrive at acceptable standards of performance in art through agreed-upon criteria seems to eliminate the notion of individual chance discovery felt to be so important in the assessment of growth and potential in the arts.

I shall attempt to describe national examinations as they currently exist in several countries and then to cite and evaluate specific examples of the differing emphases exhibited in the references contained herein. Originally representatives from twenty countries were contacted, but the returned documents represent only a portion of these and only four can be adequately discussed. Nonetheless, such an analysis will represent a start toward international understanding of the problems faced by art education colleagues worldwide in assessing not only the cultural heritage of individual groups but the more ancient artistic heritage that has about it a desired universal quality.

INTERNAL VERSUS EXTERNAL ASSESSMENT

Recent developments in England account for a general disenchantment with remote or external standards for local teachers and pupils. In 1975 the Schools Council commissioned a group to critically study the established General Certificate of Education examinations with a rubric to recommend change. Based in Newcastle upon Tyne, this Art Group found that one of the chief inadequacies of the English examination system was that there were too many exclusions of talent as the exams stood in relation to a diversity of emphases in the contemporary art world. That is, examinations at the ordinary ("O") level and the advanced ("A") level should balance between the theoretical and the practical. It was felt that there were several disadvantages to an emphasis either way, and one of these is particularly striking: "The disadvantage of an exclusively theoretical course would be [that] it would exclude from the course the concrete exploration essential to the fulfillment and reinforcement of theoretical study."[1] This assertion would suggest that a shift (or at least an acknowledgment) toward internal evaluation is essential.

National art examinations find their strength in the "Critical and Analytical" potential of art programs, but the foregoing assertion would propose that critical and analytical exclusivity would produce as much of a prejudicial examination as an exclusively practical one. The balance between the theoretical and the practical will be shown to be a universal consideration in the planning of national examinations in the countries discussed. The credibility of this distinction will be related to certain other common factors of concern in the general social attitude of the role of art in culture.

It should be noted that the same study group in England made a separate but equally strong assertion regarding the relationship of external to internal interpretation of a pupil's progress. They wrote: "It is considered that candidates in Art should be assessed internally with external moderation. This has the advantage of combining unbiased objectivity with a close knowledge of the individual circumstances of the candidate."[1]

Although this localization could be seen as an extension of a much earlier English decision to move in this direction, the study group's report proposes a more radical attempt to bring to local school systems a share in the ultimate evaluation of their own pupils. Little has been done to alter the examination precepts developed by the study group; later descriptions of examinations in Great Britain have tended to distinguish between the concept of accountability and that of examination.[2]

In Nigeria the problem of criteria localization is a social necessity, for there are regional considerations that have developed over the long history of occupation by various local and foreign powers. For example, the Islam region of Nigeria will not permit representation in art-making. Thus, there are no examples within that region that would correspond to figural or natural-life studies. It is forbidden. But the Yoruba not only produce figural sculpture and other designs, they insist upon a tradition within art instruction to insure perpetuity. Other areas work almost exclusively with ceramics. The difficulties of a national assessment of art pupils in Nigeria are, therefore, compounded, yet these examinations exist. The English and Nigerian examples may only illustrate the internal-external issue in extreme because the perpetual issue of an orientation toward social demands, as opposed to one toward individual demands, is much more deeply embedded in the world of art, artists, and art education. It is neither surprising nor disappointing to find it at the center of controversy in assessment.

No national assessment has occurred in countries such as France and Germany because of a larger history of a breach between theory and practice in those countries. In the United States attempts have been made sporadically to normalize curricula through examination, but these have only been regional—such as Regents' examinations, which are still in partial use in the state of New York—until quite recently. These examinations are exemplary of attempts in the United States to normalize instruction and are related to the larger issues of linking experimentation to curricula.

There are some apparent advantages to external evaluations, as expressed in Allison's paper: "The emphatic wish of the majority of art teachers not to be solely responsible for assessing their pupils' work is also based upon the belief that to actually act as the 'assessor' may spoil the personal relationships which they, albeit temporarily, feel they develop with their pupils. Many feel more comfortable that the 'good' or 'bad' news regarding assessment should come from 'anonymous authority.'"[3] It has been my experience that a general departmental assessment of a student's progress is considered less onerous than a personal rejection, although I have never subscribed to this view. The student is usually less upset by the judgment of a panel of judges than that of a single person, regardless of his or her prestige. This practice, however, removes itself from the very issue that many art educators feel important: that the apprenticeship of a pupil is superior to his status as a pupil.

Another real advantage in external evaluation is the elimination or the diminution of attention to trivial and uninspiring activity by poorly educated teachers. People untrained in art thinking and in productive ways of knowing the world are often placed in classrooms for strictly economic convenience. They often rely upon notions detrimental to art learning and are responsible for promoting a view of the art process as idle, time-consuming activity (for example, the prepared kits, the imitative seasonal displays, and the subservience of manual activity to the service of social studies). External evaluation affords one way of ensuring some aspects of authentic art learning not found in these situations.

The question of internal evaluation is predicated upon the assumption that the foregoing situation does not exist. However, it is clear to educators worldwide that it does.

Even when well-intended art educators are at work, there is (at least in the United States, France, and England) the pitiful relegation of art activity to a few minutes per week. This tends to reduce the quality of experience. External evaluation often has the potential to correct this reduction. No concerted effort has been made to counter the almost insidious encroachment of external controls on the affairs of the individual meanings discovered locally. Foremost among attempts must be the

Schools Council project in England, which, while attempting to decipher the program distinctions of the "not-college-bound pupil" (the "N," or normal, level, referring to a curriculum for general education) and the "college-bound" pupil (the "F" level, meaning a curriculum for "future" studies), have actually engaged the issues of local control. The attempt here is to provide dual-track national examinations that also supply regional and local determinants.

In the Nigerian program such a distinction is not so clear, for examinations are linked to a social necessity to provide designers for a growing economy similar to the earliest developments in the United States. As previously outlined, the Nigerian problem is one which must bring the indigenous diversity of a people to collectively contribute to the work force in a third-world nation.

The move toward centralization of criteria seems closely linked to the success of technology within a culture—yet glaring examples oppose this observation. In West Germany, for instance, there are no national examinations, and in Japan national examinations below the university level seem nonexistent. Still, in both of these cases, attempts are being made to centralize examinations or to determine general university entrance requirements.

The marriage between external or remote examination of progress and local, more intimate involvement in examination criteria is an issue in which the humanistic interest in subjective, individually based discovery is opposed to a social necessity enervated by social survival itself.

EXAMINATIONS AND CURRICULA

It is reasonably clear that to establish any assessment is to produce a curriculum to accommodate it. Issues raised around this fact merit some discussion. These issues are not peculiar to art; in fact, it is common to hear the accusation that pupils are being trained to score well on examinations. An examination of the pros and cons of this position is thus in order. In countries where no national examinations exist, the issue is at best pedantic and at worst absurd. However, a careful look at these countries provides only a slight clue as to national intent, for even without national examinations, a national ethos prevails. An example of this is seen in the New Asia College of the University of Hong Kong, where the entrance examinations demonstrate a national intent. While it is clear that little attention is given to the expressive qualities of a pupil's work, considerable regard is shown to evidence of an understanding of the history of the culture itself.[4] Thus, it is clear that there is a national policy with an educational goal without the necessity of a national examination.

One might suspect that in other countries (West Germany, Japan, Brazil, and Denmark, for example) where no national examinations exist, the rubric for art education is similarly disseminated. In the United States an unspecified ethos pervades. Although a current concern is to link artistic learning with cognition and the learnings which proceed from other social science areas, there remains an unspecified national intent: to provide an American art education. The question thus becomes one of patriotism: an art in the service of a country. In England art educators have made a case for the value of national examinations. The Schools Council research groups were clearly in favor of the continuation of their national system under certain specified conditions (as, for example, the triadic distribution of areas: theoretical, complimentary, and practical), wherein external examiners would join the local faculty in determining the rightness of criteria. Although the promotions of this report are postsecondary in nature, the endorsement is favorable to national assessment.

In Allison's paper the connection is made still clearer:

> External examinations, whatever their shortcomings, do have an important and influential effect on what goes on in schools throughout the whole of formal general education, particularly when teachers in schools are involved in their development. Despite this involvement at the interface of educational endeavor, however, teachers alone cannot provide the perspective from which meaningful curricula can be developed, and realization of this will bring about the most positive developments in English art and design education.[3]

Curriculum development in the United States is often linked to the potential of national assessment. The Aesthetic Education movement of the Central Midwest Regional Laboratory at St. Louis (CEMREL) attempted to specify what was to be learned in the art classroom (particularly in the primary grades) and to bring to an assessable level the learnings produced. The results of this effort are still highly controversial and are not widely used.

The United States, however, has turned its most remote bastions, including art, to servicing its national goals. This attitude is best realized in the organization called "National Assessment." This organization did not begin with art—it encompassed it. It was felt that it would be possible to identify the art values of the country and to provide a means to assure that these values were phrased in a way that would ensure perpetuity; certain historical elements were to be accommodated and linked to a notion of what young children should learn. It was clear that relationships between these notions of history would be inculcated into a social order by requiring pupils to identify relationships with their culture. It is also suggested that certain process skills would be introduced to ensure the social and cultural intent. Therefore, the curriculum proposed was to be in service of these goals.

The more intercultural aspects of assessment have not been adequately attended to as yet—but national assessment has not yet been established in America. Nonetheless, attempts continue, with the general support of the federal government. There is still the question as to whether such an assessment should come to be. On the one side, there is interest in external examination, while, on the other, there is a continued demand that accountability be reserved for regional and local authorities. It is clear that the arts are vulnerable on this score, and particularly since a general accountability is often demanded by taxpayers. Yet, as Margaret Mead once told me, "the only reason the arts have survived in America is because they have never been funded!" We must wonder whether a national accountability in the arts would be positive. Would the establishment of a national curriculum help or hinder the delicate life of art in the United States or China or West Germany?

SOME DIFFERING EMPHASES

Several "culture specific" emphases are identifiable within the national examinations currently used, and the almost dichotomous movement toward and away from centralization of criteria is of interest in certain of the examples. A look at some of these examination criteria will bring the conflicting movements into better focus.

Nigeria. The West African Examinations Council was developed under British colonial conditions and, as such, followed many of the general patterns of content. However, the 1970 West African School Certificate and the General Certificate of Education (GCE) examinations clearly demonstrate an attempt to link both content and process with cultural considerations. Examples of problems encountered in a University of London examination utilized in Nigeria and by the West African Examinations Council demonstrate these considerations.[5]

> A. University of London (GCE Ordinary level) Art 25:020. Main paper 3—"Drawing and Painting from a Theme." Six hours.

Please feel free to interpret ONE of these themes in any way you wish.

a. This house has been far out at sea all night.
The woods cracking through darkness, the booming hills.
Winds stampeding the fields under the window
Floundering black astride and blinding wet
Till day rose; then under an orange sky
The hills and new places, and wind
Blade light, luminous black and emerald,
Flexing like the lens of a mad eye.

From "Wind"
Ted Hughes

b. Fruit pickers
c. Ramps and steps
d. Urban clearway: night
e. Warm reds, cool blues
f. Boatyard

The nature of choices of themes seems linked to the experiences of the pupils under consideration. "Ramps and steps" and "Urban clearway" are particularly related to the likelihood of having encountered these urban scenes within the course of living in such a technological society (perhaps not in rural England).

These set examinations, although still used in West Africa, have been altered to accommodate the nature of life in that country.[6]

B. W.A.S.C./GCE (West African Version). Art 4. 3 hours. Original Imaginative Composition in Color.
You are required to make an original composition based on one of the subjects given overleaf below. In making your choice you should consider which subjects are best suited to your style of work. . . .
. . . (3) It is very easy to know Yekinis' pay day. He comes home in the evening unusually gay and loud. He immediately summons his friends—Jide, Sunmola, and Monsuru—with whom he sits outside on the pavement chatting loudly, singing, and drinking palm wine (or the local wine) well into the night.

The London-based examinations with cultural embellishments persist in many parts of Africa once held by the British, and current third-world attempts at curriculum reform promise to influence the general character of them. According to Felix Ekeada, if a general culture-specific intent in Nigerian curricula could be spoken of, it would be related to the governmental attempt to develop a work force. This, however, is speculation, as the current examination structure continues to reflect its colonial base.

Hong Kong. No national examinations as such exist in Hong Kong. However, the New Asia College of the University of Hong Kong is included here because its matriculation requirements show, in effect, ways in which the training toward particular goals is accomplished at the preuniversity level.

The central thrust of the matriculation examination at the New College of Asia is to identify individuals rounded in several aspects of art. Any student entering the university must pass an examination in five areas out of thirteen, and these include competencies in the Chinese and English languages and in histories of both the West and the East.

The Hong Kong example is unique in its attempt to include East-West considerations of history and practice. Although it may only reflect the East-West nature of its culture, it is exemplary at a time when international understanding is of such strong interest and urgency. While this examination is not truly a national examination, it is sufficiently tied to national interests to warrant mention here.

Typical of the concern over intercultural understanding is the attempt to understand the oriental influences among such painters as Delacroix, Monet, Manet, and Fantin La Tour. Thus, by the time he or she leaves school, the Hong Kong pupil is well versed in Western as well as Eastern art history and appreciation. This situation is unusual among the examinations reviewed for this article.

England. England's history of National Examination extends farther than that of most other countries. The relationship of the ordinary ("O" level) examinations in art and the advanced ("A" level) examinations in art to the broader program of English examination is intricate and often difficult for a foreigner to grasp. The program's growth has not always been systematic, but it continues to represent a belief that external examination of curricula is necessary to ensure quality. Some of the more recent thought on national examinations in England and Wales is innovative and interesting.

The 1964 School Council's 18+ Research Programme, through the Syllabus Steering Group, attempted to provide two levels that could eventually lead to a replacement of the older, A-level examination. This would offer an art education to pupils who intended no further (N-level) art study and to those who intended further (F-level) study. This distinction expanded the concept of art syllabus content.

One innovative dimension of the new examination proposals is the inclusion of an area referred to as "Critical and Analytical Studies," which evolved from the more specific concepts of design, environment, and visual education. The mode by which such an education would take place was also innovative. That is, through a modular structure it would be possible to integrate various areas of art and design, and possibly with other subject areas. Analysis and criticism would become legitimate content for this new modular approach.

There seems to be agreement in England that examinations and the curricula which support them, or those that are influenced by them, should be developed only with teacher participation. Still, the examination boards expect to reserve for themselves the final judgments regarding individual teacher proposals.

The Netherlands (Eindexamens).[7] Since 1968, officials in the Netherlands have been conducting experimental national examinations as a means by which to assess the four components of art education: drawing, music, arts and crafts—handicrafts, and arts and crafts—textiles. Music, drawing, and arts and crafts were established as compulsory subjects in the Netherlands in 1968. Music is considered a component of art education.

The examinations for the school types called "MAVO," "HAVO," and "VWO" are occupationally oriented. For instance, at the MAVO level, examinations given to pupils between the ages of twelve and sixteen have the lowest academic standards and prepare pupils for entrance into intermediate vocational training programs; on the other hand, the HAVO level examination, although offered to the same age group (up to seventeen years), prepares the students for higher vocational training including the colleges of Education. The VWO level examination, offered to youngsters between the ages of twelve and eighteen, prepares for university entrance. University entrance is in fact closed to those who have not successfully completed this examination.[7]

The examinations are both theoretical and practical. For drawing, handicrafts, and textiles, the theoretical component of the tests is appreciation as well as the history of art and civilization. While the MAVO exam tests primarily on nineteenth- and twentieth-century movements in art, handicraft, and textile (including industrial design), the HAVO exam includes a longer history, beginning with the Romanesque period. The VWO examination extends this history and will continue as an experiment until 1985, when it will become a standard examination.

Assessment of these examinations is based upon the use of model-answers as guidelines. The theoretical component of the examinations is considered "national" in that it is standardized throughout the Netherlands.

The practical component of the Netherland exams is generally referred to as the "school exam." Here the work produced by pupils is assessed in one of three ways: (1) over a certain period (two or three months), (2) during a specific, prearranged test period, or (3) a combination of these. The actual organization and assessment of this school exam is entrusted to the schools—a practice which thus achieves regional and local variety.

Since the examination structure in the Netherlands is both newly in place and dynamic, it is expected to develop and change. To date, the school-leaving examination has not included art education. It is projected that this examination will expand to include music, drawing, and arts and crafts in the near future. It should be noted that the actual examination brochures are visually exciting, being in full color, and the spread of content is clearly evident in them.

In summary, interest in external evaluation along standardized concepts appears to be increasing in several countries. The nature of these examinations seems to reflect new world concerns for heritage, ecology, the interrelationship of the arts, and connections with other subject areas.

It is equally interesting to find that movements toward developing national examinations are concerned with preserving regional and local influences and providing a general arts education for pupils who will not pursue further education in the arts.

NOTES

1. Schools Council 18+ Research Programme, studies based on the N and F Proposals (Fine Arts), November 1976.

2. Calouste Gulbenkian Foundation, *The Arts for Schools: Principles, Practice and Provision* (London: Calouste Gulbenkian Foundation, 1982).

3. B. Allison, "Problems and Recent Developments for Art-Design Examinations in England," *Art Education*, NAEA (December 1977).

4. Matriculation Regulations, *The Chinese University of Hong Kong* (Hong Kong, 1977).

5. University of London, *General Certificate of Education Examination*, 020/021, Art, Ordinary Level (January 1975).

6. West African Examinations Council, *Schools Certificate and G.C.E. Exams* (November 1970).

7. Guus Broeders, "Experimental Examinations in Art Education by the Netherlands," unpublished article (Utrecht, 1977).

Issues in Empirical Cross-Cultural Research in Arts Education

Frances E. Anderson

Researchers engage in cross-cultural inquiry for a number of reasons. Some wish to further the frontiers of knowledge, others to test hypotheses, to develop new theories, or to extend existing theories. There are, in particular, some mixed motives in the literature on cross-culture in some psychological research (Brislin 1975; Lonner 1975). Thus, I caution researchers in art education who are about to engage in cross-cultural research and make a strong plea for rigorous scholarship, planning, methodology, and reporting of research—especially if research is to be executed across several cultures and/or nations. For both neophyte and seasoned researchers, there are some important guidelines that can facilitate the endeavor and, most importantly, result in qualitatively outstanding cross-cultural study.

While Berry and Dasen refer specifically to the cross-cultural study of cognitive functioning, their overview of the field is particularly relevant to this discussion, especially if the word *artistic* is substituted for *cognitive*. They refer to two specific goals in a study of cognitive (artistic) functions in various cultures. Their study (1) "attempts to understand the range, the variability, [and] the differences in cognitive (artistic) processes as a function of cultures, including ecological and social variables" and (2) "attempts to understand the uniformities, the pan-human or cross-cultural consistency in cognitive (artistic) processes, so that valid generalizations may be made about human cognitive (artistic) functioning" (1975, 13). Thus, there are three aims in such study from a Western perspective: (1) "to transport our present hypotheses and laws to other cultural settings to test their applicability or generalizability"; (2) "to explore new cultural systems to discover cognitive (artistic) variations and differences we have not experienced within our own cultural context"; and (3) "to compare our prior understanding with our newer knowledge within diverse cultures to generate more universal descriptions, hypotheses, and laws of human cognitive (artistic) functioning" (Berry and Dasen 1975, 14). These worthy aims must be accomplished with research that is firmly grounded in theory and significant to each culture in question. The research should be on a problem that is either common to or shared by both cultures and has relevance to a field of study (in this case, art education) as well as to contemporary social issues (Berrien 1970). Moreover, such research should be in a well-developed area of a field to which a transcultural dimension would add needed perspective and insight.

Once the research problem is confirmed, it will be necessary to establish a common baseline of performance that is inherent in the individual organism, in the stimulus, and in the relationship between them. As with all research, it is crucial to avoid comparisons of "apples and oranges." Berry and Dasen feel that it is essential to compare more than one Western and non-Western cultural group. They recommend three as a minimal number and urge that more than three cultural groups be studied. Moreover, they suggest a combination of and balance between the *etic* and the *emic* approaches to cross-cultural study. In the etic approach the investigator's entrance into a culture is made with a method and structure for study that is *external* to that particular culture. As this approach is implemented, a concurrent empathy and comprehension for the perspective of the native who is in the culture is developed—that is, the emic approach (Pike 1966). This within-culture empathy (the emic approach) modifies the etic approach yet does not totally dissipate it. Such a combination of both approaches results in a derived etic approach, which can be used in other studies as the "initial etic" component (Berry and Dasen 1975).

In attempting to tell how comparisons are to be made among cultural groups, there are four major principles that must be acknowledged: the functional, conceptual, metric, and motivational equivalents (Berry and Dasen 1975; Triandis et al. 1972). In comparing different cultural groups, it is necessary to develop a "functional equivalence of behaviors" (Berry and Dasen 1975, 15) so that equivalent data on performances can be obtained and comparisons made. Conceptual equivalence means building in the same meaning (or lack thereof) in instruments used, concepts tested, and apparatus utilized. It also aims at a careful and sensitive language translation. This can be achieved by using the technique of back translation, in which an independent interpreter translates the already-translated language intended for use in data collection or testing. If these two translations are very similar, then there is a good possibility that conceptual equivalence has been established.

In addition to back translation, Werner and Campbell (1970) make these suggestions. In the initial version of the translation, simple sentences should be used and nouns repeated instead of using pronouns. Slang, metaphors, or other colloquialisms should be avoided. Whole paragraphs should be translated instead of individual words, and different words should be used if a series of questions is being asked about a particular situation or concept.

Metric equivalence emphasizes the necessity to study behavior within cultural groups as well as across groups. This is especially necessary before making hypotheses about group differences. The issue of motivational equivalence is also crucial in cross-cultural research (Triandis et al. 1972). While working against the clock or with great speed on a task may be a prime method of motivation in Western culture, in many parts of the world the concept of a timed performance or working with speed does not exist. Therefore, it cannot be assumed that competing against the clock is always a motivating factor. Timed tests may indeed be a totally inappropriate method of data collecting in a non-Western culture. A high level of competitiveness may exist in a group or between individuals, and this can affect motivation and even interfere with the testing and collection of responses. Also, in some cultures, individuals respond negatively to being tested anonymously, preferring instead being singled out. It is thus necessary to pretest and interview subjects to check their reactions to participating in an anonymous study (Triandis et al. 1972).

There are also some specific points to remember about collecting data. It may be surprising to realize that the body of knowledge in Western-world psychology is estimated by some researchers to be based on no more than 1% of the population of the world. The researcher must avoid a pseudo-approach to data collection where American instruments, based on American theory, are simply transposed (Triandis et al. 1972). It is essential to realize that in specific testing situations, subjects may be unfamiliar with Western methods and this in itself may produce anxiety and influence the responses of the subjects.

There also may be different reactions to the experimenter who is doing the actual collection of data. He or she may not be well received—or may be received too well, resulting in efforts on the part of the subjects to "please the researcher" and give responses they think the researcher wants to obtain. To remediate such a situation, native experimenters and other similar testing situations have been suggested (Triandis et al. 1972). An alternative to this would be to have as varying conditions and kinds of experimenters as possible. It also may make sense to use a graduating steps design if tasks are unfamiliar to the subjects. This design enables subjects to move in a systematic, gradual way into unfamiliar tasks and would look like the following suggested by Price-Williams (1975, 46):

Step	Task	Material	Content
zero level	familiar	familiar	familiar
one	familiar	unfamiliar	familiar
two	familiar	familiar	unfamiliar
three	familiar	unfamiliar	unfamiliar
four	unfamiliar	unfamiliar	unfamiliar

In data collection the response style of the subjects must also be considered. Some persons always agree with questions; others may have an extreme checking style, marking the extremes on a scale. To ameliorate this, a Q-sort technique has been suggested, in which responses are placed into three stacks: agree, disagree, and uncertain (Triandis et al. 1972).

A cross-cultural study should be a collaborative effort, including researchers from each culture who then become a team. Each member should have the support of his or her own institution and should have a chance to place his or her own interpretation on the data collected. The reporting of the findings should also be a joint endeavor in the form of an article or a presentation at a professional meeting.

A perusal of the analyses of the characteristics of the strongest and the weakest manuscripts submitted during the first three years of the *Journal of Cross-Cultural Psychology*'s publications may help recap the discussions thus far (Lonner 1975). According to the journal reviewers, a strong manuscript had explicitly stated methods, a frame of reference that was clearly established (grounded in theory from a specific field). The instruments used were established ones with tested reliability and validity. There were direct educational implications and a wedding of theory with reality in terms of the culture (clear rationale and combination of psychological and anthropological constructs). Sampling was large and there was some novelty in the design. The major weakness of manuscripts included the use of samples that were "casual," "convenient," or "accidental" (Lonner 1975, 314)—which made it impossible to generalize about the cultures studied. There was a lack of both a rigorous theory base and an established link between psychological and anthropological factors. Weak studies used instruments with poor translation and little established reliability and validity. Also, these instruments were used indiscriminately. Finally, poor manuscripts had several possible hypotheses to explain the findings and were too verbose in their discussions and analyses of the findings.

Within this discussion there is a note of reality which must be sounded. From my own experience (Anderson 1976) I have found that cross-cultural research is not as easy an endeavor to pursue as one might think. In cross-cultural research the investigator operates in a field situation and must make some sacrifice in terms of control in conducting these studies (Berry and Dasen 1975; Kerlinger 1972). There is a greater chance for generalization in a field study because a few abstractions have been made to "fit" the behavior into the laboratory setting. Research is never easy, even in industrialized nations, and is much more difficult in different cultures (Frijda and Jahoda 1966).

By taking a specific case in point and examining cross-cultural research using esthetic evaluations, some of the problems involved can be readily observed. In the discussion of work in this area, remarks will be limited to the research of I. L. Child of Yale University. His work began with the development of a test of esthetic sensitivity (Child 1962, 1965), which he initially used in research in this country. In developing this instrument, Child began with a large pool of pairs of visual examples of art, architecture, furniture, paintings, and sculptures, which were matched for subject matter but differed in their "esthetic merit" as determined by art experts. The initial pool had 3,360 paired works. When twelve of fourteen art experts agreed on a slide item in a pair, that pair was retained. In this way a smaller pool of 1,270 pairs was obtained. From this pool 120 slide pairs were randomly selected, and this made up the Child Test of Esthetic Sensitivity. This CTES was administered to adults whose mean score was 74. Agreement scores ranged from 44 to 104 agreement. The alfa coefficient of 87 indicated satisfactory reliability (Child 1965). This slide test, in varying lengths (ranging from 80 slide pairs to 130), was subsequently used in a series of cross-cultural studies which focused on attempts to answer the questions: "Is there such a construct as a universal esthetic that transcends culture barriers?" and "What personality traits are associated with sensitivity to esthetic values?"

I must admit that I have some reservations about the instrument that Child developed to measure esthetic judgments. Although it has a few slide pairs on the CTES of purely abstract visual stimuli and some visual stimuli that are culture specific to some of those cultures under study, the CTES needs more of these examples. Inclusion of stimuli such as the black and white patterns used by Ross (1976) and Berelyne (1975) would strengthen the test as a measure of universal esthetic judgment. In addition, research with the CTES would be strengthened if some of the variety of methods used by Ross and Berelyne to obtain subjects' responses were employed. It would also seem important to include examples of art and artifacts that are culture specific to *each* group, nation, or culture under study, thereby helping to build in functional and conceptual equivalence (Gordon and Kikuchi 1966). Finally, several different measures and methods of assessing esthetic judgments would be helpful in such research because the nature of making esthetic judgments is extremely complex.

In summary, then, cross-cultural research must be meticulously planned and piloted well in advance of the data collection for a particular study. I urge anyone who is contemplating cross-cultural work to adhere to as many as possible of the guidelines already discussed. Moreover, investigators are urged to thoroughly develop their testing instruments before going into foreign territory. A sound grounding in theory of a research problem is crucial. That problem should be significant to each of the three or more cultures that are going to be studied. A clear and careful collaboration of the research team is essential, as is the opportunity for investigators in each culture under study to have a chance to interpret the data (Berrien 1970). Finally, there is also a need for consistent, clear reporting of findings in a manner which enables replication.

Few studies in art education have adhered to the guidelines discussed above. One such exemplar of an outstanding cross-cultural study in art education is the Hess-Behrens study (1973). This study of the development of spatial concepts in children's drawings was grounded in the theories of Piaget and was based on collected drawings (using standardized instruction and materials) from lower- and middle-class boys and girls in nine countries. One hundred drawings were obtained from each of grades 1, 3, 5, and 7—that is, about 900 per country. Extra data from some nongraded groups pushed the final data total to 9,000 drawings. This data was carefully sorted and then judged as to Piaget's descriptors of stages in the growth of logical thought and the development of spatial concepts. The findings indicate that these stages in drawings follow a sequence that does not vary.

I would like to conclude by repeating here some of the tongue-in-cheek "advice" about the reporting of cross-cultural research given at the first meeting of the International Association for Cross-Cultural Psychology, Hong Kong, in 1972, recounted first by Lonner (1975, 315–17).

(1) Admit that a certain technique was chosen for convenience so that long, individual data-gathering sessions would not be necessary. . . .
(2) Use instruments for which the overwhelming body of evidence indicates no reliability or validity. Do not even be concerned with these two concepts. Or, alternately, develop your own measurement device because other candidates "do not quite fill your needs." Then confidently use this instrument as if it were around since the days of Archimedes. . . .
(3) For subjects, use school children in areas where school attendance is rare. Then generalize from these to the whole population, including school nonattenders. . . .
(4) [Omitted]
(5) Use only one method to measure one variable so that all the faults of

the method and the vagueness of the variable confound data interpretation. . . .

(6) [Omitted]

(7) When comparisons across variables result in significance tests that approach, or even go beyond, statistical significance, use them as a license to make any interpretation you wish. When data are in line with expectations, gloat and close the case; when data are not in line with expectations, explain them away with armchair speculation. In really tough spots, select those writings from cultural anthropologists which you know will sound convincing. . . .

(8) Choose a research topic or a specific hypothesis, not because of its importance, but because there is a convenient technique or instrument available to test it. . . .

(9) Choose topics that will yield a large number of publications rather than make a contribution to an understanding of human behavior. . . .

(10) Do one study, for instance, French-English bilinguals in Canada, and then generalize to the world's bilinguals. . . .

(11) Do not bother translating because of the hard work necessary to obtain equivalence of measures. Instead, use as subjects people who speak a language of convenience, even though such people are unrepresentative of the entire population. . . .

(12) When a number of small studies are done to investigate one hypothesis, publish each of the small studies in a separate place. When asked a question about what data are in what article, be unable to answer. . . .

(13) Do not bother doing a literature review. Do not be concerned with the work of others so that there might be a link made between one set of data and another. . . .

(14) Resist any temptation to admit that other theories or rival hypotheses may explain your data. . . .

(15) Make sure that the report is as long as possible, and that complex tables and fancy figures will exonerate you of any misinterpretation you have unknowingly made. Early in the report, be sure to tell the reader that this is perhaps the best and most important study ever done. . . .

(16) [Omitted]

Perhaps the issues, guidelines, and discussion presented in this article will save other researchers in arts education from having to follow any of these concerns. Arts education researchers may be able to learn from the past work of these less cautious predecessors and forge ahead with deliberate speed and a clear determination not to repeat (replicate) the work of others who have caused Lonner to compile such a list.

I am indebted to Dr. Rogena Degge for her critical comments on the initial draft of this manuscript.

REFERENCES

Anderson, F.E. "Aesthetic Sensitivity, Previous Art Experiences and Production of Outstanding Works of Art." Ph.D. diss., Indiana Univ., 1968.
———. "Aesthetic Sensitivity, Previous Art Experiences, and Participation in the Scholastic Art Awards." *Studies in Art Education* 10, no. 3 (1969): 4–13.
———. "Aesthetic Sensitivity, Dogmatism and the Eisner Art Inventories." *Studies in Art Education* 12, no. 2 (1975): 49–53.
———. "Esthetic Evaluations and Art Involvement in Australia, Pakistan and Thailand." *Studies in Art Education* 17, no. 3 (1976): 33–43.
Anwar, M.P., and I.L. Child. "Personality and Esthetic Sensitivity in Islamic Culture." *Journal of Social Psychology* 87 (1972): 21–27.
Berelyne, P.E. "Extension to Indian Subjects of a Study of Exploratory and Verbal Responses to Visual Patterns." *Journal of Cross-Cultural Psychology* 6, no. 3 (1975): 316–30.
Berrien, F.F. "A Super-Ego for Cross-Cultural Research." *International Journal of Psychology* 5 (1970): 33–39.
Berry, J.W., and P.R. Dasen. *Culture and Cognition: Readings in Cross-Cultural Perspectives on Learning.* New York: Wiley and Sons, 1975.
Brislin, R.W.; S. Bochner; and W.J. Lonner. *Cross-Cultural Perspectives on Learnings.* New York: Wiley and Sons, 1975.
Brislin, R.W.; W.J. Lonner; and R.M. Thorndike. *Cross-Cultural Research Methods.* New York: Wiley and Sons, 1973.
Budner, S. "Intolerance of Ambiguity as a Personality Variable." *Journal of Personality* 30 (1962): 39–50.
Bulley, M. *Art and Everyman.* London: Batsford, 1951.
Campbell, D.T., and D.W. Fiske. "Convergent and Discriminant Validation by the Multi-Trait/Multi-Method Matrix." *Psychological Bulletin* 56 (1959): 81–85.
Child, I.L. "Personal Preferences as an Expression of Esthetic Sensitivity." *Journal of Personality* 30 (1962): 496–512.
———. *Development of Sensitivity to Esthetic Values.* Cooperative Research Project No. 1748. Washington, D.C.: U.S. Office of Education, Cooperative Research Program, 1964. Mimeographed.
———. "Personality Correlates of Esthetic Judgment in College Students." *Journal of Personality* 33 (1965): 475–511.
Child, I.L., and S. Iwao. "Personality and Esthetic Sensitivity: Extension of Findings to Younger Age and to Different Cultures." *Journal of Personality and Social Psychology* 3 (1968): 308–12.
Child, I.L., and L. Siroto. "Bakwele and American Esthetic Evaluation Compared." *Ethnology* 4 (1965): 349–60.
Ford, C.S.; E.T. Prothro; and I.L. Child. "Some Transcultural Comparisons of Esthetic Judgments." *Journal of Social Psychology* 68 (1966): 19–26.
Frijda, N., and G. Jahoda. "On the Scope and Method of Cross-Cultural Research." *International Journal of Psychology* 1 (1966): 109–27.
Gordon, L.V., and A. Kikuchi. "American Personality Tests in Cross-Cultural Research, A Caution." *Journal of Social Psychology* 69 (1966): 178–83.
Haritos-Fatouros, M., and I.L. Child. "Transcultural Similarity in Personal Significance of Esthetic Interests." *Journal of Cross-Cultural Psychology* 8, no. 3 (1977): 285–98.
Hess-Behrens, B.F. *The Development of the Concept of Space as Observed in Children's Drawings: A Cross-National/Cross-Cultural Study.* Project No. R02–0611, Grant No. OEG–0–72–4524. Washington, D.C.: U.S. Office of Education, National Center for Educational Research and Development, 1973. Mimeographed.
Iwao, S., and I.L. Child. "Comparison of Esthetic Judgments by American Experts and by Japanese Potters." *Journal of Social Psychology* 68 (1966): 27–33.

Iwao, S.; I.L. Child; and M. Garcia. "Further Evidence of Agreement Between Japanese-American Esthetic Evaluations." *Journal of Social Psychology* 78 (1969): 11–15.

Kerlinger, F.N. *Foundations of Behavioral Research*. 2d ed. New York: Holt, Rinehart and Winston, 1972.

Lonner, W.J. "An Analysis of the Pre-Publication Evaluation of Cross-Cultural Manuscripts: Implications for Future Research." In *Cross-Cultural Perspectives on Learnings*, edited by R.W. Brislin, S. Bochner, and W.J. Lonner. New York: Wiley and Sons, 1975.

Miller, D. *Handbook of Research Design and Social Measurement*. New York: McKay, 1964.

Pike, L. *Language in Relation to a Unified Theory of the Structure of Human Behavior*. The Hague: Mouton, 1966.

Price-Williams, D.R. "Introduction and Part One: Theory and Method." In *Cross-Cultural Studies*, edited by D.R. Price-Williams. Baltimore: Penguin Books, 1970.

———. *Explorations in Cross-Cultural Psychology*. San Francisco: Chandler and Shoup, 1975.

Rokeach, M. *The Open and Closed Mind*. New York: Basic Books, 1960.

Ross, B. "Preferences for Nonrepresentational Drawings by Navaho and Other Children." *Journal of Cross-Cultural Psychology* 7, no. 2 (1976): 145–56.

Strodbeck, F.L. "Considerations in Meta-Method in Cross-Cultural Studies." *American Anthropologist* 66 (special issue, 1964): 223–29.

Triandis, H.; V. Vassiliou; G. Vassiliou; Y. Tanaka; and A. Shanmagan. *The Analysis of Subjective Culture*. New York: Wiley, 1972.

Valentine, C.W. *The Experimental Psychology of Beauty*. London: Metheun, 1962.

Werner, O., and D.T. Campbell. "Translating, Working Through Interpreters and the Problem of Decenterny." In *Handbook of Method in Cultural Anthropology*, edited by R. Caroll and R. Cohen. Garden City: Natural History Press, 1970.

Resources for Cross-Cultural Research in Art Education

A final word should be said regarding institutions and organizations to which one can turn for assistance in cross-cultural research. There are a number of organizations that are concerned with international art education and museum education. Several of these publish periodic bulletins and newsletters or journals, which often prove to be useful. The oldest existing forum for conferences and communication among art teachers is INSEA, the International Society for Education through Art.

INSEA is a NGO (nongovernment organization) affiliate of UNESCO (United Nations Educational Social and Cultural Organization) and has no permanent funding or headquarters. Its office resides with the president. Dues are a nominal fee, and one may join by writing Al Hurwitz, 1300 Mt. Royal Avenue, Baltimore, Maryland 21217. Newsletters are issued four times a year; regional and national conferences are held yearly; and major congresses meet every three years. The U.S. affiliate of INSEA is USSEA, the U.S. Society for Education through Art, and the current president is Al Hurwitz, Department of Art Education, Maryland Institute, College of Art. Dues, again, are a nominal fee. USSEA has two conferences a year, one in a university setting, and one at the annual conference of the National Art Education Association, with which it has a second affiliation. Conferences thus far have been held at three university centers and will continue to follow this pattern.

The director of the art education programs of UNESCO is Elena Leger. Publications, conferences, workshops, the writing of studies and reports, and the preparation of audio-visual packages and exhibitions are some of the typical tasks in which Dr. Leger has been involved in as director. Information regarding materials relevant to art education may be obtained by writing UNESCO Publications, Place de Fontenoy, 75, Paris, France.

The UNICEF program gathers children's art work for calendars, exhibitions, and holiday cards and returns the proceeds to children in the form of art supplies. Regional centers sponsor exhibitions, and these often provide the basis for the collection assembled by the Children's Culture information center, whose works now number in the thousands and represent over 130 countries. UNICEF prepares and loans exhibits from both the New York office and local UNICEF committee offices. Further information can be obtained by writing Anne Pellowski, Director, U.S. Committee for UNICEF, 331 E. 38 Street, New York, N.Y., 10016.

The major center for studying international school art is the International Collection of Child Art, which is housed at the Ewing Museum of Nations at Illinois State University, Normal, Illinois. It is director Barry Moore's responsibility to procure, organize, catalogue, and disseminate the growing number of art works that come to the center. Each piece is photographed, mounted, and cross-indexed by artist's country, age, and sex, by media, topic, and content. Descriptive brochures of the services offered by the collection are available upon request.

The most recognized and established forum for communication among museum and art educators is CECA, the Committee for Education and Cultural Action. CECA is one of the twenty or so international committees of the International Council of Museums; its headquarters are at the Masion de l'UNESCO, 1, rue Miollis, 75732 Paris-Cedex 15, France. Other committees related to the interest of art educators residing at UNESCO are the applied art, fine arts, modern art, museology, and training of personnel committees.

CECA is, however, the official education committee of ICOM (the International Council of Museums), and its offices reside with the Secretariat Mme. Th. Destree-Heymans at the Musees royaux d'art & d'historie, 10 Parc du Cinquantenaire, 1040 Brussels, Belgium. American art and museum educators may engage in a joint membership between the AAM, American Association of Museums, and ICOM by designating Education, CECA, as a requested affiliation. Such a convenient arrangement exists in many other countries as well. In the United States it is arranged with Maria Pappageorge at the American Association of Museums, P.O. Box 33399, Washington, D.C., 20033.

The most recently established and permanent division of the NAEA (National Art Education Association) is the Museum Education Division. This division meets each year at the annual conferences held throughout the United States. Membership is inclusive in the NAEA fees and information may be obtained through Charles Bleick, chairman of the NAEA Museum Education Division, 901 West Franklin Street, Richmond, Virginia, 23284. NAEA museum education offers numerous presentations by art education museum teachers each year at its national conventions, and a wide variety of museum subjects are covered. Topics range from methods to rationales and include experience workshops on museum teaching subjects. Museum education papers and articles are published in the official journal of NAEA, *Art Education,* which is included with NAEA membership dues. NAEA museum education subjects are directed to art educators at the elementary, secondary, higher education, and administrative levels.

The ICOM Committee for Education and Cultural Action (CECA) also meets annually in designated countries throughout the world. CECA is concerned with the ways in which museums meet the needs of various groups of the public and follows themes relating to such topics as: the museum and school groups; the museum and special groups such as the handicapped, the elderly, housewives, and members of industrial and business organizations; the museum and individual visitors; the museum and museum outreach programs. CECA offers an excellent opportunity to begin cross-cultural research and artistic and cultural program development because membership requires in-depth concentration within one of the areas upon which the organization is structured, including training, communication, evaluation, schools, special groups, individual visitors, and museum outreach. These organizational topics offer the advantage of being fairly small units in which discussions are held in such a way that art teachers from various countries are active in the deliberations at each international conference. At CECA meetings, art educators take part in this forum, relating their present work and experiences to others from various countries and engaging in cross-cultural sharing through meaningful discussion.

Index of Persons Cited